# Engaging with Rousseau

Jean-Jacques Rousseau has been cast as a champion of Enlightenment and a beacon of Romanticism, a father figure of radical revolutionaries and totalitarian dictators alike, an inventor of the modern notion of the self and an advocate of stern ancient republicanism. *Engaging with Rousseau* treats his writings as an enduring topic of debate, examining the diverse responses they have attracted from the Enlightenment to the present. Such notions as the general will were, for example, refracted through very different prisms during the struggle for independence in Latin America and in social conflicts in Eastern Europe, or modified by thinkers from Kant to contemporary political theorists. Beyond Rousseau's ideas, his public image also travelled around the world. This book examines engagement with Rousseau's works as well as with his self-fashioning: especially in turbulent times, his defiant public identity and his call for regeneration were admired or despised by intellectuals and political agents.

Avi Lifschitz is Senior Lecturer in European Intellectual History at University College London (UCL). He is the author of *Language and Enlightenment: The Berlin Debates of the Eighteenth Century* (2012) and co-editor of *Epicurus in the Enlightenment* (2009).

# Engaging with Rousseau

## *Reaction and Interpretation from the Eighteenth Century to the Present*

*Edited by*

Avi Lifschitz
*University College London*

CAMBRIDGE
UNIVERSITY PRESS

University Printing House, Cambridge CB2 8BS, United Kingdom

One Liberty Plaza, 20th Floor, New York, NY 10006, USA

477 Williamstown Road, Port Melbourne, VIC 3207, Australia

314-321, 3rd Floor, Plot 3, Splendor Forum, Jasola District Centre, New Delhi - 110025, India

79 Anson Road, #06-04/06, Singapore 079906

Cambridge University Press is part of the University of Cambridge.

It furthers the University's mission by disseminating knowledge in the pursuit of education, learning and research at the highest international levels of excellence.

www.cambridge.org
Information on this title: www.cambridge.org/9781108705189



First published 2016
First paperback edition 2018

*A catalogue record for this publication is available from the British Library*

*Library of Congress Cataloging in Publication data*
Lifschitz, Avi, 1975– author.
Engaging with Rousseau : reaction and interpretation from the eighteenth century to the present / edited by Avi Lifschitz, University College London.
Cambridge, United Kingdom : Cambridge University Press is part of the University of Cambridge, [2016] | Includes bibliographical references and index.
LCCN 2016017599 | ISBN 9781107146327
LCSH: Rousseau, Jean-Jacques, 1712–1778.
LCC B2137 .E54 2016 | DDC 194–dc23
LC record available at https://lccn.loc.gov/2016017599

ISBN 978-1-107-14632-7 Hardback
ISBN 978-1-108-70518-9 Paperback

# Contents

# Notes on contributors

MONIKA BAÁR is Associate Professor of History at Leiden University. She is the author of *Historians and Nationalism: East-Central Europe in the Nineteenth Century* (2010) and co-author of *A History of Modern Political Thought in East Central Europe:* Volume I, *Negotiating Modernity in the 'Long Nineteenth Century'* (2016) and Volume II, *Negotiating Modernity in the 'Short Twentieth Century' and Beyond* (forthcoming in 2017).

CHRISTOPHER BROOKE is Lecturer in Political Theory in the Department of Politics and International Studies (POLIS) at the University of Cambridge, and Fellow and Director of Studies in Politics at Homerton College. He is the author of *Philosophic Pride: Stoicism and Political Thought from Lipsius to Rousseau* (2012) and the co-editor, with Elizabeth Frazer, of *Ideas of Education: Philosophy and Politics from Plato to Dewey* (2013).

AXEL HONNETH is Senior Professor of Philosophy at the Goethe University in Frankfurt am Main and Jack C. Weinstein Professor for the Humanities at the Department of Philosophy at Columbia University. Since 2001 he has also been Director of the Institute for Social Research in Frankfurt. His publications in English include *The Critique of Power* (1990), *The Struggle for Recognition* (1995), *Redistribution or Recognition? A Political-Philosophical Exchange* (co-authored with Nancy Fraser, 2003), *Disrespect: The Normative Foundations of Critical Theory* (2007), *Reification: A New Look at an Old Idea* (2008), *Pathologies of Reason* (2009), *The Pathologies of Individual Freedom: Hegel's Social Theory* (2010), *The I in We: Studies in the Theory of Recognition* (2012), and *Freedom's Right* (2014).

JEREMY JENNINGS is Professor of Political Theory and Head of the Department of Political Economy at King's College London. He is the author of numerous books, chapters, and articles on the history of French political thought, most notably *Revolution and the Republic:*

*A History of Political Thought in France since the Eighteenth Century* (2011).

AVI LIFSCHITZ is Senior Lecturer in European Intellectual History at University College London (UCL). He is the author of *Language and Enlightenment: The Berlin Debates of the Eighteenth Century* (2012) and co-editor of *Epicurus in the Enlightenment* (2009) and *Rethinking Lessing's Laokoon* (forthcoming). He has also recently edited *Rousseau's Imagined Antiquity*, a special issue of the journal *History of Political Thought*.

NICOLA MILLER is Professor of Latin American History at University College London (UCL). She has published widely on the intellectual and cultural history of Latin America, most recently *Reinventing Modernity in Latin America: Intellectuals Imagine the Future, 1900–1930* (2008) and *America Imagined: Explaining the United States in Nineteenth-Century Europe and Latin America* (with Axel Körner and Adam I. P. Smith, 2012). She is currently working on a comparative history of knowledge in Latin America.

PHILIP PETTIT is L. S. Rockefeller University Professor of Politics and Human Values at Princeton, and Distinguished Professor of Philosophy at the Australian National University. His books include *Republicanism* (1997), *The Economy of Esteem* (with G. Brennan, 2004), *Group Agency* (with C. List, 2011), *On the People's Terms* (2012), *Just Freedom* (2014), and *The Robust Demands of the Good* (2015). *Common Minds: Themes from the Philosophy of Philip Pettit*, ed. G. Brennan, R. Goodin, F. Jackson, and M. Smith, appeared in 2007; *Philip Pettit – Five Themes from His Work*, ed. S. Derpmann and D. Schweikard, appeared in 2016.

ALEXANDER SCHMIDT is Junior Professor of Intellectual History at the Friedrich Schiller University in Jena and currently a Feodor Lynen Fellow at the John U. Nef Committee on Social Thought, University of Chicago. He is the author of *Vaterlandsliebe und Religionskonflikt. Politische Diskurse im Alten Reich 1555–1648* (2007). His work has appeared in *The Historical Journal*, *History of European Ideas*, *History of Political Thought*, *Modern Intellectual History*, *Francia*, and elsewhere. He has also edited Friedrich Schiller's *On the Aesthetic Education of Man* and co-edited a special issue of *History of European Ideas* entitled *Sociability in Enlightenment Thought*.

CÉLINE SPECTOR is Full Professor at the Philosophy Department of the University of Bordeaux (Montaigne). Her research interests include the history of political thought, particularly the eighteenth century and its legacy. Recent publications include *Montesquieu: liberté, droit et histoire* (2010), *Au prisme de Rousseau: usages politiques contemporains* (2011), and *Rousseau: les paradoxes de l'autonomie démocratique* (2015).

JEAN-FABIEN SPITZ is Professor of Political Philosophy at the University of Paris I – Panthéon Sorbonne. His latest major publication is *Le mythe de l'impartialité: les mutations du concept de liberté dans la culture politique américaine, 1870–1940* (2014).

RICHARD WHATMORE is Professor of Modern History at the University of St Andrews. He is the author of *Republicanism and the French Revolution* (2000) and *Against War and Empire* (2012). He directs the St Andrews Institute of Intellectual History.

# Preface

It has long been observed that Rousseau's works can inspire an extensive range of responses, often thoroughly contradicting one another. If for the German Romantics Rousseau was the ultimate individualist decrying an ever-corrupting social yoke, for authors from Hippolyte Taine to Jacob Talmon he represented the fundamental inspiration for a form of totalitarian democracy that crushes all forms of individuality. He has been cast as a champion of religion but also an enemy of Scripture; a promoter of Enlightenment and a beacon of Romanticism; an inventor of the modern, expanded notion of the self; and an advocate of ancient republican self-restraint. Indeed, it has been common ever since the publication of Rousseau's first works to view him as a paradoxical, inconsistent author whose different works were at odds with one another, lacking a core of unifying ideas.[1] The perplexing variety of the images and legacies of Jean-Jacques Rousseau has been attributed to the manifold character of his work itself, yet usually in an overwhelmingly negative manner. Conflicting interpretations were taken to reflect some fundamental problems and a lack of systematic rigour in Rousseau's original writings.

Throughout the twentieth century, new attempts were made – from Ernst Cassirer's to Nicholas Dent's – to view Rousseau's work as a (more or less) coherent whole. Cassirer saw the unifying idea underlying all of Rousseau's writings as the striving to make human beings self-legislating, autonomous agents – so as to ensure they did not lose their freedom by becoming wholly dependent on the law in the political realm.[2] Dent, on the other hand, saw the notion of self-love, or *amour propre*, as Rousseau's main preoccupation in his different works,

[1] On Rousseau scholarship in the twentieth century, see the contributions by Christopher Brooke (Chapter 8) and Céline Spector (Chapter 9) in this book. An overview of older accounts is available in Peter Gay's introduction and postscript to Ernst Cassirer, *The Question of Jean-Jacques Rousseau*, trans. Peter Gay (New Haven: Yale University Press, 1989), 3–30 and 131–141.

[2] Cassirer, *The Question*, esp. 55–59.

emphasising the positive as well as the notoriously negative forms it could assume.[3]

This book, by contrast, strays away from the controversies over unity in the diversity of Rousseau's writings. Most of its chapters do not propose a particular interpretation of the supposed core of these works or their author's life along specific ideological lines. Rather, they highlight the originality of Rousseau's *œuvre* by treating it as an enduring topic of intellectual controversy; the book investigates the resonance of Rousseau's work by examining the responses it has generated from the late eighteenth century to the present. The guiding assumption here is that a firm focus on subsequent engagement with Rousseau's work can highlight more resolutely its inherent tensions and ambiguities. The book therefore suggests that Rousseau's legacy does not constitute a set of immutable principles, arguments, and theories. Instead of asking who read Rousseau correctly or misunderstood the 'core' of his writings, contributors emphasise the variety of ways in which Rousseau could be, and still is, read and interpreted.

Although this book may correctly be regarded as a variation on the theme of German *Rezeptionsgeschichte*, or reception studies, it does differ substantially from accounts of intellectual influence, which we regard as a highly problematic term. Indeed, the title *Engaging with Rousseau* is deliberately chosen to highlight two main issues. First, in lieu of a study of disembodied influences based merely on textual echoes, this project is an account of reaction and interpretation by particular authors and political actors in well-defined geopolitical contexts and with specific intentions. Second, the term 'engagement' includes two subsets, as implied in the subtitle: 'interpretation' – the close reading of Rousseau's works, their analysis or elucidation, and an informed reply to them – and 'reaction' in the sense of a general response to Rousseau on various possible levels. These include images of his philosophy (what Rousseau's work came to represent) alongside his public persona, politics, and rhetoric.

Our emphasis on reception and subsequent engagement stems from the observation that the much-needed focus in recent decades on contextualised intellectual history has generated excellent work, yet largely on the circumstances and background of the *production* of renowned texts.

[3] N. J. H. Dent, *Rousseau: An Introduction to His Psychological, Social and Political Theory* (Oxford: Blackwell, 1988): on self-love, see esp. 52–56, 143–145. Cf. Frederick Neuhouser, *Rousseau's Theodicy of Self-Love: Evil, Rationality, and the Drive for Recognition* (Oxford: Oxford University Press, 2008). On this issue, see also the contributions by Alexander Schmidt (Chapter 3), Axel Honneth (Chapter 11), and Avi Lifschitz (Chapter 2).

Indeed, the focus on the intended uptake of particular texts has mostly led to the investigation of how authors secured such an uptake (what they were performing by writing specific works) rather than how readers in subsequent generations and centuries engaged with their work.[4] By way of emphasising our focus on the afterlife of texts and their authors' personae, we use the notion of 'engagement' with Rousseau by building on recent theories of cultural transfer through translation. In a series of works from the 1990s onwards, Michael Werner and Michel Espagne have pleaded for the substitution of 'transfer' for 'influence' or 'reception', since the latter terms implied a somewhat passive absorption of a static set of ideas.[5] Their emphasis on the permeability of cultural borders, historical continuities, and the active appropriation involved in cultural transfer is embedded in our notion of engagement. This term signifies active agency on the part of authors and readers who responded to Rousseau by either reinterpreting his works or reacting to them publicly in other ways.

Our concentration on engagement with Rousseau's work emphasises yet another assumption: that the intellectual potential of an author's writings is not necessarily exhausted by reading them on their own or by situating them within the immediate context of their production. Subsequent engagement may reveal much about the original work, no less than about the authors and movements interacting with it. As recently suggested by László Kontler in relation to translations of eighteenth-century texts, 'the difference of meaning emerging through translation in the recipient environment can be turned to contributing to significant discussions and to sorting out disagreements about the character and status of authors, their texts, and their concepts as they exist in their "home" culture'.[6] The chapters of this book, all dealing with different

[4] Quentin Skinner, 'Meaning and understanding in the history of ideas', *History and Theory* 8 (1969), 3–53; revised and reprinted in Skinner's *Visions of Politics*, I: *Regarding Method* (Cambridge: Cambridge University Press, 2002), 57–89, as well as the other methodological essays in Skinner's volume. An excellent recent example is J. G. A. Pocock's serial exploration of the contemporary intellectual contexts of Gibbon's *Decline and Fall* in his *Barbarism and Religion*, 6 vols. (Cambridge: Cambridge University Press, 1999–2015).

[5] See, for example, Michel Espagne and Michael Werner, 'Deutsch-französischer Kuturtransfer im 18. und 19. Jahrhundert', *Francia* 13 (1985), 502–10; Michel Espagne, *Les transferts culturels franco-allemands* (Paris: PUF, 1999); idem., 'La notion de transfert culturel', *Revue Sciences/Lettres* (online) 1 (2013), accessed on 12 March 2015. (URL: http://rsl.revues.org/219; DOI: 10.4000/rsl.219) See also Stefanie Stockhorst (ed.), *Cultural Transfer through Translation: The Circulation of Enlightened Thought in Europe by Means of Translation* (Amsterdam: Rodopi, 2010).

[6] László Kontler, *Translations, Histories, Enlightenments: William Robertson in Germany, 1760–1795* (Basingstoke: Palgrave Macmillan, 2014), 14. A recent study that corroborates this point by re-reading Rousseau through Adam Smith's intensive engagement with his works is István Hont, *Politics in Commercial Society: Jean-Jacques Rousseau and Adam*

engagements with Rousseau's works from the eighteenth century to the present and from Russia to Latin America, may serve as a demonstration of this claim.

In order to make these points, the present project necessarily had to be selective. It is extensive yet not fully comprehensive; the thematic choices were made with an eye to the overall methodological issues above, especially concerning engagement as the active agency of interpreters and respondents rather than passive reception on their part. In this respect, two particular notions guided the selection of essays published here: interdisciplinarity and an extended spatio-temporal range. Since readers may approach this book from very different disciplinary backgrounds, it includes contributions by specialists in political and cultural history, intellectual history, political theory, philosophy, and the history of political thought. Moreover, studies of Rousseau's legacy have so far mostly centred on France and Britain. The inclusion of various German themes, as well as essays on Eastern Europe and Latin America, is meant to extend this traditional focus geographically.[7] While still largely focused on European intellectual spheres and legacies, this project is meant to raise an initial contribution to a more transnational overview of the engagement with Rousseau's work. At the same time, our points concerning engagement, reaction, and interpretation are refracted though a large temporal canvas extending from Rousseau's lifetime to the present day. Beyond their historical observations, the contributions by Axel Honneth (Chapter 11) and Philip Pettit (Chapter 10) are examples of current engagement with Rousseau by contemporary political theorists.

The malleability of Rousseau's *œuvre* and its multi-faceted nature are revealed here in a number of test cases, which will now be briefly outlined (not necessarily in the order of their appearance in the book). One of the most striking contrasts in past engagement with Rousseau may be perceived in the different manners in which such notions as the general will could be interpreted during the struggle for independence in Latin America and in social conflicts taking place at the same time in Central and Eastern Europe. Monika Baár (Chapter 6) argues that in the extensive territories of the Habsburg and Russian empires, the *Social Contract* was appropriated to defend the status quo just as eagerly as to advocate reform or even revolution: the sovereign nation was often identified with largely aristocratic diets instead of the entire people. However, Baár

*Smith*, ed. Béla Kapossy and Michael Sonenscher (Cambridge, MA: Harvard University Press, 2015).

[7] On Germany, see also Jacques Mounier, *La Fortune des écrits de J.-J. Rousseau dans les pays de langue allemande de 1782 à 1813* (Paris: PUF, 1980); Herbert Jaumann (ed.), *Rousseau in Deutschland. Neue Beiträge zur Erforschung seiner Rezeption* (Berlin: de Gruyter, 1994).

shows that the *Social Contract* did not only provide inspiration for numerous (unrealised) constitutional projects; it also became common practice to examine national history in the light of Rousseau's work, for example by using it as a standard for the reassessment of various medieval and early modern pacts. The myriad ways in which the *Social Contract* penetrated local discourses ranged from translations to cursory references and from political appeals to fiction and poetry.

Nicola Miller's contribution (Chapter 7) concerns a more politically assertive appropriation of Rousseau's work. Intellectual historians have long debated the role of Rousseau in the French Revolution, but have paid far less attention to the ways in which he was read in the area where republicanism next took root. The *Social Contract* was the most important political tract of the struggle for independence in the River Plate (and also in other parts of Latin America), yet it was not necessarily Rousseau's actual arguments that played the most significant role there. What mattered above all was his vision of social transformation, as interpreted locally and distinctively by Spanish American thinkers. This radical vision mobilised both supporters and opponents of independence and made Rousseau's name emblematic of social equality, whether desired or feared. It had consequences both at the time, particularly during the early stages of the struggles for independence, and subsequently in a Spanish American legacy of egalitarian political projects.

Nowhere was Rousseau's legacy more contested and polarised than in his hometown, Geneva, as argued in Richard Whatmore's account of changing local attitudes to Rousseau's political theory (Chapter 1). Local reformers considered the renowned *Citoyen de Genève* as insufficiently democratic and too obsessed with peace to serve as an inspiration for regeneration before and during the French Revolution. At the same time, Rousseau's writings could not be ignored by critics or reformers of any stamp. His cynical perspective on contemporary Europe ensured that those dissatisfied with the present would turn to Rousseau for support. Whatmore focuses on a point Rousseau repeatedly made concerning practical reform: modern states could usually not avoid a turbulent destiny because of the forces unleashed by commerce and egoism, yet this did not mean that revolutionary doctrines would solve their problems. Rousseau believed that radical politics in Geneva would only make things worse, partly because the politics of small states were altogether different to those of their larger neighbours. This stance rendered him a complicated figure for Genevan reformers, especially those who called themselves democrats.

Such tensions were also evident in the contrasting engagements of French liberals and socialists with Rousseau in the nineteenth century.

Jeremy Jennings explores the complex readings of Rousseau's writings by liberals in France from the Revolution of 1789 until the creation of the Third Republic. In the decades immediately following 1789, the focus of liberal readings of Rousseau fell upon an alleged connection between his ideas and the turning away from liberty that was associated above all with the rise of the Jacobins and the Terror. This theme is examined primarily through a discussion of the views of Jean-Joseph Mounier and Benjamin Constant. The chapter also looks at François Guizot's criticisms of Rousseau's notions of representation, and concludes by suggesting that the preoccupation with the damaging consequences of Rousseau's ideas declined after 1848. In fact, between 1848 and 1870 Rousseau re-emerged among liberal readers as a theorist of modern democracy.

Jean-Fabien Spitz (Chapter 5) examines the changing fortunes of Rousseau's work among nineteenth-century French authors who were particularly interested in his views on redistributive justice. Rousseau was convinced that it was impossible to restore the conditions of primordial freedom once inequality has gone beyond a critical point – mainly because such inequality could only be rectified by breaching the impartiality of the law and depriving some citizens of their legally sanctioned property. Hence, the tensions in his political thought enabled it to be used to legitimise both individual freedom under a general law and the redistribution of excessive wealth. Louis Blanc, who stands at the centre of Spitz's contribution, was inspired by Rousseau in his promotion of free credit for those who had no access to the means of production. Rousseau and Blanc shared the same notion of freedom but differed in their conceptualisation of the means to realise it (a general law for all or a special legislation aimed at the wealthy). Spitz seeks to explain this difference, exploring the peculiar ways in which Blanc and fellow socialists engaged with Rousseau's writings.

Beyond such accounts of engagement with Rousseau in particular geographical and political contexts, conflicting and changing attitudes to his thought could also be found in the work of a single author or political agent. Avi Lifschitz (Chapter 2) examines the intellectual relationship between Rousseau and Frederick II ('the Great') of Prussia, which has been overshadowed by the much-advertised collaboration between the self-styled 'philosopher-king' and Voltaire. Though in this case one cannot find a close alliance, Frederick's works and his correspondence betray a long-lasting preoccupation with the themes raised by Rousseau in his *Discourses* of the 1750s. Their mutual fascination reached its peak in 1762 when Rousseau sought refuge in the Prussian territory of Neuchâtel following the outcry prompted by *Emile* and the *Social Contract*. The chapter investigates the notion of self-love, or *amour propre*, in letters exchanged between Frederick and Rousseau through George Keith, the governor of Neuchâtel, as well as in Frederick's poems and treatises. Both Rousseau and Frederick used amalgams of Stoic and Epicurean elements in their discussions of self-love, but the king identified Rousseau as a modern champion of virtue as self-denial. It is argued that despite their disagreements, there was much common ground between Frederick's notion of self-love and Rousseau's modified views, especially as elaborated in *Emile*.

Another case of uneasy personal wrestling with Rousseau's thought is described in Alexander Schmidt's account of how Immanuel Kant dealt with Rousseau's sharp distinction between nature and civilisation (Chapter 3). This distinction was expressed in Rousseau's differentiation between natural (mainly physical) needs and 'artificial' ones originating in human imagination through social interaction. Such artificial needs were repeatedly viewed in the eighteenth century as the driving engine of civilisation, yet Rousseau feared they could also spell political and moral disaster by increasing human interdependence and inequality. Rousseau's analysis of artificial needs, especially as manifested by the arts and the sciences, became a building block in Kant's rejection of eudaemonist moral philosophy and his call for moral action based on reason only. For Kant, in order to overcome the ills of unsociability in economic and political relations, the arts and the sciences had to be transformed into instruments of moral education and means of regulating human needs.

Two twentieth-century test cases reflect the growth of academic scholarship on Rousseau. Yet as demonstrated by Christopher Brooke (Chapter 8) and Céline Spector (Chapter 9), this mode of engagement was not too different from earlier, more political ways of reading and using Rousseau. The circumstances of two World Wars, followed by the Cold War, moulded academic engagement with Rousseau to a considerable extent. Brooke outlines the changing contours of mainstream interpretations of Rousseau in Britain from the First World War to the Cold War. This period was sometimes marked by overt hostility to Rousseau, as apparent in Isaiah Berlin's identification of the Genevan as one of the 'enemies of human liberty' and in Bertrand Russell's view of Hitler as 'an outcome of Rousseau'. Notwithstanding these hyperbolic judgments, significant contributions to Rousseau scholarship were made by their near-contemporaries working in British universities. The chapter surveys the arc of Rousseau scholarship in Britain from the appearance of C. E. Vaughan's edition of the *Political Writings* in 1915 until John Plamenatz's death in 1975. Brooke considers the fortunes of idealism in the interwar period, the emergence of historical scholarship on Rousseau in the 1930s, the contribution of postwar experts on French literature, and the arguments of political theorists – especially Berlin, Oakeshott, and Plamenatz – in order to provide the intellectual background to the more recent renaissance in Anglophone Rousseau studies.

Céline Spector centres on a distinct and highly influential interpretation of Rousseau emerging in another academic context, that of Harvard University after the Second World War. John Rawls regarded Rousseau as a precursor of the Kantian concept of autonomy; as such, Rousseau provided major inspiration for Rawls's own books, *A Theory of Justice* and *Political Liberalism*. Explicitly wishing to round off the tradition of Locke, Rousseau, and Kant, Rawls cited the *Social Contract* as one of the sources for his theory of the 'well-ordered society'. Spector focuses on Rawls's *Lectures on the History of Political Philosophy* given to Harvard students between the second half of the 1960s and the second half of the 1990s. In these synoptic courses, influenced to a large extent by Judith Shklar, Rawls ventures a bold interpretation of Rousseau in terms of 'realistic utopianism'. The result is a Kantian reading of the *Discourse on Inequality* combined with an ultra-rationalist exegesis of the *Social Contract*, which eventually laid the conceptual foundations for Rawls's *A Theory of Justice*.

Concluding the book are two essays by contemporary political thinkers who spell out the continuing relevance of Rousseau's ideas. Axel Honneth, a theorist of inter-subjective recognition in ethics and politics, traces in depth the roots of this discussion back to Rousseau's work (Chapter 11). Honneth zooms in on Rousseau's original insight that human beings are characterised not only by a drive for self-preservation, but also by a need for social esteem and recognition (*amour propre*). The chapter subsequently surveys the enormous impact Rousseau's bipolar conception of social recognition had on modern philosophical discourse – especially in Kant's philosophy of history and in Fichte's and Hegel's discussions of mutual respect among equals. However, Honneth does not neglect the scepticism that Rousseau always exhibited towards the dependence on others that is inherent in *amour propre*. According to Honneth, Rousseau's works exhibit two fundamental motifs that stand in constant conflict with each other and also feature in modern recognition theory: the Stoic idea of personal independence from all external attachments and the inter-subjective idea of a deep-seated dependence on others. Therefore, Honneth suggests that Rousseau's insights function as a Trojan horse in any modern account of the necessity of external recognition of our dignity.

Philip Pettit (Chapter 10), one of the foremost contributors to contemporary debates on republicanism, emphasises another 'unwelcome dilemma', which he regards as an inescapable legacy of Rousseau's political thought. Rousseau defends the traditional republican idea that freedom requires not being subject to the will of another, yet argues in an innovative way that being subject to the will of the community – the public person – is no problem: 'each by giving himself to all, gives himself to no one'. He thinks it is no problem under two conditions: first, that each member consents to being subject to the majority rule of the community; and second, that the majority rule expresses the general will of members rather than a mere majoritarian will. But what if the second condition fails, as Rousseau clearly thinks possible, even likely? Either he must declare that society is dissolved and majority rule illegitimate, or he must hold that it is still legitimate and that freedom is no longer guaranteed for all. Responding to Rousseau's work in this mode, Pettit argues that his philosophy makes the dilemma virtually inescapable.

Taken together, all of the chapters in this collection make the case that engagement with Rousseau has never been straightforward, unproblematic, or consensual – even when this engagement was limited to the mind of a single thinker or political agent. As noted above, it is precisely these challenging and often conflicting aspects of engagement with Rousseau through the ages that the present book aims to highlight. Due to their interdisciplinary character, the chapters themselves reflect the manners in which engagement with Rousseau (as reaction and interpretation) might take shape. Concern with the logic of some of Rousseau's arguments and its role in current political theory is obviously different from a historical account of its echoes in nineteenth-century France, Latin America, or Eastern Europe. And this inevitable formal diversity of our own engagement with Rousseau points to another facet of his *œuvre*, perhaps its only aspect on which there has usually been widespread agreement: its rhetorical force and stylistic uniqueness. As argued by Jeremy Jennings and Nicola Miller in particular, it was not only Rousseau's ideas that travelled from context to context; so did his persona as one of the first celebrity writers. Indeed, Madame de Staël famously depicted Rousseau in her *De la littérature* (1800) as an author of a new style rather than of brand new ideas: in her words, 'he discovered nothing but he inflamed everything'.[8] As argued below, the significant role of Rousseau's public image had already been perceived early on by contemporaries such as Frederick the Great. Rousseau's self-fashioning complemented his thinking on social recognition, the drive for

[8] 'Il n'a rien découvert, mais il a tout enflammé', in Germaine de Staël, 'De la littérature considérée dans ses rapports avec les institutions sociales', in *Œuvres complètes de la Baronne de Staël, publiées par son fils* (Paris: Treuttel and Würtz, 1820), IV, 373–374.

distinction, and the interrelations between solitary existence and political life (or between 'man' and 'citizen'). Especially in times of socio-political turbulence, Rousseau's defiant public identity, as well as his call for individual and social regeneration, was admired by intellectuals from Russia, to France, to Latin America.[9] His image as one of the first modern public intellectuals provided yet another channel of engagement with Rousseau parallel to the diverse readings and interpretations of his works.

AVI LIFSCHITZ

[9] On this point, see the recent account by Antoine Lilti, *Figures publiques: l'invention de la célébrité, 1750–1850* (Paris: Fayard, 2014), esp. ch. 5; see also Lilti, 'The Writing of Paranoia: Jean-Jacques Rousseau and the Paradoxes of Celebrity', *Representations* 103 (Summer 2008), 53–83.

# Acknowledgements

This book emerged from a long conversation that started on the occasion of an event marking the tercentenary of Jean-Jacques Rousseau's birth: 'Rousseau 300: Nature, Self, and State' (University College London, 19–21 April 2012). The editor and contributors wish to express their gratitude for the generous support provided by the following institutions, without which the event – and this book – would not have materialised: the Berendel Foundation; the French and Swiss embassies in London; the Fidelio Charitable Trust; UCL Grand Challenges and the Vice-Provost for Research, David Price; the UCL European Institute; the UCL History Department; the UCL Centre for Transnational History and its Director, Axel Körner. Thanks to Charles Peebles and University College Opera for staging an unforgettably lively performance of Rousseau's opera *Le Devin du village*. At the UCL Art Museum, Andrea Fredericksen, Nina Pearlman, George Richards, and Justin Badger offered indispensable help before, during, and after the accompanying exhibition. Emma Patten was indefatigably efficient and resourceful as the conference administrator.

At the event and thereafter we have profited from comments by and conversations with Valentina Arena, Richard Bellamy, Richard Bourke, Richard Butterwick, Gregory Claeys, Nicholas Cronk, Sean Gaston, Angus Gowland, Knud Haakonssen, Marian Hobson, Jared Holley, István Hont, Kevin Inston, Andrew Kahn, Cécile Laborde, Anthony La Vopa, Miriam Leonard, Antoine Lilti, Bill Marshall, Iain McDaniel, Véronique Munoz-Dardé, Nicholas Phillipson, Wolfgang Pross, John Robertson, Quentin Skinner, Michael Sonenscher, Gareth Stedman Jones, Tracy Strong, Georgios Varouxakis, and Jacqueline Waeber. Much of the editorial work was done during residential fellowships at the Wissenschaftskolleg in Berlin and at the Lichtenberg-Kolleg in Göttingen. The editor is grateful to staff members and to the Rector and Director of these institutions, Luca Giuliani and Martin van Gelderen, for their hospitality – as well as to Reinhart Meyer-Kalkus (formerly at the Wissenschaftskolleg) for a particularly invigorating intellectual exchange.

Another product of the conversations started at the UCL event is a special issue of *History of Political Thought* 37 (2016) entitled *Rousseau's Imagined Antiquity*.

Publishing with Cambridge University Press has been both a privilege and pleasure. We are wholeheartedly grateful to Rebecca Taylor, Liz Friend-Smith, and Michael Watson, whose guidance through the practicalities has been exemplarily helpful. Thoughtful comments and suggestions by two anonymous readers improved substantially the content of the book. Alessandro De Arcangelis professionally doctored the cover image. At the final stages of the production process, Rosalyn Scott, Claire Sissen, and Matthew Bastock provided us with invaluable support and assistance.

# Note on the texts and references

Citations from works by Rousseau and his interpreters have been translated into English in the chapters; the footnotes may contain particularly striking quotations in other languages.

Translations from French and other languages are the authors' where no published edition is referred to. The essays include abbreviated references to the following standard editions of Rousseau's works.

*OC* *Œuvres complètes*, ed. Bernard Gagnebin, Marcel Raymond, et al. (Bibliothèque de la Pléiade), 5 vols. (Paris: Gallimard, 1959–1995)
*DI* *The Discourses and Other Early Political Writings*, ed. Victor Gourevitch (Cambridge: Cambridge University Press, 1997)
*SC* *The Social Contract and Other Later Political Writings*, ed. Victor Gourevitch (Cambridge: Cambridge University Press, 1997)

# 1 'A lover of peace more than liberty'? The Genevan rejection of Rousseau's politics

*Richard Whatmore*

## I

Writing in 1836, an anonymous contributor to the *Bibliothèque de Genève* noted,

> There are few writers whose most private actions and intimate thoughts have occupied the public in the manner of J.-J. Rousseau's. There are fewer still whose life has been scrutinized to the extent that his has been; his friends and his enemies have with equal alacrity published everything they knew about his private conduct, his writings and even the least substantial of his words. Has the public curiosity been satisfied to the extent that further information about Rousseau will not be welcomed? We do not think so.[1]

Etienne Dumont was typical of many Genevans born in the latter half of the eighteenth century; he never managed to escape from Rousseau's shadow. Having seemingly been an enemy to Rousseau's politics for most of his life, acting as the editor and translator of Jeremy Bentham's incomplete manuscripts and being at the forefront of the admirers of Britain's constitution and commercial society, he was drawn back to Rousseau, both in his private reflections and in considered references in his own published work.[2] Dumont's manuscripts contain endless references to Rousseau, whose work he consistently returned to.[3] As he put it in a letter to his close friend Samuel Romilly, they were living in 'the age of Rousseau', and future generations would find it difficult to understand

[1] Anon., *Bibliothéque de Genève. Nouvelle série* (Geneva and Paris, 1836), vol. 1, 82. All translations are by the author unless otherwise stated. The French has not been modernised.

[2] Dumont edited and translated Bentham's attacks upon Rousseau in the *Traités de legislation civile et pénale*, 2 vols. (Paris, 1802), 'vol. 1, 112, 117–118.

[3] Étienne Dumont to Samuel Romilly, December 1789: 'Vous avez donc lu les Confessions de Rousseau, on voit combien son stile dépendoit de l'etat de son ame, on y cherchoit l'histoire de ses Sentiments, on n'y trouve guere que celle de son menage, la premiere lecture m'a desapointé, la seconde m'a fait plus de plaisir, il est si bon homme, si naïf, il se montre avec tant de verité, ses sentiments sont toujours si près de la nature – cet ouvrage a fait peu de sensation, mais cette sensation n'a pas été defavorable à Rousseau.': Rousseau, *Correspondance complète de Jean Jacques Rousseau*, ed. R. A. Leigh et al., 52 vols. (Oxford: Voltaire Foundation, 1965–1998), vol. 46, 150–151 (Letter 8004).

why Voltaire, who was altogether inferior, had been venerated in the same breath.[4] In addition to Dumont's history of the early years of the French Revolution, the only two essays that his literary executor believed were suitable for publication after Dumont's death in 1832 concerned Rousseau.[5]

On the surface, Dumont's continuing fascination is explicable. As a young man, he was supportive of the *représentant* rebellion against the magistrates at Geneva, culminating in the revolution of 1782. During training for Protestant ministry, his mentor was Jacob Vernes, who considered himself a disciple of Rousseau.[6] In the 1760s, Vernes was one of many who viewed Rousseau as a latter-day Calvin for the city. In an extensive correspondence with Rousseau, commenced after Rousseau returned to the Calvinist Church and thereby reclaimed his status as a citizen in 1755, Vernes pushed Rousseau to solve the problems facing the old republic. He called Rousseau the great instructor of humanity.[7] Divisions between magistrates and reformers beset Geneva. The former acknowledged the dominion of France in the affairs of the city and encouraged closer economic and political ties to their great neighbour. This strategy was eminently realistic given the growing strength of France in the region. It was also held to be paying immediate dividends in that the wealth of the city was rising while the magistrates, often investors in the French economy themselves, were respected at Versailles. The reformers' task was difficult since they had to develop an alternative future that would see the city maintain its reputation for austere morals, the protestant religion, political liberty, and commercial growth, which were held to be in jeopardy because of the policies of the magistrates; and all of this without alienating France. At the same time, concerns were expressed more generally about the fit between Protestantism and commerce, between republics and the imperial monarchies that surrounded them,

[4] Étienne Dumont to Samuel Romilly, Friday, 22 May 1789, ibid., 37–38 (Letter 7954): 'le regne de Voltaire est passé, excepté au Théatre. Rousseau s'eleve à mesure que l'autre s'abaisse. La postérité sera bien etonnée qu'on les ait regardé comme rivaux.'

[5] Dumont, 'Observations sur le caractère et les écrits de Rousseau', *Bibliothèque universelle de Genève. Nouvelle série* (Geneva and Paris, 1836), vol. 2, 128–135; 'Observations sur le style de J.-J. Rousseau', *Bibliothèque de Genève*, vol. 2, 298–313.

[6] Jacob Vernes to Jean Jacques Rousseau, July 1756: 'Vos lettres, cher philosophe, sont lues et dévorées par tous nos concitoyens.' *Correspondance complète*, vol. 4, 25–26 (Letter 417). Vernes became very close to Rousseau after the death of his wife: Jacob Vernes to Rousseau: Friday, 15 February 1760 in *Correspondance complète*, vol. 7, 37–39 (Letter 942).

[7] Jacob Vernes to Rousseau, 26 May 1761, Rousseau, *Correspondance complète*, vol. 8, 332–333 (Letter 1419): 'J'ai lu, il y a quelques jours, le Projet de Paix perpetuelle. Je crains bien, mon cher Ami, que la Musique françoise ne subsiste malgré votre Lettre, que les Sciences ne gatent les hommes malgré votre Discours, & que la guerre ne fasse ses ravages malgré votre Projet; mais enfin vous instruisés les hommes, & ce n'est pas votre faute s'ils ferment les oreilles à vos leçons.'

and between the existence of small states and modern political and economic trends. Within the Protestant community at Geneva, worries were expressed about the apparent vibrancy of Gallican Catholicism, about the capacity of Protestantism to support morality in a commercial world, and about the future of Calvinism itself.[8] Vernes was certain that Rousseau's vision of a moralised world made compatible with commerce and religion needed to be embraced; furthermore, it ought to be tested within the walls of Geneva by magistrates devoted to Rousseau's creed. Vernes at first believed that Rousseau was a Christian, and that his association of natural religion with Christianity could transform the world.[9] The Rousseau Vernes corresponded with was perceived by the latter to be a friend of the people. Rousseau was anticipated to become a mentor to advocates of democratic government in small states, being the only one to have found solutions to the problems of Protestant republics in modern times. Vernes fell out with Rousseau after the publication of the *Lettres écrites de la montagne*, which Vernes believed was critical of his own view of Christianity and of the Christian faith more generally. A split accompanied by far more vitriol followed because Rousseau was convinced that Vernes was the author of the *Sentiment du citoyen*, circulated in Geneva in early 1765, which revealed that the writer of *Emile* had abandoned his own children on the steps of the Paris foundling hospital. Despite the fact that proof that Voltaire had written it only came to light after Rousseau's death, Vernes retained a powerful sense of identification with Rousseau. Jacques-Pierre Brissot reported in 1782 on a visit to Geneva, that Vernes confessed to have sobbed on learning of Rousseau's death.[10] Brissot called Vernes a democrat, and perceived an affinity between Rousseau's religious politics and the democratic leanings of the *représentants*, in whose ranks Vernes was prominent.

A secularised version of Vernes' Rousseau, despite having few adherents among contemporary Genevans, has become the Rousseau most recognisable to scholars. In part because of the cult of Rousseau established in the French Revolution, and because of the widespread claim, these days most often associated with Benjamin Constant, that Rousseau's doctrines caused the Terror, the radical elements of Rousseau's politics are almost always to the fore.[11] Rousseau's cynical

[8] R. Whatmore, *Against War and Empire. Geneva, Britain and France in the Eighteenth Century* (New Haven and London: Yale University Press, 2012).

[9] Jacob Vernes to Rousseau, 21 July 1762, Rousseau, *Correspondance complète*, vol. 12, 76–78 (Letter 2018).

[10] Jacques-Pierre Brissot, *Mémoires*, ed. Claude Perroud (Paris: A. Picard & Fils, 1912), vol. 1, 277–279.

[11] See Jeremy Jenning's discussion of Rousseau and French liberalism in Chapter 4 of this volume.

perspective upon the contemporary world, and especially upon placemen, politeness, commerce, and public credit, ensured that those dissatisfied with the state of the present would turn to Rousseau for inspiration. When it comes to Rousseau's ideas about practical reform, however, a point that Rousseau made time and time again needs to be underscored. Almost every modern state could not avoid a turbulent destiny because of the forces unleashed by commerce and egoism. States like France were straightforwardly doomed, with a future certain to include social collapse and civil war. This did not mean, though, that revolutionary doctrines would solve the problems modern societies faced. As will be made clear in this chapter, Rousseau believed that radical politics at Geneva would only make things worse. The only states that had a chance of survival were those that had already turned their backs on the modern world. Rousseau was, therefore, a complicated figure for reformers, and especially those who were attracted to democratic politics or called themselves democrats.

This is made plain when Dumont's experience is considered. When Dumont became a leading figure within the Genevan diaspora that was established after the invasion of the city by French, Bernese, and Savoyard troops, he came into contact with *représentants* who were much more critical of Rousseau. One such was Etienne Clavière, the merchant and Genevan bourgeois agitator, who only ever referred to Rousseau's writings in an ad hoc fashion, deeming them to be largely irrelevant to his causes and interests.[12] Clavière had been one of those who turned to Voltaire rather than Rousseau for aid in the crisis of the late 1760s.[13] As a political economist who saw Adam Smith's *Wealth of Nations* as the best book written on the subject, Clavière had no time for Rousseau's critique of commercial society, and did not see any overlap between Rousseau's ideas and those of Smith.[14] François d'Ivernois was another prominent *représentant* who came to know Dumont in London in the late 1780s. A citizen of Geneva from a family that had long had strong ties with Rousseau, d'Ivernois inherited from his father and other *représentants* their voluminous correspondence with Rousseau during

[12] Clavière and Brissot, *De la France et des États-Unis* (London, 1787), 159; *De la foi publique envers les créanciers de l'Etat: lettres à M. Linguet sur le N° 116 de ses Annales* (London, 1789), 63.

[13] Jacob Vernes to Voltaire, 17 November 1768, Voltaire, *Correspondence and Related Documents: XXXIV: August 1768–May 1769, letters D15164–D15672*, 2nd ed., ed. Theodore Besterman, *Les Œuvres complètes de Voltaire*, 51 vols. (Geneva, Banbury & Oxford: Institut et Musée Voltaire & Voltaire Foundation, 1968–[ongoing]), vol. 34, 139–140 (Letter D15320).

[14] Clavière, *Opinions d'un créancier de l'état. Sur quelques matières de finance importantes dans le moment actuel* (Paris, 1789), 56, 90, 103.

the travails of the 1750s and 1760s. D'Ivernois took advantage of this – and other manuscripts he was granted access to by Marie Thérèse Levasseur and the friends to whom Rousseau had presented his manuscripts – and brought to the world the Geneva edition of Rousseau's works from 1782.[15] Detailed knowledge of Rousseau's private writings led d'Ivernois to the conclusion that the sage had loved peace more than liberty, and was no model for any reformist politician in the modern world. A third critic of Rousseau among Dumont's close friends and advocates of change at Geneva, although he was equally critical of the *représentants*, was Jacques Mallet du Pan, who ultimately blamed Rousseau's imprecision and over-general prophetic pronouncements for the political explosions in Paris and Geneva in the mid 1790s. As du Pan put it, 'The innocent blood which has been shed for these four years past spurts back upon, and attaints [Rousseau's] memory; and I fear not to tell his enthusiastic admirers, if any yet remain beyond the bloody limits of Paris, that he ought to be solemnly branded with public infamy, if the goodness of his intentions, and his inconsequential conclusions from his own principles, did not dictate to us some tenderness for his genius.'[16]

With such influences close at hand, Dumont might have been expected to reject Rousseau altogether as a traitor to the radical cause within their native city – the line that d'Ivernois took during the following decades. But Dumont, like other friends such as the Pastor Étienne Salomon Reybaz, always considered Rousseau to be worth taking seriously, and kept returning to Rousseau's books for sustenance during his own intellectual journey.[17] One example was described in Dumont's *Souvenirs sur Mirabeau*, where he recalled reading Rousseau's *Contrat Social* and *Considérations sur le gouvernement de Pologne* and giving Mirabeau the idea of graduated elections. Dumont advised forcing would-be legislators to serve in lower echelons of government, in the manner of the ranks of the armed forces, prior to standing for elections carrying significant national power. All of this was in order to prevent the worst excesses of democracy. Mirabeau embraced the idea, but was not sufficiently conversant in the minutiae of the Rousseau-Dumont proposal to repel the criticisms of

[15] François d'Ivernois to René Louis de Girardin, marquis de Girardin, 24 December 1779 in Rousseau, *Correspondance complète*, vol. 44, 121–122; d'Ivernois to *Journal de Paris*, 30 May 1779; no. 150, 602–603 in Rousseau, *Correspondance complète*, vol. 43, 300–301.

[16] Mallet du Pan, *Considerations on the Nature of the French Revolution: And on the Causes which Prolong Its Duration* (J. Owen, London, 1793), 8. Mallet continued, 'The English, who are far-advanced beyond the rest of Europe in political knowledge, always despised the *Social Contract.*'

[17] Étienne Salomon Reybaz to René Louis de Girardin, marquis de Girardin, 14 February 1779, in Rousseau, *Correspondance complète*, vol. 43, 141–144 (Letter 7475).

Antoine Barnave and other members of the National Assembly.[18] In his contribution to the book he wrote with Samuel Romilly and James Scarlett, the *Account of the Late Revolution in France*, Dumont also praised 'the masculine genius of Rousseau' for propagating important principles and for being prescient about the future of France.[19]

This chapter will not consider one of the central conundrums of late-eighteenth and early-nineteenth-century politics, the relationship between Rousseau and Bentham; rather, it will focus on some of the Genevan perspectives upon Rousseau in order to give substance to the claim that Rousseau was considered insufficiently democratic, and too obsessed by peace, in order to serve as inspiration for the reform-minded before and during the French Revolution. At the same time, Rousseau's writings could not be ignored by critics or reformers of any stamp.

## II

Rousseau's involvement with the Genevans from the late 1750s and into the 1760s has been well documented. Rousseau, through his friendship with the De Luc family, among others, was directly involved with the reformist cause within the city and gradually became associated with the longstanding critique of magistracy. The response of the magistrates was marked, condemning Rousseau's books and seeking to arrest him in 1762, and organising a campaign against Rousseau in which he was vilified as an enemy of Christianity and an advocate of anarchy. Rousseau became the bugbear of the critics of reform. They accused him of favouring 'pure democracy', the destruction of social order, and of plotting for equality and the abandonment of wealth. This line, said to be evident in all of Rousseau's works, but especially in the *Contrat social* and *Lettres écrites de la montagne*, was commonplace in anti-*représentant* tracts over the following decades. Rousseau had become a notorious rebel who had been hounded out of so many states that it was natural to tarnish the cause of reform at Geneva through his name. Isaac Cornuaud, perhaps the most vigorous and vitriolic opponent of the *représentants* in the 1780s, repeatedly invoked Rousseau to blacken the reputation of his enemies and to associate their politics with extremism.[20]

[18] Dumont, *Souvenirs sur Mirabeau et sur les deux premières assemblées législatives* (Paris, 1832), 238–240.

[19] Henry Frederic Groenvelt, [Dumont, Romilly and James Scarlett], *Letters Containing an Account of the Late Revolution in France* (London, 1792), 166, 176.

[20] Isaac Cornuaud, *Le natif interrogé, ou confession morali-politique d'un patriote* (Geneva, 5 April 1782), in Emile Rivoire, *Biographie historique de Genève au XVIIIie siècle*, 2 vols. (Geneva, 1897), vol. 1, 299 (entry 1899).

Significantly, Rousseau's response was not to embrace the reformist cause. Historians have not sufficiently appreciated this. Rather, Rousseau saw the reformers at Geneva as excessively democratic and made clear his opinion in the *Lettres écrites de la montagne*. His advice, over the three years between the publication of the *Lettres* and the settlement of the constitutional turmoil within the city, was to accept that nothing could be done about increasing French dominion. The reformers at Geneva had to accept the existing constitution and the status quo. Democratic rebellions would result in civil war and would then be crushed by France. This fact was problematic for the *représentants* because so many of them had believed Rousseau to be on their side. Many of the better informed tracts authored by the enemies of the *représentants* took pleasure in reminding their opponents of the fact that Rousseau had not been of their party. Rather, he had accepted that Geneva enjoyed an aristocratic government modelled on that of Venice. He had not only seen this to be of benefit to the state but had explicitly followed the argument that the existing form of government was the best possible for Geneva. While the *représentants* sought to dismantle the constitution ratified by France, Bern, and Zurich in 1738, Rousseau always declared himself in favour of it.[21]

Rousseau's stance was rejected by the reformist *représentants*, for whom he became a complicated figure. They drew upon his renown and associated him in general terms with their cause, while making clear that they were not following his political prescriptions. Rousseau the martyr unfairly oppressed by the magistrates at Geneva was the oft-relayed message. Some of the *représentants* continued into the late 1760s to turn to Rousseau for advice in the hope that he would come closer to their position. But in his letters to the leaders of the movement he clung to the position he had articulated in the *Lettres écrites de la montagne*, that they had no chance of standing against France and had no possibility of creating a better future for Geneva without working out means of replacing both the magistrates and the influence of France in Genevan counsels. The reformers at Geneva were utopian dreamers. In his correspondence with the pastor Paul Moultou, to whom Rousseau was especially close during these years, he ridiculed *représentant* politics for being naïve and impractical.

Recognising that Rousseau was not a natural friend to them, the new generation of *représentants* who began to lead the movement after 1767, many of whose fathers had associated with Rousseau in the 1750s and

[21] Anon., *Adresse des membres constitutionnaires du magnifique conseil des deux-cent, au magnifique petit-conseil, présentée aux seigneurs syndics Le 24 Février 1780* ([Geneva], 1780), 22, 42.

1760s, responded to Rousseau's work in a different manner. A case in point is François d'Ivernois, the young lawyer who became increasingly prominent within the *représentant* movement from the late 1770s. In his writings, d'Ivernois condemned the magistrates for their behaviour towards Rousseau and described Rousseau as a victim of a grotesque violation of liberty and law. D'Ivernois called himself a democrat. While he argued that democracy in a pure form was suited to states based on agriculture and arms, in which citizens laboured on the soil and fought to defend the state, in a commercial society a tempered form of democracy was necessary.[22] It had to be based on a distinction between sovereignty and government. This was not derived from Rousseau's *Contrat social*, but was rather a product of domestic discussion of the relationship between the small and large councils of state within Geneva. Rousseau had justified aristocratic government in the *Contrat social;* this was exactly what d'Ivernois wanted to avoid. He warned the French foreign minister Vergennes that while aristocracy might be suited to large monarchies like France, it would always destroy a small commercial city.[23] The need to avoid the establishment of aristocracy meant it was necessary to elect magistrates at Geneva annually. The General Council of citizens also had to consent to every new law proposed to them by the small councils every year, once again in order to prevent aristocrats from emerging. D'Ivernois did not go to Rousseau for such arguments, but rather drew on longstanding concerns about the establishment of aristocratic government at Geneva, which was in his view on the verge of destroying Calvinism, commerce, and liberty. As long as the magistrates at Geneva had the support of France, d'Ivernois was concerned that the *représentants* could do little to combat them. His attempt to persuade the French of the benefits of tempered democracy in small republics came to nothing.

In the aftermath of this failure, d'Ivernois, like all of the younger generation of reformers, had to combat the French destruction of democracy at Geneva, which meant the French assault, culminating in 1782, upon a constitution which they believed had been stable since the

[22] D'Ivernois, *Lettre à son Excellence Monsieur le Comte de Vergennes* ([Geneva], 3 November 1780), 6: 'La pure Démocratie pouvoit être un régime salubre pour les Genevois, tant qu'ils ne formerent qu'une société d'agriculteurs & de soldats, uniquement occupés de leur défense; mais il ne pouvoit plus convenir à une société tranquille, industrieuse & commerçante, & il fallut le tempérer, quand la paix, cimentée au-dehors, nous eut forcé à chercher dans notre activité les ressources que nous refussoit notre local. Les richesses & l'instruction publique furent les fruits de ce développement d'industrie, & l'on en vit bientôt résulter, au milieu de nous, les talens de l'ambition & les vertus de l'égalité.'

[23] D'Ivernois, *Lettre à son Excellence Monsieur le Comte de Vergennes*, 10: 'Une sage Aristocratie peut convenir à de grands États; mais son poids seroit insupportable dans une petite Ville où l'on ne rencontre que des Négocians & des Artistes.'

Reformation because 'almost every member of the community has, and any member of it may easily have, a share in the Government'.[24] By this time Rousseau was seen to have become an opponent of the cause of liberty rather than a source of arguments to sustain it. In composing the *Lettres écrites de la montagne*, Rousseau had written a book that 'deserved to be admired for its general principles, and the closeness of its reasoning'. At the same time, however, it erred in 'circumstantial details, because he was not in possession of particular facts'.[25] In short, Rousseau was no guide to the problems of Geneva because he did not understand the nature of the civil war within the city nor the nature of the democratic constitution that the reformers were defending. Rousseau's ignorance was confirmed when d'Ivernois's father, François-Henri, obtained Rousseau's verdict upon the increasingly violent struggles of 1767. Rousseau then advised the *représentants* to leave Geneva to 'seek liberty under another climate', on the grounds that it had been 'lost to their country'. D'Ivernois called this 'timid advice' and stated that 'fortunately it did not prevail'. Furthermore, he printed Rousseau's letter in a note to the text.[26] D'Ivernois also made explicit Rousseau's non-involvement in the struggles of the reformers within the republic leading up to the partial settlement of 1768, stating that 'I have not spoken of Rousseau since his abdication, because he took no share whatever in the duration of the troubles.' Rather than supporting the reform cause, Rousseau, from 1765, had 'exerted all his persuasion to induce [the *représentants*] to yield to the force that threatened them'. Abandoning Geneva, d'Ivernois claimed that Rousseau 'retired to England, to forget the injustice of his country, and to hear of her misfortunes no more'. In correspondence with the older d'Ivernois, however, and as confirmed by the printed letter, Rousseau 'often bewailed the fate of his fellow

[24] D'Ivernois, *A Short Account of the Late Revolution in Geneva, and of the Conduct of France towards That Republic, from October 1792, to October 1794: In a Series of Letters to an American* (London: T. Spilbury and Son, 1795), 3.

[25] D'Ivernois, *Tableau historique et politique des révolutions de Genève dans le dix-huitième siècle* (Geneva, 1782), 193.

[26] D'Ivernois, *Tableau historique et politique*, 393. The offending passage, from the letter Rousseau sent to François-Henri d'Ivernois on 29 January 1768, read: 'Oui, Messieurs, il vous reste dans le cas que je suppose un dernier parti à prendre, et c'est j'ose le dire, le seul qui soit digne de vous: c'est, au lieu de souiller vos mains dans le sang de vos compatriotes, de leur abandonner ces murs qui devoient être l'azile de la liberté et qui vont n'être plus qu'un repaire de tirans. C'est d'en sortir tous, tous ensemble, en plein jour, vos femmes et vos enfans au milieu de vous, et puisqu'il faut porter des fers, d'aller porter du moins ceux de quelque Grand Prince, et non pas l'insupportable et odieux joug de vos égaux. Et ne vous imaginez pas qu'en pareil cas vous resteriez sans azile: vous ne savez pas quelle estime et quel respect votre courage, votre moderation, votre sagesse ont inspiré pour vous dans toute l'Europe': Rousseau, *Correspondance complète*, vol. 35, 62–65 (Letter 6225).

citizens'. This drew the ire of d'Ivernois, who attacked Rousseau for preferring peace to liberty:

Unfortunate man! Instead of fanning the fire of discord amongst them, an imputation he did not escape, he employed in his correspondence with d'Ivernois all the arts of eloquence and friendship to persuade the *représentants* that tranquillity was yet more precious than liberty, and that they ought to think themselves happy to purchase peace by any sacrifice.[27]

The view that Rousseau's politics were ill suited to addressing the problems of Geneva was reiterated in d'Ivernois's later work. In 1789, he noted that the inspiration for the *représentants* of the 1780s had been the Pastor Reybaz's *Défense Apologétique*, published on 10 November 1779, the style of which was as good as Rousseau's and the substance clearly superior.[28] But d'Ivernois's focus altered significantly with the advent of the French Revolution. He began to praise Rousseau in his letters.[29] Rousseau was henceforth an ally in the war against the Revolution. The image of Rousseau the lover of peace was then used to taunt the violent revolutionaries at Paris who were making a cult of the Genevan sage. D'Ivernois, like so many who considered themselves to be committed republicans and democrats at Geneva, were altogether opposed to the attempts to turn France into a democratic republic. For d'Ivernois, the republican movement in France was a smokescreen for imperial designs on surrounding states. From this perspective, the Revolution was altogether continuous with the policies of Vergennes, the French foreign minister under Louis XVI who had been responsible for the invasion of 1782 and the destruction of the *représentants* within the city. Associating Rousseau with the French Revolution was, in d'Ivernois's view, entirely bogus. As he put it in a further defence of the reform movement at Geneva, which contrasted sharply with the ideas of the Girondins at Paris, the French idolisation of the memory of Rousseau was an affectation. For Rousseau, it had become clear in the 1760s that 'the most perfect

[27] D'Ivernois, *Tableau historique et politique des deux dernieres révolutions de Genève* (London, 1789), 162, translated as *An Historical and Political View of the Constitution and Revolutions of Geneva* (London: T. Cadell, 1784), 177, 330–331.

[28] D'Ivernois, *Tableau historique*, 162: 'Cette premiere *défense apologétique*, & celle qui la suivit sous le même titre, sont infiniment supérieures à tout ce qui s'est écrit sur la Constitution de Genève, & ne le cèdent en rien, pas même pour le style, aux *Lettres de la Montagne* de J-J. Rousseau. Dans tous les tems elles seront dignes de servir de modèles aux peuples libres, assez malheureux pour avoir à plaider la défense de leurs droits, & assez sages pour ne vouloir y employer que les armes de la raison & du sentiment. Le Ministre *Reybaz* était l'auteur de ces deux chefs-d'œuvre.'

[29] François d'Ivernois to Pierre Alexandre Du Peyrou, 13 December 1789 in Rousseau, *Correspondance complète*, vol. 46, 128–131 (Letter 7987).

liberty is dearly purchased by the effusion of a single drop of blood'. By contrast, violence and bloodshed were the watchwords of the revolutionaries, and the symbol of liberty and progress. D'Ivernois asked, 'What would [Rousseau] have thought of his worshippers, had he lived to see the object of his greatest reverence and most affectionate attachment, made the first sacrifice on the bloody altars of a system of which they call him the author?'[30]

It was also the case that the equality vaunted in Paris as the fount of democratic politics was the antithesis of the Genevan practice Rousseau lauded. Genevan politics rested upon an explicit social hierarchy that established gradations of political involvement. It precluded ordinary people from direct involvement in politics, in order to prevent demagoguery. Like Dumont, and following the argument of Rousseau, d'Ivernois was convinced that democracy necessitated a graduated politics in which only those who were sufficiently enlightened to govern were able to stand for election. In violating this principle, the French, and the Genevans who followed them, were making sure that disorder and the rule of the demagogue would follow.[31] D'Ivernois made the argument that Rousseau too had made. The politics of small states were altogether different to those of large states, and that in confusing the two, and applying what worked in small states to 'a great empire', the French were behaving in a politically stupid fashion.[32] Rousseau was henceforth employed to attack the revolutionaries who claimed to be inspired by his works and deeds. Rousseau had predicted that if they achieved power, the French *philosophes* would be more intolerant than any priest, d'Ivernois claimed, and exactly this was being proven by the events at Paris in the mid 1790s.[33] In short, Rousseau's arguments against democracy were being employed to condemn revolutionary activity across Europe.

[30] D'Ivernois, *A Short Account*, 3.

[31] D'Ivernois, *La Révolution française à Genève: tableau historique et politique de la conduite de la France envers les Genevois* (London, 1795), 149: 'La Convention Genevoise rejeta avec mépris toutes ces gradations qu'avaient établies nos loix antiques & répétant en chorus avec les Révolutionnaires Français que le patriotisme valait mieux que les lumières.'

[32] D'Ivernois, *La Révolution française*, 150, 165–166.

[33] D'Ivernois, *Histoire de l'administration des finances de la république française pendant l'année 1796* (London, 1797), 2nd ed., 154. The way that d'Ivernois used Rousseau is illustrated by a later comment upon Napoleonic centralisation: 'Combien est devenu juste ce mot exagéré de Rousseau: Je ne vois pas élever à Paris un palais qui ne me signale quelque province tombant en ruine': *Napoléon administrateur et financier; pour faire suite au Tableau historique et politique des pertes que la Révolution et la guerre ont causees au peuple Français* (London, 1812), 242.

## III

In the aftermath of the French Revolution, and with the establishment of the First French Empire firmly in mind, attitudes among the Genevans to Rousseau altered once again. The association of democracy at Paris with Terror, combined with the successive failures of republican constitutions to establish domestic stability, made political scepticism rife. In such circumstances, Dumont and many other Genevans were attracted by the creation of social sciences that might operate independently of political controversy. This is what inspired his turn to Benthamism from the middle of the revolutionary decade. As he put it in his letter to the editors of the *Bibliothèque britannique* of 1797, Bentham alone had established a science of legislation separate from the discussion of forms of government, the irresolvable issue that had caused such dreadful upheaval in civil life across the European mainland. This made Bentham the most important philosopher of the age, and a potential antidote to revolutionary doctrine everywhere.[34] In turn, this caused Dumont to develop a different view of Rousseau. The surest evidence for this comes from two essays written about Rousseau that were posthumously published in 1836 in the *Bibliothèque de Genève*. The first essay, 'Observations sur le caractère et les écrits de Rousseau', addressed the question of Rousseau's personality and view of the world; the second essay, 'Observations sur le style de J.-J. Rousseau', dealt with Rousseau's identity as a writer. The dating of the essays is altogether uncertain. Dumont may have written them at the same time as he was most intimately engaged with Bentham's first manuscripts. At the same time, the lofty tone of the essays would indicate that Dumont was writing in the 1820s, and passing a final judgement upon Rousseau after a lifetime of engagement with his writings.

Dumont made clear in the 'Observations sur le style de J.-J. Rousseau' that he was intimately acquainted with all of Rousseau's works in addition to his letters. He considered Rousseau to be the greatest of modern writers. Parts of Rousseau's works, such as the 'Confession de foi du vicaire savoyard' in *Emile*, he considered impossible to better. Dumont stated that Rousseau had most admired Tacitus, Tasso, and Racine, although his acknowledged literary master was Diderot, whose *Pensées philosophiques* Rousseau had scrutinised with singular care. In Dumont's

[34] Dumont, 'Lettre aux rédacteurs du Bibliothèque britannique sur les ouvrages de Bentham', *Bibliothèque britannique*, ed. Marc-Auguste Pictet, Charles Pictet de Rochemont, and Frédéric Guillaume Maurice (Geneva, 1797), vol. 5, 155–164; 'Principes du Code Civil après les manuscrits de Jeremy Bentham', *Bibliothèque britannique*, vol. 5, 277–302, vol. 6, 4–25.

opinion Rousseau the pupil had far surpassed his teacher. Like so many other writers of the first rank – Dumont named Plato, Cicero, Bossuet, Fénelon, Burke, and Buffon – Rousseau had combined clarity with colour and force of argument. But the purpose of Dumont's essay was to identify Rousseau's particular characteristics. The first Dumont found was that Rousseau had laboured over every line that he had written. While Voltaire 'found pleasure in writing', even a letter by Rousseau 'was a work in itself'. Rousseau took pains to avoid rhetoric in his utterances. Yet his writing was full of assertions, 'abandoning a cold and impartial manner of reasoning and throwing himself into the most passionate style'. This weakened the coherence of Rousseau's claims; Dumont noted that 'Turgot appears to me to be very much Rousseau's superior when it comes to philosophical discussion.' The best of Rousseau's writing lay in his descriptions of people and places, so that the reader was transported into a particular setting, and altogether convinced by the argument that accompanied the depiction. Dumont gave examples of the condemnation of Epicureanism through a portrait of a person adhering to such a philosophy, and of the collapse of the simple and virtuous life that would follow the introduction of a theatre at Geneva. Rousseau convinced because he illustrated exactly the evils that followed from a specific course of action. The reader saw the future in the portrait Rousseau painted. In describing nature, Dumont stated that Rousseau was the equal of Milton. The key was that in arguing in favour of a moral maxim, Rousseau sought to illustrate it in action, such that it was forever graven on the heart of the reader. His achievement was to have combined the advocacy of austere Spartan morals with a sense of gentler and more substantial life that would result from adhering to them.[35] Rousseau had to be taken seriously as a literary giant. The tragedy lay in the fact that what he was advocating was, in Dumont's eyes, altogether unpalatable.

Dumont gave his verdict upon Rousseau's message for the moderns in the 'Observations sur le caractère et les écrits de Rousseau'. In Dumont's view, Rousseau had launched a more devastating attack upon social institutions than any other person. Rousseau had described and decried the loss of liberty and equality in modern times. He had deployed the voice of nature to reveal the extent to which the moderns lived at odds with the natural world, which was at once more real and profound. In doing so, he straightforwardly assaulted contemporary manners,

[35] Dumont, 'Observations sur le style de Rousseau', 311: 'Fénelon est presque toujours tendre, il manque d'énergie; Labruyère est presque toujours amer, il est dépourvu de sensibilité. Rousseau semble avoir combiné deux qualités opposées avec plus d'art qu'aucun écrivain. Il en a tire des effets surprenants; c'est en lui l'humanité qui s'irrite, et l'austérité qui s'attendrit.'

calling them fake and listing their abominable consequences for the individual and for society. Rousseau's ideas justified an extreme form of democracy, because he called only such a state free. Following the logic of his own general argument, Rousseau condemned all of the existing states of the earth. For Dumont, such arguments amounted to 'more declamation than philosophy'. Rousseau's 'exaggerated opinions' had produced 'no positive good' in the world, were 'irreconcilable with the constitution of humanity', and 'truly destructive of all government'. In imbibing Rousseau's philosophy, the minds of a large number of persons had been ruined. The exception to this rule was the work where Rousseau 'returned to the actual world', in Dumont's opinion. The best concerned the government of Poland, which was unlike his more general works in recognising that reform 'can only take place by degrees'.

It was evident in the 'Observations' that Dumont blamed Rousseau for the horrors of the French Revolution. Rousseau had unleashed a form of republican pride that was uncompromising and ultimately demanded the abolition of ranks, the removal of kings, and the rejection of any ethic associated with honour on the grounds that it smacked of aristocratic baseness. Rousseau had been so remarkable a writer that he had convinced his readers to embrace a revolutionary philosophy. He had given the masses hope that there might be justice in this world, by shattering the icons of nobility and monarchy. Dumont believed that Rousseau's writings conveyed the possibility of an alternative future in which people became independent of all of the shackles imposed by social hierarchies and all of the corruption associated with commerce and luxury. Those who followed Rousseau's script would begin to see themselves as beings more profound, more honest, and more admirable. Rousseau demanded no less than the transformation of the self, involving an absolute dedication to the pursuit of the virtues associated with equality. Dumont recognised that raising the possibility of a world transformed had enormous appeal among the large numbers who lived under the yoke of a ruling class:[36]

> The fierce sentiment of equality which breathes through all of his writings, this hatred towards the dominant classes of society, made the multitudes respond to Rousseau, sensing in his writings the possibility of vengeance on behalf of the people, and the reparation of the ruins of human nature.

Although Rousseau had been true to his own vision, Dumont was convinced that his philosophy, rather than providing an alternative manner of

[36] On this aspect of Rousseau's appeal in Latin America, see Nicola Miller's discussion in Chapter 7 of this volume.

living, amounted simply to the restoration of the republics of the ancient world. In other words, the world transformed towards equality was not a new or altered world, but resurrected and transposed from altogether different times to the present. Dumont was withering in his criticism of such advocacy.

Rousseau's first failing as a political writer, according to Dumont, was that he greatly exaggerated the qualities of the ancients. He saw their republics as 'a species of epic poem'. He described the life lived in the ancient republics as one which enhanced human nature. Sparta, although a dual monarchy, was the exemplar of ancient republican values. By contrast, the moderns were 'shadows and pigmies'. All of this was so much balderdash for Dumont. There was no evidence that human nature had been different in the ancient world. The same problems bedevilled ancient as well as modern states. No golden age or utopia could be found by looking backwards. Yet Rousseau's writing style was so attractive that the young especially had been entranced by his portrayal of what Dumont called 'an imaginary republic'. Rousseau had made youth feel that they could undertake great deeds, become more independent and more profound as individuals, and contribute to the magnificent goal of restoring ancient liberty and equality. The urge to light a republican flame that represented true liberty was the central cause of the French Revolution, according to Dumont. The duty to change the world had been called such a noble cause by Rousseau that those who took it upon themselves to follow his lead were free to ignore all of the petty and major crimes that accompanied the reacquisition of liberty. This meant that they felt no guilt when they participated in the Terror. Unlike Bentham, the philosopher of the real and the practical who articulated an alternative future and described exactly how to create it, Rousseau had been a fool. His politics had been impractical and dangerous. He had been a republican who did not know how to create a republic.

Dumont's verdict on Rousseau had moved very far from the expectations of the first generation of *représentants*, for whom Rousseau might have maintained the liberty of Geneva where so many others had failed. By contrast, Dumont's verdict was almost as harsh as that of Rousseau's enemies among the magistrates. If Dumont venerated Rousseau as a writer, he agreed with Rousseau's enemies about the consequences of his politics. Indeed, if the Dumont of the 'Observations' was transported back to 1762, when *Emile* and the *Contrat social* had been condemned at Geneva for being destructive of social order and government, he might have supported the actions of the magistrates and gone against *représentants* who wanted to turn the burning of Rousseau's books into a *cause célèbre*. The irony was that Rousseau himself had attacked the very doctrines espoused by the younger Dumont and his fellow *représentants*. In Rousseau's letters to friends of the late 1760s he warned that democratic ideas at Geneva would result in war, death, and extremism. For Dumont, however, to remain devoted to maintaining liberty in small republics like Geneva entailed steering clear of all of Rousseau's best-known books. In his effort to influence the new constitution after Geneva became a canton in 1815, and to create penal and civil laws compatible with republican liberty and manners, Dumont turned to Bentham rather than to Rousseau.

# 2 Adrastus versus Diogenes

## Frederick the Great and Jean-Jacques Rousseau on self-love

*Avi Lifschitz*

A portrait of Frederick the Great adorned Jean-Jacques Rousseau's study at Montmorency. It stood on his desk, accompanied by the epithet: 'He thinks as a philosopher, and behaves like a king' (*Il pense en philosophe, et se conduit en Roi*). Yet before Rousseau's guests could be duly impressed by this potentially laudatory sentence, most of them were treated to the complementary rhyming line, inscribed on the back of Frederick's portrait: 'Glory, self-interest – that is his God, his law' (*La gloire, l'intérêt, voilà son Dieu, sa loi*).[1] This couplet, which Rousseau feared would cost him a desired asylum in Prussian-ruled Neuchâtel, testifies to the crucial role of self-regarding notions in the largely unconsummated intellectual relationship between the Genevan author and the Prussian king.

By contrast to the widely advertised collaboration between Frederick the Great and Voltaire, the king's attitude towards Rousseau has not been the focus of much scholarly attention.[2] Indeed, in this case one can find neither a close alliance nor an enduring mutual appreciation. Yet several of Frederick's philosophical works and his correspondence betray a long-lasting preoccupation with the themes discussed by Rousseau in the 1750s. The Genevan, for his part, had already become captivated by

Helpful comments on earlier versions of this chapter were provided by audiences at a conference on Frederick the Great and the Republic of Letters at Jesus College, Oxford, in July 2012 (organised by Katrin Kohl and Thomas Biskup) and at the fellows' seminar at Lichtenberg-Kolleg, the Göttingen Institute for Advanced Study (November 2014).

1 Jean-Jacques Rousseau, *The Confessions and Correspondence (The Collected Writings of Rousseau*, vol. 5), ed. Christopher Kelly, Roger D. Masters, and Peter D. Stillman (Hanover, NH: University Press of New England, 1995), Book 12, 496; *OC* I, 592–593.

2 Emil du Bois-Reymond saw them in the late nineteenth as paragons of an outdated Gallo-Roman classicism (Frederick) and a new form of Romantic literature (Rousseau): Du Bois-Reymond, *Über das Nationalgefühl; Friedrich II. und Jean-Jacuqes Rousseau* (Berlin: Dümmler, 1879), 33–86. A recent essay by Jörn Sack, *Friedrich der Grosse und Jean-Jacques Rousseau – Eine verfehlte Beziehung und die Folgen* (Berlin: Berliner Wissenschaftsverlag, 2011), erects a largely conjectural edifice on the basis of the few known facts, while misrepresenting Rousseau as a founding father of parliamentary liberalism.

Frederick's public persona in his youth.[3] Both Frederick and Rousseau were, moreover, among the most effective masters of public self-fashioning in the eighteenth century.

Though our protagonists never met one another, their mutual fascination reached its peak in 1762 in their indirect correspondence through George Keith, the Jacobite governor of Neuchâtel on Frederick's behalf, when Rousseau sought refuge in the Prussian enclave. Thereafter, well into the 1770s, Frederick continued to tackle the themes that had preoccupied Rousseau. He was acquainted with the renowned discourses Rousseau wrote for the Academy of Dijon, although there is no conclusive evidence of the king's sustained engagement with Rousseau's later works. To a large extent, Frederick's interest in Rousseau's works fits the more general pattern of his involvement with contemporary French philosophy. After the end of the Seven Years War, his interest in and enthusiasm for contemporary French authors gradually waned.

Given Frederick's engagement with the main themes of Rousseau's early career, this chapter focuses on the problematic notion of self-love, or *amour propre*. Self-love is not only a major theme in the *Discourse on Inequality* (*Second Discourse*, 1755), but also in the preceding *Discourse on the Arts and the Sciences* (*First Discourse*, 1750), where Rousseau traced the origins of different scholarly pursuits back to hubris and the desire for self-promotion.[4] The notion of self-love, with its background in various strands of ancient and early modern Epicureanism and Stoicism, is particularly salient in Frederick's correspondence with George Keith and in the king's essays on the topics highlighted in Rousseau's discourses: the *Essay on Self-Love as an Ethical Principle* (1770) and *Discourse on the Usefulness of the Sciences and the Arts within a State* (1772). These items are closely linked to what Frederick saw as the defining features of human nature and the sort of happiness available to human beings in this world.

Over the last generation self-love, or *amour propre*, has increasingly come to the fore as the unifying thread running through Rousseau's different works, mainly due to a new approach to this thorny term (suggested in Nicholas Dent's 1988 interpretation of Rousseau and elaborated in Frederick Neuhouser's more recent book of 2008).[5] Self-love is

[3] Rousseau, *Confessions*, Book 5, 179; *OC* I, 214.

[4] Jean-Jacques Rousseau, 'Discourse on the Sciences and Arts', in *DI*, 1–28; here 16; 'Discours sur les sciences et les arts', in *OC* III, 1–30 (17–18).

[5] N. J. H. Dent, *Rousseau: An Introduction to His Psychological, Social and Political Theory* (Oxford: Blackwell, 1988), esp. 52–56, 143–145; Frederick Neuhouser, *Rousseau's Theodicy of Self-love: Evil, Rationality, and the Drive for Recognition* (Oxford: Oxford University Press, 2008). For an overview of the changing views on the unifying core of Rousseau's philosophy, see particularly the contributions to this volume by Axel Honneth (Chapter 11), Christopher Brooke (Chapter 8), and Céline Spector (Chapter 9).

indeed a key term in Rousseau's various writings, linked as it is to the origins of social interaction especially through the wish for mutual recognition. Traditionally, it had been common to emphasise Rousseau's strict distinction in the *Discourse on Inequality* between *amour de soi-même*, a benign care of the self or basic self-preservation – which he deemed one of the essential characteristics of the man of nature – and the inflamed, socially generated *amour propre*, seen as an excessive drive for recognition and domination. According to the *Discourse on Inequality*, while the former was a natural instinct leading both animals and human beings to care for their self-preservation, '*amour propre* is only a relative sentiment, factitious, and born in society, which inclines every individual to set greater store by himself than by anyone else, inspires men with all the evils they do one another, and is the genuine source of honour'.[6] Since Rousseau's state of nature is pre-social and pre-political, self-love in its negative guise could not have been present there. As he noted more rhetorically towards the end of the *Discourse on Inequality*: 'The Savage lives within himself; sociable man, always outside himself, is capable of living only in the mind of others and, so to speak, derives the sentiment of his own existence solely from their judgment'.[7] Indeed, self-love as the constant need for recognition by others, a competitive zero-sum game, had already been recognised by Hobbes as a major characteristic of human beings in the absence of natural sociability.[8]

Yet, as Dent has suggested, one can distinguish not only between *amour de soi-même* and *amour propre* in Rousseau's works, but also between two different kinds of *amour propre* itself: its basic form as a natural need for recognition which accords others the acknowledgement one seeks for oneself, and its corrupt version, consisting in a malignant desire for preference over others. Following Dent, Neuhouser examined Rousseau's use of self-love in its positive version, especially in *Emile* (1762), by contrast to its inflamed appearance in the *Discourse on Inequality*. These changes in Rousseau's use of the term *amour propre* have also been highlighted by Christopher Brooke, who has argued that Rousseau's initial Epicurean approach to self-love in the *Discourse on Inequality* was tempered by Stoic impulses in later works, most manifestly

[6] Rousseau, 'Discourse on the origin and foundations of inequality among men', in *DI*, 111–222, here 218 (Note XV); 'Discours sur l'origine et les fondemens de l'inégalité parmi les hommes', in *OC* III, 109–223 (219).

[7] Rousseau, *DI*, 187; *OC* III, 193.

[8] On this notion in Hobbes see, recently, Philip Pettit, *Made with Words: Hobbes on Language, Mind, and Politics* (Princeton, NJ: Princeton University Press, 2008); István Hont, *Politics in Commercial Society: Jean-Jacques Rousseau and Adam Smith*, ed. Béla Kapossy and Michael Sonenscher (Cambridge, MA: Harvard University Press, 2015), 6–12.

in *Emile*.[9] Drawing on this new interpretative framework concerning self-love, I shall try to situate Frederick's views on the interaction between the care of the self and the common good against the background of Rousseau's works, and conclude with a discussion of the synthesis between Epicureanism and Stoicism that underlay much of the king's *œuvre*.

## The Môtiers triangle: Rousseau, Keith, Frederick

The distant relationship between Rousseau and Frederick the Great intensified in 1762 when Rousseau asked for Frederick's protection in Môtiers, within the territory of Neuchâtel. Following the uproar, censure, and official ban provoked by his publications of the same year, the *Social Contract* and *Emile*, Rousseau saw Neuchâtel – sufficiently close to Geneva and France, yet governed by Brandenburg-Prussia – as a viable refuge. In the *Confessions*, Rousseau related his hope that Frederick would grant him asylum despite the mocking couplet on his portrait; Rousseau was certain that Frederick had heard of it through his Parisian correspondents. A second problem was Rousseau's unflattering if indirect reference to Frederick in his recently published *Emile*. In Book V, the protagonist Emile reads Fénelon's *Télémaque* with his tutor while discussing international relations and various arrangements of civil society. In this context, the tutor mentions that Adrastus, the bellicose and treacherous king of the Daunians in Fénelon's novel, could be identified in present-day Europe; this was probably a reference to the Silesian Wars of the 1740s and the still raging Seven Years War, in which Frederick played a major role. The barely concealed allusion to the Prussian king would not have been lost on most contemporary readers. Though the tutor immediately adds that links between the novel and contemporary Europe are 'invidious comparisons that the author himself dismisses or makes in spite of himself', Rousseau's retelling of the Môtiers episode in his *Confessions* makes it clear that this comparison was precisely and deliberately intended. To make things worse, the subsequent paragraph is a much more explicit attack on eighteenth-century kingship, following a rhetorical dissociation of Emile from Fénelon's princely protagonist, Telemachus:

[9] Christopher Brooke, *Philosophic Pride: Stoicism and Political Thought from Lipsius to Rousseau* (Princeton, NJ: Princeton University Press, 2012), 183–202. See also John Rawls's view that *amour propre*, prior to its corruption, made it possible to reconcile self-interest and justice: Rawls, *Lectures on the History of Political Philosophy*, ed. S. Freeman (Cambridge, MA: Harvard University Press, 2007), 198–200; cf. Céline Spector's contribution to the present book (Chapter 9).

Emile does not travel as an idle man, and he does more good than if he were a prince. If we were kings, we would no longer be beneficent. If we were kings and were beneficent, we would do countless real evils without knowing it for the sake of an apparent good that we believed we were doing. If we were kings and were wise, the first good thing that we would want to do for ourselves and others would be to abdicate our royal position and become again what we are.[10]

Retrospectively, having been granted asylum by a king who was much more concerned with the ongoing Seven Years War than with philosophical squabbles, Rousseau changed the royal comparison. In the *Confessions*, he recast himself as another ancient hero, Coriolanus, exiled from Rome and looking for refuge among his erstwhile enemies, the Volscians. Arguing he knew all along that Frederick's generosity would not disappoint him, Rousseau exclaimed: 'When Jean-Jacques raises himself up next to Coriolanus, will Frederick be beneath the General of the Volscians?'[11] In fact, the situation in 1762 was much more prosaic. Frederick granted Rousseau asylum fairly easily, as he had done in the case of La Mettrie and other authors whose views he did not necessarily share. While the protection of Rousseau cost Prussia next to nothing, this magnanimous gesture towards the renowned Citizen of Geneva enhanced Frederick's carefully managed credentials as a philosophically inclined king and an enemy of religious persecution. Indeed, d'Alembert subsequently argued that Frederick was glad to strike a pose against the Protestant clergymen who attacked Rousseau's publications in Geneva and beyond.[12] Furthermore, it was a unique opportunity for the self-fashioned philosopher-king to prove that his own monarchy was much more tolerant and clement than Rousseau's republican *patria*.

While in Môtiers, Rousseau forged a close friendship with the Scottish Jacobite exile George Keith (the tenth Earl Marischal), governor of Neuchâtel and one of Frederick's most trusted companions. Rousseau regarded this fellow exile as a father figure; Keith became the mediator between Frederick and Rousseau, transmitting their views and requests in both directions. Approving Rousseau's request of asylum, Frederick also

[10] Rousseau, *Emile, or on Education*, trans. and ed. Allan Bloom (New York: Basic Books, 1979), Book V, 467; *OC* IV, 849. Cf. Rousseau's *Confessions*, Book 12, 496; *OC* I, 593. See also Rousseau's critical comments on monarchs in the *Social Contract* of 1762 (*SC* 96–98; *OC* III, 409–411). On the role of Fénelon's *Télémaque* in Frederick's education, see Ernst Bratuscheck, *Die Erziehung Friedrichs des Großen* (Berlin: Georg Reimer, 1885), 27–28; Eduard Spranger, *Der Philosoph von Sanssouci*, 2nd edition (Heidelberg: Quelle & Meyer, 1962), 29–30.

[11] Rousseau, *Confessions*, Book 12, 497; *OC* I, 593.

[12] Jean le Rond d'Alembert, *Éloge de Milord Maréchal* (Paris: Libraires Associés, 1779), 68–75.

proposed to provide the fugitive with an allowance. He noted that if Prussia had not been ruined by the contemporary war, he would have built Rousseau a hermitage with a garden where the Genevan could re-enact the state of nature. Yet Rousseau 'would never persuade me to graze the grass and walk on all fours', Frederick added, replicating Voltaire's misrepresentation of the argument of the *Discourse on Inequality*.[13] Keith augmented Frederick's offer with corn, grain, and other supplies, which Rousseau resolutely declined in a letter to Frederick:

> You wish to give me bread; is none of your subjects in need of it? Take away from my eyes that sword which dazzles and wounds me; it has done only too much of its duty, and the royal sceptre is abandoned. There is a grand career in wait for kings of your mettle, and you are still far from its end; nevertheless time is running out, and even a spare moment is not left for you to proceed towards the goal. If I could see Frederick the just and the dreaded covering his lands with a numerous populace and becoming their father, then J.-J. Rousseau, the enemy of kings, will come to die at the foot of his throne.[14]

While paying tribute to his benefactor, Rousseau unapologetically uses here the same anti-monarchical language he employed in *Emile*, and for the same reasons. On both occasions, before and after finding refuge in Neuchâtel, Rousseau charged Frederick with extreme bellicosity, grounded in excessive self-love and a pathological pursuit of glory which undermined not only the European peace but also the domestic welfare of Prussia itself. Rousseau's allusion here is to the ancient Cynic philosopher Diogenes of Sinope, who allegedly told the warmongering Alexander the Great to stand out of his sun.[15]

Frederick retorted that making peace was not such an easy task, and that the political leaders with whom he had to deal were as intractable as the philosophers with whom Rousseau had fallen out. Apparently impressed by Rousseau's rejection of his offer of financial and material aid, Frederick wrote to Keith that Rousseau exhibited the apex of virtuous disinterestedness. Yet just like Rousseau's compliment to Frederick, this was a double-edged remark. For Frederick, every virtue had its value in moderation – which applied equally to self-love and disinterestedness. Frederick admitted in the same letter to Keith that excessive voluptuousness, or what he called 'Asiatic luxury', was not at all necessary. But he

[13] Frederick II to Keith, 1 September 1762, in *Œuvres de Frédéric le Grand*, ed. Johann D. E. Preuss, vol. XX, 322.

[14] Rousseau to Frederick, 30 October 1762, ibid., 333–334.

[15] On Rousseau and Diogenes, see Michael Sonenscher, *Sans-culottes: An Eighteenth-Century Emblem in the French Revolution* (Princeton, NJ: Princeton University Press, 2008), 134–201; Louisa Shea, *The Cynic Enlightenment: Diogenes in the Salon* (Baltimore, MD: Johns Hopkins University Press, 2010), 89–105.

immediately qualified this point by wondering why we should renounce most of the conveniences of modern life as long as they could be innocently enjoyed without detriment to society. 'The true philosophy', Frederick argued, 'is the one that does not proscribe luxury but limits itself to the condemnation of its abuse'. And where could one find this 'true philosophy'? Frederick confided in Keith that he always remained faithful to John Locke, Marcus Aurelius, 'my friend Lucretius', and the physics of Epicurus – everything, in his words, 'that can make us moderate, good, and wise'.[16]

This sound philosophy seemed to Frederick to be the direct opposite of what he interpreted as Rousseau's call for austere self-denial in the *Discourses*, enhanced by the philosopher's rejection of his offer of material help. The king argued that his own philosophical heroes would reject the claim that because we were all born equal, we had to live like savages without law, or that the arts and the sciences had actively damaged morality. Writing to Keith in Neuchâtel, Frederick contrasted his own moderate philosophy with what he saw as Rousseau's pitiable rehearsal of Diogenes's Cynicism:

> I believe that your Rousseau has missed his vocation. He was undoubtedly born to become a famous Cenobite monk, a Church father of the desert, celebrated for his austerity and self-maceration, a Stylite. He would have performed miracles, he would have become a saint, and would have enlarged the enormous catalogue of any martyrologist. But at present he cannot be seen as anything but a peculiar philosopher who resuscitates the sect of Diogenes after two thousand years.[17]

Frederick added that disinterestedness is no doubt the foundation of virtue, but in Rousseau's case it was highly exaggerated: one should know how to do without various things while renouncing nothing. Therefore, if Rousseau seemed to Frederick to exhibit abstract morality by renouncing his natural self-love, this very quality made his philosophy inconsequential in the real world.[18] Several years later, Frederick would elaborate this argument in his own essays on the topics that stood at the centre of Rousseau's *Discourses*.

## The benign effects of natural self-love

In his *Discourse on the Usefulness of the Sciences and the Arts within a State*, Frederick referred only briefly and in a veiled manner to Rousseau, though it was clear that this essay was the royal reply to the Genevan's

[16] Frederick to Keith, 1 September 1762, *Œuvres*, XX, 323. [17] Ibid.

[18] 'Ce grand désintéressement est sans contredit le fond essentiel de la vertu; ainsi je juge que votre sauvage a les mœurs aussi pures que l'esprit inconsequent.' (Ibid.)

*First Discourse*. True to the utilitarian tones of the title, the king sought to demonstrate the close alliance between cultural progress and national greatness. For this purpose, he turned Rousseau's narrative of ancient and modern history upside down. In Rousseau's *Discourse on the Sciences and the Arts*, Sparta was the glory of Greece rather than Athens; the *Discourse* ended with a distinction between a people who knew how to speak well, and another who acted well. Among the Romans, 'all was lost' when instead of practising virtue they started studying it. For Frederick, on the other hand, the Greek heroes were not only Pericles and Alexander but also Thucydides, Euripides, Xenophon, and Plato; the Romans truly came into their own when Cicero, Varro, Virgil, and Livy produced their 'brilliant' masterpieces.[19]

Yet the difference between these texts runs much deeper than a disagreement on the historical links between political and intellectual greatness. For Rousseau, the problem with the arts and the sciences lay right at their source: an excessive desire for self-aggrandisement. Eloquence was born out of ambition, hatred, flattery, and lying; geometry originated in greed; and physics was the offspring of vain curiosity. In a nutshell, all forms of scholarly inquiry owed their emergence to human pride and self-love; they were intellectual and social luxuries, widening the gap between appearance and essence while generating inequality. In Rousseau's cultural critique, the arts and the sciences were the closest collaborators of political usurpers and arbitrary rulers, pacifying their exploited subjects. As Rousseau famously argued, the arts and the sciences 'spread garlands of flowers over the iron chains with which they are laden, throttle in them the sentiment of that original freedom for which they seemed born, make them love their slavery, and fashion them into what is called civilized Peoples'.[20]

Frederick celebrated, by contrast, the most renowned scientists and artists as national heroes. He too saw a close link between the arts and politics – obviously not in a conspiratorial alliance of despots and their scientific advisors, but through a quasi-cameralist view of scientific progress as enhancing the size of the national population, contributing to manufacture, and creating budgetary surplus and military superiority. As Frederick summed up his utilitarian vision of science, 'all enlightened princes have protected those whose savant works honour the human mind; now things have come to the point that if a government failed only slightly in its promotion of the sciences, it would soon find itself

[19] Rousseau, *DI*, 10–11, 28; *OC* III, 10–11, 30; Frederick II, 'Discours de l'utilité des sciences et des arts dans un état', in *Œuvres*, IX, 195–207; here 205–206.

[20] Rousseau, *DI*, 6; *OC* III, 6–7.

a whole century behind its neighbours'.[21] (As usual, Poland was Frederick's example of this sorry state of affairs.) In Frederick's account, scientists and artists acted for the common good. If self-love fired up their intellectual pursuits or if they wished to excel in order to outshine their peers, this only promoted the lustre and greatness of their homeland. As real patriots, their self-interest was perfectly aligned with that of the state, according to Frederick's *Discourse*: detrimental self-interest was ascribed to those sects and individuals who delayed the progress of science or prohibited experimentation and the publication of new discoveries. Only swindlers, impostors, and religious zealots were harmed by scientific progress, not public or individual morals. Intellectual self-love was in Frederick's eyes the source of patriotic pursuits rather than a cause of personal and national corruption.[22]

Frederick's *Essay on Self-Love Considered as an Ethical Principle* was read at the Berlin Academy in January 1770 and published later that year.[23] Despite the much-touted collaboration between Voltaire and the Prussian king, the treatise was much longer and substantially different from Voltaire's '*amour propre*' entry in his *Dictionnaire philosophique* of 1764.[24] Both Voltaire and Frederick saw self-love as a natural instinct, yet the latter presented a wider overview of its workings (with no reference to Voltaire's examples of a Spanish beggar and an Indian fakir). In fact, Frederick probably replied here to recent works by Helvétius and d'Alembert, while keeping in mind both Rousseau's *Discourse on the Arts and the Sciences* and his *Discourse on Inequality*, where self-love played a pivotal role within the overall argument.[25]

Frederick's view of self-love in the essay is fairly similar to Rousseau's modified theory in *Emile* (1762). In this work, Rousseau revised his dichotomous distinction in the *Discourse on Inequality* between the

[21] Frederick II, *Œuvres*, IX, 206.

[22] A rare point of agreement between Frederick and Rousseau is the significance of scientific academies as promoters and regulators of genuinely useful knowledge. Both discourses were addressed to such institutions: Rousseau's treatise won the prize of the Dijon Academy, while Frederick's essay was first read at a public session of the Berlin Academy in the presence of his sister Ulrike, the dowager queen of Sweden (27 January 1772). On this topic, see Alexander Schmidt, 'Scholarship, Morals, and Government: J. H. S. Formey's and J. G. Herder's responses to Rousseau's *First Discourse*', *Modern Intellectual History* 9.2 (2012), 249–274.

[23] Frederick II, 'Essai sur l'amour propre envisagé comme un principe de morale', in *Histoire de l'Académie royale des sciences et belles-lettres, Année 1763* (Berlin: Haude & Spener, 1770), 341–354. References here are to the Preuss edition: *Œuvres*, IX, 99–114.

[24] *Œuvres complètes de Voltaire*, vol. XXXV, ed. Christiane Mervaud (Oxford: Voltaire Foundation, 1994), 334–336.

[25] Frederick to Voltaire, 17 February 1770, in *Œuvres*, XXIII, 169–170. Frederick's interest in the natural aspects of self-love is already apparent in his *Réfutation du Prince de Machiavel* (*Œuvres*, VIII, 311).

positive *amour de soi-même* and its inflamed relation, *amour propre*, as well as their separation from pity, which he had described as the source of all fellow-feeling. In *Emile*, Rousseau argued that the same self-love could be the source of both 'humane and gentle' passions and 'cruel and malignant' ones, depending on context and education. He now proclaimed that 'love of men derived from love of self is the principle of human justice'.[26] Indeed, *Emile* can be read as a guide to the transformation of one's self-love into benign social and civic sentiments rather than inflamed self-preference; this is the direction in which the tutor tries to channel the child's mental development. The point is to make us genuinely linked to other human beings in such a way that their interests would approximate our natural self-love or become its extension.

> But when the strength of an expansive soul makes me identify myself with my fellow, and I feel that I am, so to speak, in him, it is in order not to suffer that I do not want him to suffer. I am interested in him for love of myself, and the reason for the precept is in nature itself, which inspires in me the desire of my well-being in whatever place I feel my existence.[27]

Frederick too regards self-love as a most natural human inclination, and hence the most durable hinge on which virtue and civic behaviour could turn. As he puts it, human beings are usually the secret object of all the good they perform: 'Through a hidden and barely perceptible sentiment, men trace everything back to themselves, placing themselves at the centre where all lines of circumference end.'[28] Frederick then anticipates the objection that equates virtue with perfect disinterestedness – which he had already mentioned in the 1762 letter to Keith concerning Rousseau's rejection of royal assistance. In a similar manner to Emile's tutor, Frederick's task here is to rectify the human judgement of what was natural about self-love and what constituted its corruption. Drawing on examples from Roman history, Frederick claims that 'our greatest examples of disinterestedness are provided to us by the principles of self-love'.[29] One had to regulate self-love, showing human beings that others' interests could be conceived as their own.[30] Yet how could such a regulation of self-love be achieved? Frederick suggests here the adoption of the Hellenistic view of happiness as a perfect tranquillity of the mind. Once we opted for it as the ultimate goal of our actions, there could be no contradiction between disinterestedness and self-love. Such mental

[26] Rousseau, *Emile*, Book IV, 235; *OC* IV, 523. [27] Ibid.
[28] Frederick II, *Œuvres*, IX, 111. [29] Ibid., 110–111.
[30] Ibid., 104–105. One crucial difference between the two accounts of benign self-love is Frederick's pronounced emphasis on military glory and fear for one's reputation as major extensions of natural self-love.

tranquillity would teach us not to attach ourselves vehemently to tempestuous passions, unhealthy debauchery, or excessive anger.

Frederick's use of a term so similar to the ancient Epicurean *ataraxia* or its Stoic version, *apatheia*, is telling. It is complemented by a fascinating enumeration of those who had not properly understood how to reconcile self-love and love of one's fellows or fatherland. One of the authors who allegedly went astray was La Rochefoucauld, whose Epicurean emphasis on self-love as the font of all social action dismayed Frederick because it slandered virtue and presented it as a fig leaf covering merely egotistical sentiments.[31] But first and foremost among Frederick's targets were the monotheistic faiths – Judaism, Christianity, and Islam – which, together with Confucianism, were charged with advocating the wrong sort of ethics. According to Frederick, their anchoring of morals in a transcendental God and divine rewards and punishments was a serious obstacle to the proper motivation of virtuous action. Virtue, for Frederick, could only be based on natural self-love. Though he claims that errors on this front were made equally in pagan antiquity as well as in Christian times, the gist of the argument is clearly directed against Christianity:

> How the Christians degenerated and corrupted the ancient purity of morals! Cupidity, ambition, and fanaticism filled those hearts that made their vocation the renunciation of this world, and perverted what simple virtue had established. History is teeming with similar examples. With the exception of a few hermits, as pious as they are socially useless, the Christians of our day are eventually not preferable to the Romans of Marius's and Sulla's times; I limit this parallel, of course, only to the comparison of morals.[32]

Apart from the unsurprisingly joyful condemnation of Christianity, one may identify here a serious issue that specifically bothered Frederick in Christian ethics, and which he saw epitomised by hermits and other recluses: the interpretation of virtue as self-denial. This is the crux of his attempt to rehabilitate self-love as a moral principle, or to derive socially beneficial actions from a healthy care of the self. Like Emile's tutor, Frederick tries to get rid of an ethics of dependence on external factors, be they priests or divine rewards and punishments. Self-love could lead to all the sociable and patriotic actions usually deemed virtuous; it is

[31] Ibid., 105. This did not prevent Frederick from including in 1780 La Rochefoucauld's *Maxims* in the list of exemplary works to be translated into German in order to enrich the language. ('De la littérature allemande', in *Œuvres*, VII, 119.) See Louis Hippeau, *Essai sur la morale de La Rochefoucauld* (Paris: Nizet, 1967), Jean Lafond, *La Rochefoucauld: augustinisme et littérature*, 3rd ed. (Paris: Klincksieck, 1994); Michael Moriarty, 'La Rochefoucauld on Interest and Self-Love', in *Fallen Nature, Fallen Selves: Early Modern French Thought II* (Oxford: Oxford University Press, 2006), 225–248.

[32] Frederick II, *Œuvres*, IX, 102.

disinterestedness in the guise of self-denial and withdrawal from this world that Frederick saw as detrimental to both individual health and the social fabric.

Such self-denial is precisely what the king had criticised in Rousseau's behaviour in 1762, when he described the Genevan as a potential Christian saint or a philosopher whose disinterestedness was thoroughly useless in the modern world. Frederick formed this view on the basis of the letters he received from Rousseau and Keith in 1762, as well as on an all-too-common interpretation of the *Discourse on Inequality*. Ironically, Frederick did not realise how close his understanding of the benign effects of natural self-love was to Rousseau's own revised stance in *Emile*. His only direct reference to this book is in a letter of February 1763, where he indicates he has just started reading it. Disrupted as his reading must have been by the negotiations leading to the Peace of Hubertusburg, it does not seem likely that Frederick ever made it to Book IV of *Emile*, where Rousseau elaborated his theory of the careful, positive extension of *amour propre* from its natural basis in the self onto others.[33]

## Frederick's pagan synthesis

The king's combination of ethical principles from different Hellenistic schools is hardly surprising. After all, already in the 1762 letter to Keith about Rousseau, Frederick confessed that the Stoic emperor Marcus Aurelius and 'my friend Lucretius' were among the very few sources of his 'true philosophy'. Indeed, when Frederick used *De rerum natura* as his breviary, especially during the Seven Years War, he was particularly interested in its consolatory effects against the fear of death and what he saw as its exhortation to moral self-sufficiency given the absence of divine providence. One of his most extensive meditations on Lucretius's poem is the work known as the Epistle to Keith, which bore the title *On the Futile Terror of Death and Fear of Another Life* (1752); in its 1760 edition, a subtitle was added to indicate that this was 'an imitation of the third book of Lucretius'.[34] Yet even towards the end of this largely Epicurean poem, Marcus Aurelius makes a grand appearance (together with Julius Caesar, Virgil, and Newton) to

[33] Frederick to Luise-Dorothea of Saxe-Gotha, 10 February 1763, in *Œuvres*, XVIII, 248–250.

[34] Frederick II, 'Épître XVIII. Au maréchal Keith', in *Œuvres*, X, 226–237. It first appeared in the 1752 private edition of *Œuvres du philosophe de Sans-Souci*. On the Epicurean overtones of this work, see Reinhart Meyer-Kalkus, '"Mein Freund Lukrez." Friedrichs "XIII. Epistel an den Marschall von Keith: Über die leeren Schreckens des Todes und die Angst vor einem anderen Leben"', in *Friedrich der Große als Leser*, ed. Brunhilde Wehinger and Günther Lottes (Berlin: Akademie Verlag, 2012), 121–142.

recommend a full recognition of the transitory nature of human existence and the mortality of the soul.[35]

In the Epistle, Frederick tries to console Keith by recourse to the same argument he would use in 1770 in his essay on self-love. Keith and Frederick, made wiser by their constant confrontation with death, learned to appreciate what Lucretius and Marcus Aurelius had taught: the reward of a benevolent act is in the act itself, and its proper motive is natural self-love. Frederick contrasts this mode of action to the behaviour of Christian believers, deemed cowardly criminals whose illicit desires are blocked only by the external bulwark of divine damnation. As in the *Essay on Self-Love*, the king sees here Christian virtue as mere illusion, for instead of flowing from the natural self it depends on outward factors. By contrast to the Christians, Frederick depicts Keith and himself as unsullied by artificial interests precisely because they have renounced any hope for future rewards in another life. Their Epicuro-Stoic synthesis leaves them with no other motivation for virtuous action than the here and now. Keith and I, Frederick argues, can bestow benevolent actions on the world because we stare death in the eye with no regrets, having acted solely from a love of humankind generalised from natural self-love. In the Epistle (part of which is reproduced below in the original rhyming French) 'interest' is the opposite of the healthy extension of self-love: *amour propre* as a moral principle is not the same as the pursuit of excessive self-interest at the expense of others.[36] Frederick was not, of course, the only author to distinguish between self-interest and love of self: at the beginning of this chapter we witnessed Rousseau accusing Frederick of placing glory and 'interest' before the

[35] The Stoic emperor also rode to the rescue of the ill-informed moderns in the conclusion of Frederick's *Essay on the Forms of Government* of 1777 (*Œuvres*, IX, 239).

[36] Allez, lâches chrétiens, que les feux éternels
Empêchent d'assouvir vos désirs criminels,
Vos austères vertus n'en ont que l'apparence.
Mais nous, qui renonçons à toute récompense,
Nous, qui ne croyons point vos éternels tourments,
L'intérêt n'a jamais souillé nos sentiments:
Le bien du genre humain, la vertu nous anime,
L'amour seul du devoir nous a fait fuir le crime;
Oui, finissons sans trouble et mourons sans regrets,
En laissant l'univers comblé de nos bienfaits.
(Frederick II, *Œuvres*, X, 235–236)

In the 1760 edition, the sensitive 'lâches chrétiens' was replaced by a more neutral 'mortels craintifs'; on this modification, see Meyer-Kalkus, 'Mein Freund Lukrez', 122–124. For the instrumental use of this poem and the entire *Œuvres du philosophe de Sans-Souci* by the French government during the Seven Years War, see Thomas Biskup, 'Die Schlacht von Sanssouci: Der roi-philosophe und die klandestine Literatur im Siebenjährigen Krieg', in *Krieg und Frieden im 18. Jahrhundert: Kulturgeschichtliche Studien*, ed. Stephanie Stockhorst (Hanover: Wehrhahn, 2015), 75–92.

common good. Both Rousseau and Frederick thus contrasted the unbridled pursuit self-interest to the socially benevolent aspects of benign self-love.[37]

Frederick's 'true philosophy', if he ever had a coherent one, is hard to pin down as an appropriation of a particular intellectual school or trend. Well acquainted with seventeenth-century French works in which either a Christianised Epicureanism or its more ancient versions played a major role (such as La Rochefoucauld's), he did not follow wholeheartedly the fashionable fusion between Epicurean elements and the Augustinian notion of fallen man.[38] This intellectual amalgam had been manifest in the work of Jansenists like Pierre Nicole and Blaise Pascal, yet, as we have seen, Frederick refused to temper the arbitrariness of the Epicurean universe, or its lack of any teleological principle, with the Augustinian view of original sin or a belief in the Christian God.

If the traditional image of Frederick the Great as a staunch neo-Stoic is due for reappraisal, it seems that the king cannot be considered as an all-out Epicurean either. Indeed, Frederick's admiration for Marcus Aurelius – which probably had much to do with the desired image of a philosopher-ruler – was accompanied by his enthusiastic appropriation of major Epicurean themes and an almost instinctive aversion to metaphysics. The Epistle to Keith actually points to a volatile mélange of Epicurean physics and Stoic ethics. The total dissolution of the soul upon one's death, the lack of rewards and punishments, and the denial of any grand design or meaning of life fit the Epicurean worldview. Happiness as tranquillity of the mind could be associated either with the Epicurean *ataraxia* or with the Stoic *apatheia*. Yet it was Frederick's pagan ethics of action that exuded a particularly strong Stoic aroma. His treatment of self-love is redolent of Cicero's account of *oikeiosis* in Book III of *De finibus*, as well as of Seneca's similar stance in Letter 121 to Lucilius.[39] This synthesis may be grounded in Frederick's double distaste for grand metaphysical systems and for Christian ethics. Towards the end of the *Essay on Self-Love*, Frederick suggested that his views on virtue and love of the self could be promoted by studying the

[37] For Rousseau's distinction between 'vulgar' Epicureanism and an Epicureanism true to its sources, which closely resembled Stoicism, see Jared Holley, '*In verba magistri*? Assessing Rousseau's Classicism Today', in *History of Political Thought* 37 (2016).

[38] Jean Lafond, 'Augustinisme et épicurisme au XVIIe siècle', *XVIIe Siècle* 34 (1982), 149–158; Pierre Force, *Self-Interest before Adam Smith* (Cambridge: Cambridge University Press, 2003), 48–90; John Robertson, *The Case for the Enlightenment: Scotland and Naples 1680–1760* (Cambridge: Cambridge University Press, 2005), 127–130; Neven Leddy and Avi Lifschitz (ed.), *Epicurus in the Enlightenment* (Oxford: Voltaire Foundation, 2009), 5–10.

[39] Cicero, *De finibus bonorum et malorum*, ed. H. Rackham (Loeb Classical Library) (London: Heinemann, 1914), Book 3, V, 233–237; Seneca, Epistle CXXI, in *Ad Lucilium epistulae morales*, ed. Richard M. Gummere (Loeb Classical Library), vol. III (London: Heinemann, 1925), 397–411.

ancients and prioritising ethics over metaphysics. Even theologians should change their focus, Frederick argued, and instead of 'unintelligible dogmas' teach what we might call applied ethics – or, in his words, 'practical morals'.[40] Generally, instead of metaphysics Frederick recommended reading the *Essay Concerning Human Understanding* by John Locke, another member of the pantheon of 'true philosophy' in the Epistle to Keith.[41]

If this specific philosophical fusion was peculiar to Frederick, it was far from bizarre or exceptional in the mid eighteenth century. Christopher Brooke has pointed out the malleability of the Stoic legacy in the early modern period, while Neven Leddy and I have argued that the seventeenth-century baptism of Epicurean atoms and their presentation as moved by God entailed a confusion of philosophical tenets, which was exacerbated by the Epicurean-Augustinian blend. Eighteenth-century Epicureanism was an amalgam in constant evolution through its interaction with different philosophical traditions. Given the creative transformation of Epicureanism by Enlightenment authors, we argued it was time 'to substitute the notion of selective appropriation for the traditional concepts of reception and influence'.[42] This term may well apply to Frederick's Epicuro-Stoic synthesis. Dispelling some of the long-lasting debates over the king's identity as an Epicurean *or* a Stoic, it may also direct us back to the texts themselves and their sources, or towards an identification of the themes that remained relatively stable throughout Frederick's life. It is clear that the king used (and at times abused) his philosophy for political purposes, maintaining in the public sphere an intellectual persona that yielded tangible benefits.[43] It may also be the case that Frederick's self-identification with the advocates of moderate luxury and natural self-love,

[40] Frederick II, *Œuvres*, IX, 113.

[41] See, for example, 'Instruction pour la direction de l'académie des nobles à Berlin' (1765), *Œuvres*, IX, esp. 93–94; 'Lettre sur l'éducation' (1769), ibid., esp. 137–138.

[42] Leddy and Lifschitz (ed.), *Epicurus in the Enlightenment*, 3–5; cf. Thomas Kavanagh, *Enlightened Pleasures: Eighteeenth-Century France and the New Epicureanism* (New Haven: Yale University Press, 2010), 4–9.

[43] On Frederick's self-fashioning, see recently Jürgen Luh, *Der Große. Friedrich II. von Preußen* (Munich: Siedler, 2011); Jürgen Luh and Andreas Pečar, 'Repräsentation und Selbstinszenierung Friedrichs II. von Preußen', in the online proceedings of the Halle-Potsdam conference of 28–29 September 2012: www.perspectivia.net/content/publikationen/friedrich300-colloquien/friedrich_repraesentation/pecar_repraesentation (accessed 2 March 2015). For some of the attempts to categorise Frederick's philosophical creed, see Eduard Spranger, *Der Philosoph*, 50–53; Wolfgang Bernard Fleischmann, 'Frederick the Great and Lucretius: A Revaluation of a Relationship', *Comparative Literature Studies* 2.2 (1965), 153–159; Meyer-Kalus, 'Epikureische Aufklärung in Deutschland. Johann Georg Sulzers Gespräch mit Friedrich II. von Preußen am 31.12.1777', *Hyperboreus* 9 (2003), 191–207; Reid Barbour, 'Moral and Political Philosophy: Readings of Lucretius from Virgil to Voltaire', in *The Cambridge Companion to Lucretius*, ed. Stuart Gillespie and Philip Hardie (Cambridge: Cambridge University Press, 2007), 149–166 (esp. 161–166).

coupled with his denial that virtue consisted in self-renunciation, was aimed at undermining some tenets of republican ideology. Yet the constant wrestling with these themes in his correspondence, poetry, dialogues, and treatises could also point to genuine fascination and an open-ended engagement with such issues. This may be attested by Frederick's enduring suspicion of Christian morality as a dishonest ploy, generating self-alienation and dependence on external forces in lieu of a confident and self-reliant confrontation with a meaningless universe. His essays of the 1770s on self-love as the motor of the arts, sciences, patriotism, and virtue are testimony to the long but steady trajectory he had traversed since his Epistle to Keith in the early 1750s on the futile fear of death.

Rousseau's *Discourses* of the 1750s were an important medium through which Frederick developed his own understanding of self-love in relation to the common good. His reading of the *Discourses*, alongside his correspondence with Rousseau via George Keith, made Frederick classify the Genevan as a modern champion of virtue as self-denial. However, one cannot help wondering whether more direct contact between Rousseau and Frederick might have prompted a thicker – if no less problematic – intellectual (and musical) exchange. Unlike Voltaire, Frederick did appreciate Rousseau as a person and a philosopher: rebuking Voltaire in a letter of December 1766, the king wrote that Rousseau was unfortunate – and only perverse souls would heap abuse on such people rather than respect them.[44] In his own last letter to Frederick, sent in 1766 from Wootton, Rousseau seems to have regretted his rejection of the king's offer of residence in a Huguenot village next to Berlin (probably Buchholz). Having left for England despite his naturalisation in Prussian-ruled Môtiers, Rousseau thanked Frederick and Keith for their protection and benevolence, noting that he wished to remain Frederick's protégé and most loyal subject.[45] The avowed 'enemy of kings' may have after all identified some similarities between the ruler he had vilified as Adrastus and his own unresolved conflicts between *amour propre*, public self-fashioning, and authentic social interaction.

[44] Frederick to Voltaire, December 1766, in *Œuvres*, XXIII, 131. See also Tim Blanning, *Frederick the Great: King of Prussia* (London: Allen Lane, 2015), 326–329.

[45] Rousseau to Frederick, 30 March 1766, Nr. 5136 in *Correspondance complète de Jean-Jacques Rousseau*, ed. R. A. Leigh, vol. XXIX (Oxford: Voltaire Foundation, 1977), 76–77. Cf. Du Bois-Reymond, *Friedrich II. und Jean-Jacques Rousseau*, 41–42.

# 3 Sources of evil or seeds of the good?
## Rousseau and Kant on needs, the arts, and the sciences

*Alexander Schmidt*

## I Introduction

The ancient problem of the emergence and extent of human needs became a crucial question in Enlightenment thought, providing a deeply divisive key to the origins and the cultural progress of society and the state. The issue of needs linked together debates on theology, psychology, natural law, history, and political economy.[1] Yet it also increasingly challenged governments, magistrates, and princes all across Europe. By restraining or stimulating the needs of their subjects, they sought to police morals and to enlarge the income and power of the state. What troubled many eighteenth-century minds was where to draw a line between real needs and superfluous desires. Furthermore, at which point would the progressive extension of needs become a source of social ills? And what would be the best ways of managing spiralling needs? The aim of this chapter is to understand and situate Immanuel Kant's early engagement with Jean-Jacques Rousseau within this wider discussion of human needs as a driving factor of civilisation.

Following Josef Schmucker's classical study on the origins of Kant's ethics, scholars in recent years seem to outrival one another in stressing the importance of the early Kant's encounter with Rousseau, which reshaped his understanding of the aims of philosophy in general and of

I wish to thank David James, Avi Lifschitz, Paul Sagar, and Lea Ypi for their encouragement and comments on earlier versions of this chapter.

[1] Cf. Utta Kim-Wawrzinek and Johann Baptist Müller, 'Bedürfnis', in *Geschichtliche Grundbegriffe: Historisches Lexikon zur politisch-sozialen Sprache in Deutschland*, ed. Otto Brunner, Werner Conze, and Reinhart Koselleck, vol. 1 (Stuttgart: Klett, 1972), 440–489; István Hont and Michael Ignatieff, 'Needs and Justice in the Wealth of Nations', in Hont, *Jealousy of Trade: International Competition and the Nation State in Historical Perspective* (Cambridge, MA and London: Harvard University Press, 2005), ch. 6; Michael Sonenscher, *Sans-Culottes: An Eighteenth-Century Emblem in the French Revolution* (Princeton: Princeton University Press, 2008), *passim*; Michael Ignatieff, *The Needs of Strangers* (London: Chatto and Windus, 1984). For a suggestive systematic account, see Lawrence A. Hamilton, *The Political Philosophy of Needs* (Cambridge: Cambridge University Press, 2003).

his own role as a scholar in the mid 1760s.[2] The Genevan occasioned, Frederick Beiser claims, 'a complete revolution' in Kant's orientation, a redefinition of his engagement with metaphysics as a 'science of the limits of human reason'.[3] Kant discovered an Archimedean point in Rousseau, Susan Meld Shell argues in a similar vein, 'from which the laws of nature and those of freedom can be made to work in tandem'.[4]

Thanks to studies by Reinhardt Brandt and John Zammito, we can now trace some of the sources of Kant's critical project back to a concern with 'pragmatic' anthropology or 'the science of man', to employ David Hume's coinage.[5] Kant's engagement with Rousseau here opens up an important and disputed question in Kant scholarship: What is the exact position of Kant's anthropology within his critical philosophy, especially in relation to his moral philosophy? How can the determinism of anthropology, as expressed in human physiology, character, sex, and race, be matched with Kant's case for human freedom as spontaneity and self-determination? This issue already puzzled the early readers of Kant's anthropology.[6]

By comparison, the aim of this chapter is more modest. It seeks to show that the problem of human needs provides an overlooked yet important point of access to Kant's engagement with Rousseau's sharp distinction between nature and civilisation. This ancient distinction in its specifically Rousseauvian mould became a recurring theme in Kant's thought,

[2] Josef Schmucker, *Die Ursprünge der Ethik Kants* (Meisenheim am Glan: Hain, 1961), esp. 199ff. Cf. Klaus Reich, *Rousseau und Kant* (Tübingen: Mohr, 1936) and Ernst Cassirer's classic, *Rousseau, Kant, Goethe: Two Essays*, trans. James Gutmann, Paul Oskar Kristeller, and John Herman Randall, Jr. (Princeton: Princeton University Press, 1945). The impact of Rousseau on Kant was emphasised early on by Karl Vorländer, a prominent neo-Kantian socialist, in 'Kant und Rousseau', *Die Neue Zeit: Wochenschrift der Deutschen Sozialdemokratie* 37.1 (1919), 465ff.

[3] Frederick C. Beiser, 'Kant's Intellectual Development: 1746–1781', in *The Cambridge Companion to Kant*, ed. Paul Guyer (Cambridge: Cambridge University Press, 1992), 43. See also Richard Velkley, 'Freedom, Teleology, and the Justification of Reason. On the Philosophical Importance of Kant's Rousseauvian Turn', in *Rousseau in Deutschland. Neue Beiträge zur Erforschung seiner Rezeption*, ed. Herbert Jaumann (Berlin: de Gruyter, 1995), 181–196.

[4] Susan Meld Shell, *Kant and the Limits of Autonomy* (Cambridge, MA: Harvard University Press, 2009), 55. On the early Kant's engagement with Rousseau and contemporary thought see Rischmüller's excellent commentary, to which I am much indebted: Immanuel Kant, *Bemerkungen in den Beobachtungen über das Gefühl des Schönen und Erhabenen*, ed. Marie Rischmüller (Hamburg: Meiner, 1991).

[5] Reinhardt Brandt, *Die Bestimmung des Menschen bei Kant* (Hamburg: Meiner, 2007); John H. Zammito, *Kant, Herder, and the Birth of Anthropology* (Chicago: University of Chicago Press, 2002).

[6] See Patrick R. Frierson, *Freedom and Anthropology in Kant's Moral Philosophy* (Cambridge: Cambridge University Press, 2003); Allen Wood, 'Kant's Doctrine of Right: Introduction', in Kant, *Metaphysische Anfangsgründe der Rechtslehre*, ed. Otfried Höffe (Berlin: Akademie Verlag, 1999), 19–39, esp. 23f.

shaping his concepts of history, anthropology, and morality. The problem of human needs leads us back to the origins of Rousseau's intellectual project, namely his account of the psychological mechanisms that complement the rise of the arts and sciences and their role in human history. This was the subject of Rousseau's scandalous *Discours sur les sciences et les arts* of 1750 and the *Discours sur les origines et les fondemens de l'inégalité parmi les hommes* of 1755, otherwise known as the *First* and *Second Discourses*.[7] The claims of the *citoyen de Genève* about the corruption of natural goodness in the history of civilisation presented Kant with a disquieting challenge when it came to the question of the character of mankind as a whole and its destiny in history. Here the Königsberg philosopher was faced with a puzzle: how could Rousseau's shockingly persuasive analysis of the ills of modern monarchical societies and his unhappy narrative of human *perfectibilité* be squared with the destination of man to perfect himself as a moral and free rational being? The human duty to perfect oneself was indeed a leitmotif in natural law, theology, and anthropology in eighteenth-century Germany. As will be sketched out below in greater detail, Kant appropriated some of Rousseau's key claims for these debates. Yet he did so by radically shifting the focus of the teleological question about the *Bestimmung des Menschen* from the purpose of the individual to the aim of humanity as a historically perfectible collective.[8]

Like most of Rousseau's contemporary readers, Kant viewed the Genevan as an author of paradoxes.[9] However, in contrast to Rousseau's many critics, he did not read these paradoxes as mere rhetorical fireworks intended to draw public attention. Instead, Kant believed they would reveal a central conundrum of humanity: how could a moral and peaceful civil society be achieved – despite a sea of seemingly self-inflicted evils – by a race of crooked, discontented, self-deceptive, yet rational and free creatures? This conundrum, Kant maintained, was the result of a characteristic human tension: we are, on the one hand, individuals with certain physical and intellectual needs, but we are also, on the

[7] See Rousseau, *DI*. The best critical edition of the French text of the *Second Discourse* is Meier's: Rousseau, *Diskurs über die Ungleichheit/Discours sur l'inégalité: Kritische Ausgabe des integralen Textes*, ed. Heinrich Meier, 5th ed. (Paderborn: Schöningh, 2001).

[8] Reinhardt Brandt, 'The Guiding Idea of Kant's Anthropology and the Vocation of the Human Being', in *Essays on Kant's Anthropology*, ed. Brian Jacobs and Patrick Kain (Cambridge: Cambridge University Press, 2003), 85–104.

[9] Kant, *Bemerkungen*, 37–8; *AA* XX, 43. In the following, all references to the *Bemerkungen* are given to both Rischmüller's edition and the *Akademie Ausgabe*: Kant, *Gesammelte Schriften*, ed. Wilhelm Dilthey et al. (Berlin: Reimer, De Gruyter, 1900-) – hence *AA*, followed by volume number. On the contemporary reception of Rousseau, see Raymond Trousson, *Jean-Jacques Rousseau jugé par ses contemporaines. Du 'Discours sur les sciences et les arts' aux 'Confessions'* (Paris: Champion, 2000).

other hand, members of the human species, whose aims in history and society go beyond the individual striving for happiness and perfection.

Considering the two *Discourses* together with *Emile*, Kant identified three paradoxes in Rousseau. The first concerned the 'harm caused to culture through the sciences (because of the barbarism of culture)', the second pertains to the damage inflicted on civil society by inequality, and the last consisted in the harm done to human nature by (false) moralisation and education.[10] In tracing the genealogy of these paradoxes, I argue that the problem of human needs lies at their core.[11]

## II Natural versus unnatural needs and the origins of the arts and sciences

Following Aristotle's *Nicomachean Ethics*, theorists of natural law and political economists repeatedly stressed the centrality of human needs for stipulating the price of goods and commodities.[12] Other eighteenth-century thinkers, however, rather emphasised the role of needs in man's sensuous economy, thus linking them to the sensations of pain and pleasure. Need was a *sentiment desagréable* 'occasioned by the perceived absence or desired presence of an object', maintains the brief *Besoin* entry in the second volume of the *Encyclopédie* (January 1752).[13] Its author, Denis Diderot, at this point perhaps Rousseau's closest interlocutor, distinguishes between two kinds of needs: 'those of the body, called appetites; and others of the mind (*de l'esprit*), called desires'.[14] Without these needs, there would be neither well-being nor unhappiness in human life, nor the respectively accompanying feelings of pleasure and pain.

In line with much of the contemporary literature on natural law, but especially with Montesquieu,[15] Diderot further sketches out how isolated individuals, seeking to satisfy their needs in a state of nature, would

[10] Kant, *AA* XV, 889.

[11] The problem of needs is a recurring but rather scattered theme in Rousseau scholarship. There is no entry on it in Nicholas Dent, *A Rousseau Dictionary* (Oxford: Blackwell, 1992), nor in the *Dictionnaire de Jean-Jacques Rousseau*, ed. Raymond Trousson and Frédéric S. Eigeldinger (Paris: Champion, 2001).

[12] See the entry 'Bedürfnis' in *Grosses vollständiges Universal-Lexicon aller Wissenschaften und Künste*, ed. Johann Heinrich Zedler, vol. 3 (Halle and Leipzig: Zedler, 1733), 437–439.

[13] [Denis Diderot], 'Besoin', in *Encyclopédie, ou dictionnaire raisonné des sciences, des arts et des métiers*, ed. Denis Diderot and Jean le Rond d'Alembert, vol. 2 (Paris: 1752), 213.

[14] [Diderot], 'Besoin', 213. On their intellectual exchange, see Robert Wokler, 'The Influence of Diderot on the Political Theory of Rousseau: Two Aspects of a Relationship', *Studies on Voltaire and the Eighteenth Century* 132 (1975), 55–111.

[15] Charles-Louis de Secondat, Baron de Montesquieu, *The Spirit of the Laws*, trans. Anne M. Cohler, Basia C. Miller, and Harold S. Stone (Cambridge: Cambridge University Press, 1989), 6–7 (I.1.2).

overcome their mutual fear and create society. However, the eventual results of this coming together are ambivalent.

Society ensures [the first men] of, and facilitates [for them] the possession of things, of which they have a natural need. But it provides them at the same time with the idea of infinite chimerical needs, which press on them a thousand times more vividly than their real needs, and which render them perhaps more miserable when they are gathered together than when they were dispersed.[16]

Diderot's cool assessment of human progress foreshadows the conclusion of Rousseau's *Second Discourse* a few years later. One can even read the *Second Discourse* as a comprehensive comment on Diderot's short entry. By introducing a second distinction between man's natural needs and his infinite, socially conditioned needs, Diderot's article specifically encapsulates one of Rousseau's principal arguments about the fatal effects of society on human happiness and natural equality. According to a common notion at the time, man in the state of nature was weak, naked, without natural weapons, and hence in need of support against predators and protection from harsh weather conditions. Rousseau powerfully challenged this claim. Man in the state of nature was self-sufficient and had powers that exactly matched his needs. Because his imagination was extremely limited, he never cared about the future – nor could he develop the boundless desires characteristic of civilisation. He was thus happy and content.[17]

The later chimerical needs of society, Rousseau argues in the *Second Discourse*, were the result of man's *perfectibilité*, especially his evolving aptitude to distinguish between sizes and between things similar and dissimilar. In a social context, and driven by imagination, this leads to a state of permanent comparison between himself and others, creating sociable feelings of affection, such as love, but also triggering competition and with it envy and hatred. Such (un-)sociable feelings were unknown to the self-sufficient, isolated first human beings in the state of nature, Rousseau maintains as he argues against Hobbes's account of the state of nature as a condition of war.[18] Instead, it was the introduction of private property at the first stages of society, tied to these unsociable passions, which sparked social conflict and war. In line with Montesquieu's account of the first human beings as timid, non-aggressive animals, Diderot's article led the way to this noteworthy

[16] [Diderot], 'Besoin', 213.

[17] On Rousseau's concept of imagination, see Laetitia de Rohan Chabot, 'Le rôle de l'imagination dans la naissance du sentiment moral chez Rousseau', *Astérion* 11 (2013): http://asterion.revues.org/2393 (last accessed 22 March 2016).

[18] Rousseau, *DI*, 149–150.

rejection of Hobbes: 'Therefore they unite, losing within society the sentiment of their weakness, and the state of war begins.'[19]

The external causes of increased needs in human history, Rousseau claims, lay in abandoning a solitary life in favour of permanent settlement and family life, providing humans with leisure to invent new conveniences.[20] The growth of needs thus coincided with the beginnings of sociability and property. Rousseau terms this the first revolution in human history. The *Second Discourse* further expands Diderot's distinction between man's few natural needs and his chimerical needs in society. The latter were part of a novel, unnatural needs cycle resulting from the invention of metallurgy with its ultimate outcome – urban luxury production. Luxury was both the consequence and cause of the spiralling desires that resulted from the infinite capacity of the human mind to imagine Rousseau's new *besoin(s) de fantaisie* – or Diderot's *besoins de l'esprit.*[21] 'Fantasy, which demands endlessly more for its satisfaction than nature . . . and man's purer, less artificial happiness,' writes an anonymous German author in a Rousseauvian vein in 1786, 'creates by these means a thousand more needs and an equal number of skills and proficiencies to satisfy those needs.'[22]

Such a desire-driven economy, in contrast to one based on natural needs, was the subject of fierce controversy in the eighteenth century. Most notoriously, Bernard Mandeville, but also Voltaire and other neo-Epicurean thinkers, made the case that only an economy fired by the inventive power of human desires, and hence luxury, could create wealth, cultural refinement, and an internationally competitive state.[23] For Rousseau, however, it was this infinite feature of luxury that was guaranteed to destroy society by outbalancing natural needs with limitless desires. Luxury, as both a source of income and a sign of social

[19] [Diderot], 'Besoin', 213; cf. Montesquieu, *Spirit of the Laws*, 6–7.

[20] Rousseau, *DI*, 164–165.

[21] See Rousseau's distinction between natural needs and illusory needs in *Emile*: 'Alors il faut distinguer avec soin le vrai besoin, le besoin naturel, du besoin de fantaisie qui commence à naitre, ou de celui qui ne vient que de la surabondance de vie dont j'ai parlé.' (*OC* IV, 312).

[22] Anon., 'Nothwendigkeit encyclopädischer Kenntnisse, aus dem Grunde vervielfältigter Bedürfnisse', *Journal aller Journale* 2 (1786), 174–175. This text can be accessed at www.ub.uni-bielefeld.de/diglib/aufklaerung (last accessed 22 March 2016).

[23] See István Hont, 'The Early Enlightenment Debate on Commerce and Luxury', in *The Cambridge History of Eighteenth-Century Political Thought*, ed. Mark Goldie and Robert Wokler (Cambridge: Cambridge University Press, 2006), 379–418; E. J. Hundert, *The Enlightenment's Fable: Bernard Mandeville and the Discovery of Society* (Cambridge: Cambridge University Press, 1994), ch. 4; Christopher Berry, *The Idea of Luxury: A Conceptual and Historical Investigation* (Cambridge: Cambridge University Press, 1994).

distinction, dramatically widened inequalities in commercial societies. Higher wages in luxury production led to migration into cities and hence to the neglect of agriculture and to depopulation. In Rousseau's eyes, this would shake up current property relations, destroy liberties, and eventually give rise to a new Leviathan of all-levelling despotism.[24] As is well known, many of the physiocrats' efforts were directed at setting right the natural hierarchy of agriculture and luxury production in France, which they viewed as having been profoundly distorted by Colbert's industrialism.[25] Various other eighteenth-century authors agreed with Rousseau on this alleged distortion of the relationship between agriculture and industry. The German anonymous author located historically this inversion of primary (natural) needs and secondary (artificial) needs in the rise of cities:

> Principally, the city dweller is the servant of the countryman and supports him who cultivates the field in order that the latter will not let him perish by famine. Yet habit and a refined ease made the invention of the arts little by little necessary. Even the farmer cannot dispense of them anymore. As a result, the original relation has been reversed, and he who cultivates the land to feed the artisan and the skilled worker has become their slave. He sweats behind his plough and in the field under his sickle in order to purchase superfluous handicrafts with the noblest and most indispensable food; he works as a serf for the spirit of new inventions, which do not nourish the body but chiefly fantasy.[26]

The author identified three crucial upshots of this development. One was global trade, 'the selfish servant of new innumerable needs', satisfying a craving for commodities and ornaments. It was followed by the second result of increasing artificial needs – the striving for domination, glory, and conquest (*Herrsch- und Ruhmsucht*) in order to secure the supply of commodities through political rule and cheap (or slave) labour.[27] The third consequence was the rise of the sciences, which were indispensable for the former two developments (as attested by astronomy, shipbuilding, or political science). Their triangular relationship was almost symbiotic, for the sciences not only supplied global trade and imperial conquest with the necessary technologies and knowledge, but also further evolved as a result.

[24] Rousseau, *DI*, 185ff. and 201ff. Cf. István Hont, 'Luxury and the Route to Revolution in Rousseau's *Discourse on Inequality*', unpublished manuscript of a lecture held on 28 February 2011 at the Cambridge Political Thought and Intellectual History Research Seminar.

[25] Cf. Reinhard Bach, 'Rousseau et les physiocrates: une cohabitation extraordinaire', *Etudes J.-J. Rousseau* 10 (1999), 9–82.

[26] Anon., 'Nothwendigkeit encyclopädischer Kenntnisse', 174. [27] Ibid., 175–177.

This link between trade, luxury, and aggressive power politics refers us back to Rousseau's cutting criticism of the sciences, the arts, and monarchical politics in the *First Discourse*.[28] Despite Rousseau's later claims about his sudden, near mystical insight into the banes of society and the goodness of human nature on the road to Vincennes in summer 1749, his argument about the role of needs in human history had not been fully developed by then. Its kernel can, however, be identified in the *First Discourse* of 1750 and even more so in the ensuing debate. As Robert Wokler has pointed out, it was the reaction of his critics that made Rousseau sharpen and further develop his rather muddled criticism of modern civilisation in the *First Discourse* into a powerful argument about social inequality.[29]

## III Ill or cure? The sciences in modern society

When Kant took up the subject of the social effects of the sciences, he was probably not only acquainted with Rousseau's major works but also with the debate about the *First Discourse* (which had repeatedly been published together with critical reviews and Rousseau's responses). The handwritten *Remarks on Observations Concerning the Feeling of the Beautiful and the Sublime* of 1765 reveal how Kant struggled with Rousseauvian themes in this crucial phase of his intellectual development. Together with the lecture notes of his students from this period, they not only testify to a personal crisis and to self-redefinition as a philosopher; they should be read more generally as part of the politicisation of German enlightened thinkers in the wake of the Seven Years War, to which Rousseau supplied some crucial spurs.[30] Taking up Rousseau's *Second Discourse* together with the *First Discourse* and *Emile*, Kant phrased his reflections on the social role of scholarship in terms of the problem of human needs and social inequality. His account rests on a distinction between man in the state of nature and civilised man, as well as between the individual and mankind as a whole. According to Kant, socially conditioned needs had made man more dependent and hence more miserable, selfish, and potentially malevolent than

[28] On the *First Discourse* as a rejection of monarchical politics see Leo Strauss, 'On the Intention of Rousseau', *Social Research* 14 (1947), 455–487, and Paul A. Rahe, 'The Enlightenment Indicted: Rousseau's Response to Montesquieu', *The Journal of the Historical Society* 18 (2008), 273–302.

[29] Robert Wokler, 'The *Discours sur les sciences et les arts* and Its Offspring: Rousseau in Reply to his Critics', in *Reappraisals of Rousseau: Studies in Honor of R.A. Leigh* (Manchester: Manchester University Press, 1980), 250–278.

[30] See *Aufklärung als Politisierung – Politisierung der Aufklärung*, ed. Hans Erich Bödecker and Ulrich Herrmann (Hamburg: Meiner, 1987).

man in his natural state.[31] Kant was therefore very well aware of the ease with which superfluous pleasures could become needs, and how, conversely, such basic needs as food could be refined into pleasures and luxuries.[32]

Many eighteenth-century accounts of the sciences and scholarship emphasised their origins in man's rational nature, his curiosity and wonder at surprising events in nature.[33] By contrast, Kant argued that their pursuit was not natural, since they were neither part of man's original needs nor prerequisites for his happiness.[34] On the contrary, the sciences and their source, reason, were questionable guides to happiness and satisfaction, which could be better achieved by following our natural instincts.[35] Here Kant repeatedly pointed both to the individual and to the history of the human species in general. In contrast to the vital task of procreation, the sciences could not be perfected in an individual's lifetime. Even in his late works, such as the *Anthropology from a Pragmatic Point of View* of 1798, Kant stressed the disproportion between a scholar's lifetime and the pursuit of knowledge.[36] A similar case was the sufferings of the young bachelor, a fate with which both Kant and his Königsberg students were rather familiar. Though physically able to produce an offspring, civil law would not allow the bachelor to enter wedlock before he was ready to support a family. Thus 'the age of manhood is incomparably far longer delayed', Kant claims in his anthropology lectures of 1775–1776, 'than in the natural condition, because the needs of his wife and children are greatly multiplied, and in order to be able to meet this multitude of needs he will have to have acquired the capacity to be able to provide for them all over the course of many years'.[37] In this conflict between nature and civilisation, our animal and our moral characters were pitted against one another – often resulting in vice and pain.

This effect of cultural progress already featured prominently in Kant's argument against the naturalness of the sciences and their relation to human happiness in the *Remarks* of 1765. In a passage very much in tune with the outline of human progress in Rousseau's *Second Discourse*,

[31] Kant, *Bemerkungen*, 109; *AA* XXVII, 63 (Praktische Philosophie Herder): 'Je eigennütziger, desto mehr bedürftig'. Cf. *AA* XXVII, 65.

[32] Kant, *Bemerkungen*, 76: 'Von den Annemlichkeiten die man zum Bedürfnis macht und umgekehrt'.

[33] Jean le Rond D'Alembert, 'Discours préliminaire', in *Encyclopédie*, vol. 1 (1751), iv. Cf. Adam Smith, 'The History of Astronomy' (1746), in *Essays on Philosophical Subjects*, ed. W. P. D. Wightman and J.C. Bryce (Indianapolis: Liberty Fund, 1982), 31–32.

[34] See Kant, *AA* XXVII, 63 (Praktische Philosophie Herder).

[35] Cf. Kant, *AA* IV, 396–367.

[36] *AA* 325; cf. *AA* VII, 116.

[37] Kant, 'Anthropology Friedländer (1775–1776)', trans. G. Felicitas Munzel, in *Lectures on Anthropology*, ed. Allen Wood and Robert B. Louden (Cambridge: Cambridge University Press, 2012), 218; *AA* VII, 116 and *AA* XXV, 683.

he stressed the contingency, the slow development of the sciences, and their local and cultural limitations:

> When something is not in keeping with the length of a human lifetime, nor with its epochs, nor with the larger part of mankind, but is ultimately a matter very much of chance and only possible with the greatest difficulty, it does not belong to the happiness and perfection of the human race. How many centuries went by before the first real sciences appeared and how many nations are in the world which will never possess them.[38]

In contrast to the army of Rousseau's critics, Kant thus basically agreed in 1765 with the Genevan on the corrupting effects of the sciences. He viewed their current, glory-conditioned pursuit as intrinsically connected to luxury and as leading to idleness, melancholy, and bad health, thereby weakening human morality and virtue. According to Kant, in a passage that almost literally rephrases Rousseau, the pursuit of the sciences takes 'away so much time that the moral education of youth is neglected'; the sciences habituate 'minds [so much] to the sweetness of speculation that good actions are not done'.[39] This critical account of the deterioration of moral energies in civil society is consistent with Herder's notes of Kant's moral philosophy lectures. According to them, the 'fantastical' increase of human needs through luxury would impede moral feelings like pity from taking practical effect as solidarity and charity. The result was somewhat paradoxical: true philanthropy was less common in a society of superfluities with its extended inequality, where charity was actually more desirable than in man's original state (the 'state of innocence'). Instead of providing help to the poor, civilised human beings would merely indulge in cosmopolitan moralising without action.[40] Kant's later emphasis on acting from pure moral duty alone can be seen as a powerful response to this modern dilemma.

He also repeated Rousseau's attack on the harmful effects of scholarship on the majority of those pursuing it: 'The poor accommodation of science with mankind is primarily to be seen in this: that the vast majority of those who wish to ornament themselves with learning achieve not a whit of improvement of the understanding but rather a perversion of the same, not to mention that for the majority science only serves as a mechanism for vanity.'[41] Given this conundrum, one could wonder why so many pursue the sciences, seeking to become scholars. The answer to this question was implied above. Their motivation was,

[38] Kant, *Bemerkungen*, 34; *AA* XX, 38, Zammito's translation in *Kant*, 95f.
[39] Kant, *Bemerkungen*, 37; *AA* XX, 43 ; cf. Rousseau, *DI*, 17.
[40] Kant, *AA* XXVII, 64–65; *Bemerkungen*, 101.
[41] *AA* XX, 35, Zammito's translation in *Kant*, 96.

in Rousseau's words, 'a craving for distinction' which was the mainspring of modern commercial societies based on inequalities of power, wealth, and reputation. 'Anyone', Rousseau maintained in the *Preface to Narcissus*, 'who cultivates the agreeable talents wants to please, to be admired, and indeed wants to be admired more than anyone else is.'[42]

Kant understood this argument very well. In his *Remarks* of 1765, he re-described *amour propre* as an outward-looking striving for honour. Its result was the system of sharply distinguished ranks in commercial monarchies. People would hence tend to identify intellectual talents, wealth, and privileges of birth with moral worth, leading thereby to the corruption of our moral feelings. 'In the manner that one holds the arts and the sciences in such high regard', Kant asserts, 'one makes contemptible those who are not in possession of them and this leads us to injustice.'[43] Thus 'scholars think everything is made for their sake, like aristocrats'.[44] According to the early Kant, a pure inclination to the sciences out of a love for truth, with no regard to honour, was an illusion. The scholar was the 'most ambitious' (*ehrgeizigste*) of all, working tirelessly for honour and distributing honour and glory to others at the same time.[45] Without love of honour, the poorly paid Kant told his students, there would be no incentive to pursue the sciences.

These remarks certainly reflect the eighteenth-century promotion of scholarship through academic positions, princely pensions, and prize contests. They also allude to the quasi-aristocratic rules of conduct within the Republic of Letters and to the common meritocratic self-image of the eighteenth-century scholar.[46] The centrality of glory in intellectual activity posed, however, some very disturbing questions concerning the virtue of the scholar, whose life was usually hailed in a Stoic fashion in numerous academic *éloges* as characterised by ascetic self-renunciation and the conquest of the passions.[47]

Kant and Rousseau were not the only authors who questioned this Stoic notion of the scholar. In particular, authors mixing Epicurean and Augustinian elements in their analysis of human nature and the socially beneficial results of self-interest, like Mandeville and the

[42] Rousseau, *DI*, 99. [43] Kant, *Bemerkungen*, 33–34; *AA* XX, 37.

[44] Kant, *Bemerkungen*, 34; *AA* XX, 38.

[45] Kant, *AA* XXVII, 45 (Praktische Philosophie Herder).

[46] Anne Goldgar, *Impolite Learning: Conduct and Community in the Republic of Letters 1680–1750* (New Haven: Yale University Press, 1995).

[47] See Charles B. Paul, *Science and Immortality: The* Eloges *of the Paris Academy of Sciences, 1699–1791* (Berkeley: University of California Press, 1980); Alexander Schmidt, 'Scholarship, Morals and Government: Jean-Henri-Samuel Formey's and Johann Gottfried Herder's Responses to Rousseau's First Discourse', *Modern Intellectual History* 9 (2012), 249–274.

Marquis D'Argens, were eager to point out that the sciences originated in self-love and related passions like pride, greed, and a striving for glory.[48] In his *Lettres juives* of 1737 (translated into English as *The Jewish Spy*), the Marquis D'Argens ridiculed Stoic and Platonic notions of scholarly motivations. 'Philosophers, and Men of Learning', he wrote, 'are incessantly talking of the Contempt of Glory, of Wisdom, and the Tranquillity of the Soul. Notwithstanding all their fine and magnificent Harangues 'tis certain that were it not for Glory and Vanity, Ignorance would extend its Empire over all mankind.'[49] D'Argens himself was involved in the renewal of the Berlin Academy in 1746 as king Frederick the Great's confidant, and used the example of scholars to reject the claim that man was the gentlest and most peaceful animal. In terms of the ancient association between wisdom and virtue, one would expect scholars to be the most virtuous of men. Yet in reality, loud-mouthed courtesans and savages were more restrained in their quarrels and wars than prideful *gens de lettres*.[50] The aim of D'Argens's mockery was a serious and sceptical one, modelled on Pierre Bayle's account of the *République des Lettres* as a Hobbesian sphere of jealousy and perpetual war.[51] How could scholars and philosophers be trusted authorities when they could not agree on the slightest issue and conducted their disputes in the most vicious ways? D'Argens and other *hommes de lettres* repeatedly drew up plans to regulate the seemingly anarchic sphere of letters through government intervention and expert tribunals.[52] Kant's later claim that the *Critique of Pure Reason* would function as a quasi-sovereign tribunal pacifying such philosophical wars through a rational procedure, allowing for a true competition between arguments, was his ingenious Hobbesian solution to this wider debate.[53]

[48] On this blend of Augustinianism and Epicureanism, see: Jean Lafond, *L'homme et son image: Morales et littérature de Montaigne à Mandeville* (Paris: Champion, 1996), esp. 345–368 and 441–458; Pierre Force, *Self-Interest before Adam Smith: A Genealogy of Economic Science* (Cambridge: Cambridge University Press, 2003).

[49] Jean-Baptiste de Boyer Marquis D'Argens, *The Jewish Spy: Being a Philosophical, Historical and Critical Correspondence* [...], 3rd ed., vol. 3 (London, 1766), 26 (Letter 84); cf. Lorraine Daston, 'The ideal and reality of the Republic of Letters in the Enlightenment', *Science in Context* 4 (1991), 367–386.

[50] Jean-Baptiste de Boyer Marquis D'Argens, *Ocellus Lucanus en grec et en françois: avec des dissertations sur les principales questions de la métaphysique, de la phisique, et de la morale des anciens* (Utrecht: Libraires associés, 1762), 181–191.

[51] 'C'est la liberté, qui règne dans la République des Lettres. Cette République est un état extrêmement libre. On n'y reconoit que l'empire de la vérité et de la raison; et sous leurs auspices on fait la guerre innocement à qui que ce soit. Les amis s'y doivent tenir en garde contre leurs amis, les pères contre leurs enfants, les beaux-pères contre leurs gendres: c'est comme en siècle de fer.' (Bayle, 'Catius', in *Dictionnaire Historique et Critique*, 3rd ed., vol. 2 (Rotterdam: Michel Bohm, 1720), 812 a-b).

[52] See Schmidt, 'Scholarship, Morals and Government'.

[53] Kant, *AA* III, 492–493.

Like Rousseau, Kant took up what could be seen (with some hesitation) as the Augustinian and Epicurean analysis of modern society, while attacking some of their moral consequences. Following Rousseau, Kant identified the drive to compare ourselves with others as the main root of civilised society and an economy of honour, of which the pursuit of the sciences was an integral part.[54] Kant's complex notion of honour, his distinction between pride and craving for honour (*Ehrbegierde*) on the one hand and a more natural love of honour (*Ehrliebe*) on the other, cannot be fully analysed here.[55] Yet it is noteworthy that despite its potential for corruption, he did not entirely condemn honour. Instead, Kant – like Hobbes, Rousseau, and Adam Smith – understood profoundly the paradox of honour: the drive to acquire it originates in our notion of equality.[56] We naturally want others to recognise our worth as human beings. In society we thus need, to a certain extent, external honour as a means of recognising our inner worth. According to Collins's lecture notes of 1785, Kant linked this to a drive to submit our ideas to the judgment of others. It implied a sense of recognition of their intellectual and moral authority.[57] Therefore, allowing others to judge us functioned as a check on our moral self-love (*Philautie*), preventing it from turning into the empty pride of moral egoism.[58] Kant thus only criticised the illusions human beings received from taking external honour as an end in itself, resulting in arrogance (*Arrogantia*). Furthermore, it is often overlooked that Kant's case for a free public sphere in his famous essay *What Is Enlightenment?* was grounded in a certain concept of sociability and meant as a check against (intellectual) vainglory, especially that of religious and political authorities.

Under civilised conditions, honour and the sciences can thus bring about both positive and negative effects. 'Softness in morals, idleness, and vanity bring forth the sciences. These lend new decoration to the whole, deter much evil and if they are raised to a certain height, ameliorate the evil which they themselves have brought about.'[59] Again, this

[54] Kant, *AA* XX, 95: 'Die Gesellschaft macht daß man sich nur vergleichungsweise schätzt'. Cf. *AA* XX, 97 and *AA* XX, 166.

[55] Kant, *AA* XXVII, 409–412 (Moralphilosophie Collins); cf. *AA* VII, 272–273.

[56] Kant, *Bemerkungen*, 123: 'Der Trieb der Ehre ist gegründet auf den Trieb zur Gleichheit und dem Trieb zur Einheit'. Cf. *AA* XXVII, 63 (Praktische Philosophie Herder).

[57] *AA* XXVII, 411 (Moralphilosophie Collins). Cf. Kant's similar earlier claim in the *Bemerkungen*, 124: 'Die Ehrbegierde welche ein Sporn der Wissenschaft ist entspringt aus der Vergleichung unseres Urtheils mit dem Urtheil anderer als ein Mittel setzet also Hochachtung vor anderer Urteil voraus'.

[58] *AA* XXVII, 357–360 (Moralphilosophie Collins). On mutual recognition in Rousseau, Kant, and subsequent philosophers, see Axel Honneth's chapter in this volume (Chapter 11).

[59] *AA* XX, 42–43, trans. Shell in *Kant and the Limits of Autonomy*, 78.

argument was not too different from Rousseau's. Replying to the critics of his *First Discourse*, Rousseau insisted that he did not want to abolish the arts and sciences; for under already corrupt conditions they would prevent greater evil. As he wrote in the fragment on *Luxury, Commerce and the Arts*, the best use one could make of philosophy is its employment to destroy the defects it had caused.[60]

Yet Kant was even more confident about the social role of the sciences under civilised conditions: 'Among all ranks none is more useless than the scholar under the conditions of natural simplicity and none more necessary [to society] in the state of oppression by superstition and force.'[61] But what would this distinctive social role of the scholar consist in? The *Remarks* merely offer some scattered ideas. What seems clear is that the early Kant believed that *Wissenschaften*, correctly understood, would instruct us about our real needs, making us more moderate without turning to asceticism, the perverted reaction to luxury. The sciences would also show us how to properly fulfil our duties in society.[62] This programme is in many ways similar to what recent scholarship identifies as some of the neo-Stoic aspects of Rousseau's *Émile* and Adam Smith's *Theory of Moral Sentiments*.[63] While questioning the role of scholarship, Kant thus developed the kernel of a vision of the critical scholar as a public figure who would bring about enlightenment and help to mend social ills through instruction.[64]

He was, however, under no illusion that the road was anything but long and tortuous – and that from a moral perspective no improvement seemed to have been achieved by the progress of affluence and refinement brought about by our ('fantastic') needs. In his *Idea for Universal History with a Cosmopolitan Purpose* of 1784, Kant notes:

> Human nature endures the hardest ills under the deceptive appearance of external welfare; and Rousseau was not so wrong when he preferred to it the condition of savages, as long, namely, as one leaves out this last stage to which our species has yet to ascend. We are cultivated in a high degree by art and science. We are civilized, perhaps to the point of being overburdened, by all sorts of social

[60] Rousseau, *OC* III, 516. [61] Kant, *AA* XX, 10.
[62] Kant, *Bemerkungen*, 10, 18, and 39.
[63] Christopher Brooke, *Philosophic Pride: Stoicism and Political Thought from Lipsius to Rousseau* (Princeton: Princeton University Press, 2012), ch. 8; Ryan Patrick Hanley, *Adam Smith and the Character of Virtue* (Cambridge: Cambridge University Press, 2011).
[64] Cf. Shell, *Kant and the Limits of Autonomy*, 86. On how Johann Gottlieb Fichte responded to Rousseau by expanding this idea into a new vision of society, see Alexander Schmidt, 'Self-Cultivation (*Bildung*) and Sociability between Mankind and the Nation: Fichte and Schleiermacher on Higher Education', in *Ideas of Education: Philosophy and Politics from Plato to Dewey*, ed. Christopher Brooke and Elizabeth Frazer (London: Routledge, 2013), 160–177.

decorum and propriety. But very much is still lacking before we can be held to be already moralized. For the idea of morality still belongs to culture; but the use of this idea, which comes down only to a resemblance of morals in love of honor and in external propriety, constitutes only being civilized.[65]

With respect to happiness and the good life, the comparison between primeval and civilised man thus turns out unequivocally in favour of the former. Here the problem of evil and ills in human history and current society is raised with powerful political implications. In the next section, I will discuss how Kant's analysis of human ills deviated from its Rousseauvian roots.

## IV Rousseau and Kant on the dialectic of evil in human history

Let us briefly resume Rousseau's position on the relationship between the sciences and human needs with respect to the problem of evil. Rousseau's attack on the sciences and the arts in the *First Discourse* displayed no systematic philosophical foundation. However, in his responses to the critics of this essay and in his subsequent writings, Rousseau developed this critique into a more general argument about the limited role of reason in human nature in general and as a basis for moral agency in particular. 'Science is not suited to man in general', he wrote in the *Preface to Narcissus*:

He forever goes astray in his quest for it; and if he sometimes attains it, he almost always does so to his detriment. He is born to act and to think, not to reflect. Reflection only makes him unhappy without making him better or wiser.[66]

And in one of the most controversial statements of the *Second Discourse*, Rousseau maintained that 'the state of reflection is against Nature, and the man who meditates is a depraved animal'.[67] The paradox of reason, and its more refined manifestations in the arts and the sciences, Rousseau believed, was that the very quality that elevated man above (other) animals threatened to drag him below them with respect to happiness and health. Reason alienated man from the animal-like slumber within the moment by creating an unnatural concern for the future, the past, and the opinions of others. In a more fundamental understanding of luxury,

[65] Kant, 'Idea for universal history with a cosmopolitan aim' (1784), in *Kant's Idea for a Universal History with a Cosmopolitan Aim: A Critical Guide*, ed. Amélie Oksenberg Rorty and James Schmidt (Cambridge: Cambridge University Press, 2009), 18; *AA* VIII, 26.

[66] Rousseau, *DI*, 102.

[67] Rousseau, *DI*, 102; Cf. *Discours*, ed. Meier, 88, and Rousseau's 'Des mœurs', *OC* III, 554.

the arts and sciences exceeded what was naturally needed for human existence. For Rousseau, they thus stood at the origins of evil. As he wrote in the *Dernière Réponse à Bordes*, 'everything beyond the physical necessary is a source of evil [*mal*]'.[68] Here the link between needs and evil is laid bare. For it was one of Rousseau's most important insights in his analysis of needs that superfluous conveniences could easily degenerate into real needs, forming 'the first source of evils', since 'it became much more cruel to be deprived of them than to possess them was sweet, and men were unhappy to lose them without being happy to possess them'.[69] For Kant, this position had a clearly identifiable lineage in ancient moral philosophy. Rousseau, 'that subtle Diogenes', was a refined heir of the Cynics in his emphasis 'that nature would have provided us with everything, if we did not create new needs'.[70] Kant could not agree more:

> [T]he more a cultivated reason gives itself over to the aim of enjoying life and happiness, the further the human being falls short of true contentment . . . for after reckoning all the advantages they draw, I do not say from the invention of all the arts of common luxury, but even from the sciences (which also seem to them in the end to be a luxury of the understanding), they nevertheless find that they have in fact only brought more hardship down on their shoulders than they have gained in happiness. . . . [R]eason is not sufficiently effective in guiding the will safely in regard to its objects and the satisfaction of all our needs (which in part itself multiplies), and an implanted natural instinct would have guided us much more certainly to this end.[71]

Yet this did not lead Kant to a form of irrationalism or 'misology', a position that has been frequently and, I believe, incorrectly attributed to Rousseau. Instead, Kant employed this Cynic analysis of the effects of reason on human happiness in order to refute eudaemonistic positions in Enlightenment moral philosophy. Such positions, often eclectically blending various Hellenistic schools in moral philosophy with Wolffian notions of human perfection, claimed that reasonable conduct, virtue, and human well-being would work in tandem.[72] Against this, Kant

[68] Rousseau, *DI*, 84; *OC* III, 95. On the problem of evil and natural goodness in Rousseau see P. Hoffmann, 'Mal' in *Dictionnaire de Jean-Jacques Rousseau*, 579–581; Alexis Philonenko, *Jean-Jacques Rousseau et la pensée du malheur* (Paris: Vrin, 1984); Victor Gourevitch, 'Rousseau on Providence', *The Review of Metaphysics* 53 (2000), 565–611.

[69] Rousseau, *DI*, 165.

[70] Kant, *Lectures On Ethics*, trans. Peter Heath, ed. J. B. Schneewind and Peter Heath (Cambridge: Cambridge University Press, 1997), 45; *AA* 27, 248–249 (Moralphilosophie Collins).

[71] Kant, *Groundwork for the Metaphysics of Morals*, ed. and trans. Allen W. Wood (New Haven: Yale University Press, 2002), 11–12; *AA* 4, 395–396.

[72] See esp. Johann Georg Heinrich Feder, *Lehrbuch der praktischen Philosophie*, 4th ed. (Göttingen: Dieterich, 1776).

famously insisted on the absolute autonomy of reason and its expression in the good will, independently of any considerations of human happiness or well-being. That reason was not too conducive to meeting our natural needs, or to a satisfied life, demonstrated emphatically that man's purpose as a rational being was not happiness but freedom and moral action from duty. Again, Kant's suggestion here was somewhat disheartening. For moralisation could not be fully achieved in an individual's lifetime under the conditions of current society, with its multiple dependencies on both persons and material things. It could only be approximated by mankind as a social collective throughout history.

Nevertheless, Kant sought from the outset to demonstrate that nature was coming to the aid of mankind's moral self-perfection with the spurs of physical and moral evil (*die Übel* and *das Böse*).[73] This distinctly Kantian version of theodicy can be first identified in the Friedländer notes of Kant's anthropology lectures of winter 1775–1776.[74] While the 1770s are usually referred to as Kant's 'silent years', it was in this decade that he first developed the dialectic between the disadvantages and the benefits of the sciences and civilisation into a providential history of the progress of mankind from nature via corruption to moral perfection. This condition was to be approximated in the perpetual peace of a cosmopolitan league of nations, in which the moral actions of citizens followed the force of conscience. The Königsberg professor thereby retold in important ways the narrative of the *Second Discourse*, partly to correct the Genevan. Kant's conjectural history of civil society was also familiar from eighteenth-century readings of the book of Genesis, the natural law tradition, and especially Mandeville.[75]

Within his system of anthropology, Kant engaged with Rousseau under the aspect 'of the character of mankind in general', a subject which in this explicit form was strikingly absent from most physico-theological

[73] Cf. Allen Wood, 'Kant and the Intelligibility of Evil', in *Kant's Anatomy of Evil*, ed. by Sharon Anderson Gold and Pablo Muchnik (Cambridge: Cambridge University Press, 2010), 144–172; Jeanine M. Grenberg, 'Social Dimensions of Kant's Conception of Radical Evil', ibid., 173–194; David James, *Rousseau and German Idealism: Freedom, Dependence and Necessity* (Cambridge: Cambridge University Press, 2013), ch. 2.

[74] These notes are not verbatim records of Kant's lectures but rather revised manuscripts for an exclusive market of readers. This implies that there was indeed a growing demand for a record of Kant's thought outside the classroom. See Werner Stark, 'Historical Notes and Interpretive Questions about Kant's *Lectures on Anthropology*', in *Essays on Kant's Anthropology*, ed. Jacobs and Kain, 15–37. The Friedländer manuscript is also remarkable because here Kant first makes the case for a league of nations to prevent all future wars and to allow for reform: see *AA* XXV, 696.

[75] See Bernard Mandeville, *The Fable of the Bees*, ed. Frederick B. Kaye, 2 vols. (Indianapolis: Liberty Fund, 1988); John Robertson, 'Sacred History and Political Thought: Neapolitan Responses to the Problem of Sociability after Hobbes', *Historical Journal* 56 (2013), 1–29.

textbooks on anthropology of his time. 'This was an important item', Kant emphasised, however, 'about which many authors have already ventured to write, among whom Rousseau is the most distinguished.'[76] Kant here first followed Carl Linnaeus in placing the animal aspect of the human being in one class with apes. By nature, man was thus a dexterous and strong, even if not a handsome and kind, animal. By contrast to Rousseau, Kant stressed the aggressively unsociable character of original man:

> Yet with respect to his own species, with respect to other human beings ... he is mistrustful, violent and hostile toward his own kind, which is no longer as manifest in the civil state, since the human being is there held under constraint, but which still does very much sprout up, and a great deal from the animal state still adheres to us.[77]

In Kant's view, the tendency of human beings to harm others was not the pure result of society and of man's *perfectibilité*, as Rousseau maintained, but rather a natural human trait. Yet his slightly puzzling formulation of the problem of human evil does not really amount to a rejection of Rousseau's natural goodness hypothesis. In another passage, Kant stresses that human beings in the state of nature were innocent and morally good in a negative sense, possessing neither virtues nor vices.[78] The latter were the result of the countless needs in civil society. How should we then understand Kant's repeated claim about man's original malevolence? One of the most comprehensible answers is provided in the Pillau lecture notes of winter 1777–1778. It is here that Kant describes human evil (*das Böse*) as concomitant with reason and thus with human beings' capacity for freedom, rejecting the orthodox theological interpretations of original sin.[79] For Kant, evil originates in the problematic combination of man's animalistic features with his rational nature, allowing him to wrest himself away from natural laws and impulses. This capacity could be transformed into moral evil or 'radical evil', i.e. action based on an evil maxim, as he was later to argue in *Religion within the Limits of Mere Reason* of 1793. In a Hobbesian vein, the much earlier Pillau notes especially emphasise the problem of choice and the fundamental disagreement about goods and values, which led to dissent and conflict.[80]

[76] Kant, *Lectures on Anthropology*, 212; *AA* XXV, 675.

[77] Kant, *Lectures on Anthropology*, 214; *AA* XXV, 678. On the problem of unsocial sociability, see Allen Wood, 'Kant's Fourth Proposition: The Unsociable Sociability of Human Nature' and Paul Guyer, 'The Crooked Timber of Mankind', in *Kant's Idea*, ed. Rorty and Schmidt, 112–128 and 129–149.

[78] Kant, *AA* XXV, 685 and 687. [79] Kant, *AA* XXV, 844.

[80] *AA* XXV, 844; cf. Thomas Hobbes, *On the Citizen*, ed. Richard Tuck and Michael Silverthorne (Cambridge: Cambridge University Press, 1997), 11. Very illuminating on the relationship between reason, opinion, and aggression is Tuck's introduction to this edition, xix–xxvii.

According to Kant's blend of Christian and Stoic versions of teleology, primeval man's unsociable malevolence was hence not an evil *per se*. It had to fulfil a crucial purpose in human history, which was captured in the myth of the confusion of tongues at Babel.[81] Divine Providence wanted mankind, according to the Friedländer lecture notes, to disperse across the globe, and to settle even in the most infertile, harsh, and isolated places. Since the earth abounds in habitable space, this could only be achieved through 'intolerance, jealousy, and disagreement with regard to property'.[82]

In a further step, civil society had to be erected against the 'maliciousness of human nature'. There, the multiplying needs of human beings prompted them to further develop their skills in the arts and the sciences.[83] Human needs were here socially conditioned by the division of ranks and its accompanying other-regarding feelings. Contentment no longer depended on the absolute satisfaction of our natural needs of food, shelter, and so on. Instead it was defined relatively, i.e. in comparing our happiness with that of other people – mainly of the same social station.[84] The multiplication of needs and desires equally created infinite new vices unknown to savages. In terms of physical well-being, health, and happiness, the latter were far superior to their civilised brothers and sisters, who were dissatisfied by their real or imagined constant competition with others and by their concern for tomorrow's needs. In contrast to neo-Epicurean defenders of the unsociable origins of modern commercial society, and especially to Mandeville, Kant was reluctant to praise the security, ease, and pleasures created by civilisation. He rather reminded his students of the loss of natural freedom in civil society, occasioned by our dependence on ranks, governmental authorities, and the delusions of social status (*Wahn des Standes*).[85]

Yet while civilised society and its unsociable origins were harmful to our animal nature, they were essential for our perfection towards humanity and virtue. Everyone, Kant told his students, would ask where evil came from, while one ought rather to enquire how the good arose.[86] This

[81] For Kant's account of teleology and providence in history, see Genevieve Lloyd, 'Providence as Progress: Kant's Variations on a Tale of Origins', in *Kant's Idea*, ed. Rorty and Schmidt, 200–215; Paul Guyer, 'Kant's Teleological Conception of Philosophy and Its Development', in *Teleology*, ed. Dietmar H. Heidemann (*Kant Yearbook* 1 (2009), 57–97); Pauline Kleingeld, *Fortschritt und Vernunft: zur Geschichtsphilosophie Kants* (Würzburg: Königshausen & Neumann, 1995).

[82] Kant, *Lectures on Anthropology*, 215 (translation modified); *AA* XXV, 679.

[83] Kant, *Lectures on Anthropology*, 216; *AA* XXV, 680.

[84] Kant, *Lectures on Anthropology*, 220; *AA* XXV, 685.

[85] Kant, *Lectures on Anthropology*, 221; *AA* XXV, 686.

[86] Kant, *AA* XXV, 682. For a standard (quietist) attempt to explain evil in terms of the good, underlining Kant's stark change of focus, see Pierre Villaume, *Von dem Ursprung und den Absichten des Uebels*, 3 vols. (Leipzig: Siegfried Lebrecht Crusius, 1784–1787).

change of focus turned upside down the problem of what theodicy should explain – namely God's goodness given the numerous evils in the world. Kant broadly followed Mandeville in claiming that ills and desires would act as spurs to overcome man's natural sloth and apathy, and turn him into a sociable and industrious animal – thereby kicking off a process of civilisation.[87] Kant mixed this emphasis on man's unsociability with neo-Stoic accounts of how man's original drive for self-preservation was increasingly transformed into moral judgment based on reason, a process that also provided the blueprint for various eighteenth-century histories of mankind.

However, as explained above, Kant took extremely seriously Rousseau's criticism of the enslaving mechanisms of sociability. In a move to correct the Genevan, the Friedländer manuscript sketches out the trajectory from our mere dependence on 'the judgment of others' in civil society to moral autonomy.[88] From this interdependence, Kant notes,

> arises the concept of honour; he [man in general] becomes inspired to undertake a great deal, not only with regard to his needs, but with regard to the common good of life; Arts emerge from this ... The human being refines himself with regard to taste, prosperity and propriety. All these perfections emerged from the maliciousness of the human mind, which first produced civil constraint.[89]

This passage evokes the transformative social mechanism of honour as analysed by Mandeville and the French moralists, especially La Rochefoucauld. In order to gain public praise, genuinely selfish men conquer their egoistic passions by following the rules of propriety and working for the common good. Kant, however, was not content with how 'the Witchcraft of Flattery', to borrow Mandeville's coinage, transformed human beings into civilised and publicly orientated members of society (as long as this remained a mere outward conformity with social conventions).[90] How could such human beings, ensnared in and fearful of the opinion of their fellows, know themselves and cultivate a personality? Compared to the ignorant innocence of savages, civilised men – bound by burdensome masquerades of propriety – were thus worse off with respect to moral freedom. Further advancement was much

[87] Kant, *AA* XXV, 844–846.

[88] Kant's argument here displays a striking similarity to Adam Smith's concept of the impartial spectator in the *Theory of Moral Sentiments*, which Nicholas Phillipson identifies as the Scot's answer to Rousseau's *Second Discourse*. See Phillipson, *Adam Smith: An Enlightened Life* (London: Allen Lane, 2010), ch. 7, and Axel Honneth's chapter in this book (Chapter 11).

[89] Kant, *Lectures on Anthropology*, 216; *AA* XXV, 680.

[90] Mandeville, *The Fable of the Bees*, I, 51.

needed. The next stage would be 'the moral constraint, which consists in every human being fearing the moral judgment of the other, and thereby being necessitated to perform actions of uprightness and of pure moral life'. To achieve this, moral concepts had to be purified by reason; 'Then everyone would consider it to be an honor that he is regarded as an upright man by everyone, and not that he could ride in a carriage.'[91] Yet this conversion of moral judgment was still in a sense external, based on the heteronomous views of (educated) others. Kant henceforth projects a further and final stage of moralisation. At this stage, one is constrained solely by one's conscience and, 'in accordance with the moral law, passes judgment about his moral conduct through his conscience, and also acts likewise'.[92] The imposition of a moralised conscience as our supreme judge would make every external constraint redundant.

With its arrival at this stage of morality, humanity's historical development had run full circle. Mankind regained (natural) freedom on a higher level through the power of reason, prompted by human malevolence and wants. And it was this idea that Kant recognised as the legacy and true meaning of Rousseau's thought, to be rescued from common misapprehension. 'Rousseau', he continually stressed to the audiences of his anthropology lectures,

> did not really want the human being to go back to the state of nature, but rather to look back at it from the stage where he now stands. He assumed that the human being is good by nature (as far as nature allows good to be transmitted), but good in a negative way; that is, he is not evil of his own accord and on purpose, but only in danger of being infected and ruined by evil or inept leaders and examples.[93]

## V Conclusion

We can conclude by further locating the problem of needs and its consequences, the arts and the sciences, in Kant's (regulative) idea of a teleological trajectory of human history. As we saw in broad outline, Rousseau's moral and political philosophy is centrally concerned with human needs. In the *Second Discourse*, he identifies the origin of the loss of natural freedom and goodness in the intertwined process of *perfectibilité* and the expansion of needs beyond self-sufficiency – which leads to the

[91] All quotes from Kant, *Lectures on Anthropology*, 226; *AA* XXV, 692–693.

[92] Kant, *Lectures on Anthropology*, 227; *AA* XXV, 693.

[93] Kant, *Anthropology from a Pragmatic Point of View* (1798), trans. Robert B. Loudon, in *Anthropology, History, and Education*, ed. Günter Zöller and Robert B. Loudon (Cambridge: Cambridge University Press, 2007), 422. For earlier and quite similar formulations of this claim, see *Lectures on Anthropology*, 223; cf. *AA* XXV, 689, 684, and 846.

banes of civilisation, corrupt politics, and moral evil. In Kant's view, Rousseau's *Discourses* had shown, as he writes in *Conjectural Beginning of Human History*, 'quite correctly the unavoidable conflict of culture with the nature of the human species as a physical species in which each individual was entirely to reach his vocation'. For Kant, however, the *Discourses* were only the diagnosis of the disease. The cure was outlined in Rousseau's other writings, especially the *Social Contract* and *Émile*. For it is here that Rousseau 'seeks again to solve the harder problem of how culture must proceed in order properly to develop the predispositions of humanity as a moral species to their vocation, so that the latter no longer conflict with humanity as a natural species'.[94] Kant leaves open the question of whether Rousseau had actually succeeded in this attempt. He also seems to miss the fact that according to Rousseau's *Social Contract*, the prevention of man-made evil in modern society was not the task of mankind as a moral collective but of the legislator and political artifice. The republican state, founded on contract and a civil religion, had to regulate needs in order to secure its citizens against dependence on an arbitrary will. This could be achieved through laws, taxation, the regulation of property relations, and public education.

As David James points out, Kant, while proposing a much darker picture of human nature than Rousseau, puts greater faith in the workings of history and 'commercial sociability' (as István Hont called it).[95] It is here, I argue, that Kant decisively deviated from Rousseau with respect to the role of the arts and sciences in human history. Rousseau called for keeping them in check without endowing them with a positive role in society. As sketched out above, Kant too viewed the arts and sciences as part of the multiplication of needs in a luxury-driven economy, always prone to reinforce social and moral inequalities. Yet he also made the case that 'the sting of needs' was an essential motor of the process of civilisation (characterised by the division of labour and the emergence of the state), which provided the prerequisites for moralisation.[96] Only through the cultivation of reason and taste, i.e. aesthetic education, driven by imaginative (or unnatural) needs, could human beings eventually overcome the ills of unsociability in economic, moral, and political relations.

To fully understand Kant's rejection of Rousseau, it is important to note that he believed from early on that Rousseau was mistaken in his

[94] All quotes: Kant, 'Conjectural Beginning of Human History (1786)', trans. Allen Wood, in Kant, *Anthropology, History, and Education*, 169; *AA* VIII, 116.

[95] James, 'Evil and Perfectibility in Kant's Liberalism'; István Hont, *Politics in Commercial Society. Jean-Jacques Rousseau and Adam Smith*, ed. Béla Kapossy and Michael Sonenscher (Cambridge, MA: Harvard University Press, 2015).

[96] Kant, *AA* XV, 891.

single emphasis on negative education to preserve our natural characteristics, such as our original drive to abstain from cruelly harming others. By contrast, Kant sided here with David Hume's stress on man's aptitude to moral cultivation, achieved through the conventions of modern society. The cultivation of taste especially provided a model of how to make men sociable and overcome ideological and other forms of moral dissent in modern society. 'Rousseau and Hume quarrelled', Kant told the audience of his anthropology lectures, 'about whether virtue was a gift from nature or must be acquired. Rousseau claims the former, but Hume rightly refutes him; for if we do not educate ourselves, virtue will not emerge, even if we possess the disposition to it.'[97]

As Kant writes in the final version of his anthropology lectures, 'The human being is destined by reason to live in a society with human beings and in it to cultivate himself, to civilize himself, and to moralize himself by means of the arts and sciences.'[98] Here the pursuit of the sciences and the development of taste become almost a moral imperative, a way of realising our humanity. One could ask whether Kant ever succeeded in harmonising this Humean vision of sociable politeness with his Rousseauvian principles, for in many ways he was convinced that the unnatural needs culminating in and maintained by the sciences and the arts merely tamed human beings, making them peaceful and law-abiding but not necessarily moral.[99] This claim resonated with the memorable opening paragraphs of the *First Discourse*. Rousseau traced there the trajectory from human needs to government and to the 'iron chains' of civilised societies, over which 'the Sciences, Letters, and Arts ... spread garlands of flowers'.[100] Friedrich Schiller, I believe, understood Kant's difficulty very well when he sought to answer the *citoyen de Genève* with the idea of aesthetic education.[101]

[97] Kant, *AA* XXV, 1107.

[98] Kant, *Anthropology From a Pragmatic Point of View*, 420.

[99] Kant, *AA* XIX, 94.

[100] Rousseau, *DI*, 6.

[101] See my 'Introduction' in Friedrich Schiller, *On the Aesthetic Education of Man and Letters to Prince Frederick Christian von Augustenburg*, trans. Keith Tribe, ed. Alexander Schmidt (London: Penguin, 2016), vii–xxxiv.

# 4 Rousseau and French liberalism, 1789–1870

*Jeremy Jennings*

There was no single reading of Jean-Jacques Rousseau among French liberal writers. Three short quotations can be cited to illustrate this point. The first is taken from a text written by Jean-Joseph Mounier in 1792. Having declared that Montesquieu's *The Spirit of the Laws* was 'one of the most beautiful works that has ever honoured human intelligence',[1] Mounier went on to assert that Rousseau's *Social Contract* was 'the worst book ever written on government'.[2] The second quotation comes from Benjamin Constant and is taken from his famous lecture comparing the liberty of the ancients to that of the moderns. Distancing himself from those he describes as 'the detractors of a great man', Constant here refers to Rousseau as a 'sublime genius, animated by the purest love of liberty'.[3] The final quotation comes from a letter written by Alexis de Tocqueville to one of his closest friends, Louis de Kergorlay, in November 1836 as he worked on the second volume of *Democracy in America*. 'There are three men', Tocqueville wrote, 'with whom I live on an almost daily basis, and these men are Pascal, Montesquieu, and Rousseau.'[4] In brief, among French liberals – as elsewhere[5] – Rousseau was subject to a complex, incomplete, and often contradictory reading by those who were to read his works from the late eighteenth century onwards.

How Rousseau was read before the Revolution of 1789 by those we would now see as being of a liberal disposition was given its clearest and most articulate expression by Germaine de Staël in her *Lettres sur les Écrits*

[1] Mounier, *Recherches sur les causes qui ont empêché les français de devenir libres et sur les moyens qui leur restent pour acquérir la liberté* (Geneva, 1792) I, 148.

[2] Ibid., 150.

[3] 'The Liberty of the Ancients Compared to That of the Moderns', in Benjamin Constant, *Political Writings*, ed. Biancamaria Fontana (Cambridge: Cambridge University Press, 1988), 318.

[4] 'Correspondance d'Alexis de Tocqueville et de Louis de Kergorlay', in Tocqueville, *Œuvres complètes* (Paris: Gallimard, 1977), XIII (1), 418.

[5] See Jean Roussel, *Jean-Jacques Rousseau en France après la Révolution*, 1795–1830 (Paris: Armand Colin, 1972) and Didier Masseau, *Les Ennemis des philosophes: L'antiphilosophie au temps des Lumières* (Paris: Albin Michel, 2000), 373–376.

*et le Caractère de J.J. Rousseau*, published in 1788.[6] This was one of Madame de Staël's earliest writings and, as she commented in the preface to the first edition, 'is it not in youth that we owe the greatest debt of gratitude to Rousseau?' He, after all, was the man who had 'turned virtue into passion'.[7] What followed was a work largely of literary criticism in which pride of place was given to *La Nouvelle Héloïse* and *Émile* – the latter being described as 'the glory of Rousseau' – and where Rousseau's explicitly political writings were dealt with in less than ten pages (marginally more than the five pages devoted to Rousseau's passion for music and his love of botany). Above all, what Madame de Staël captured was the strong sense of empathy and sentimental stimulation that Rousseau was able to inspire in his readers. As we finish our reading of *La Nouvelle Héloïse*, she wrote, 'we feel ourselves more animated by a love of virtue ... we cleave more firmly to our duties ... simple customs, charity, withdrawal from a public life, are more attractive to us'.[8] Equally familiar to the readers of her day would have been Madame de Staël's discussion of Rousseau's troubled personality. Of all the reproaches that could be levelled against him, she conceded, the greatest was that he had abandoned his children. But Madame de Staël would have nothing of the charges of hypocrisy and ingratitude. Wounded by injustice and lies, she wrote, Rousseau's despair and melancholy was such that he had taken his own life.[9]

Madame de Staël's essay, published when she was only twenty-two, did, however, establish certain themes that were to figure not only in her own later writings but also in those of fellow liberals. At a minimum, there were three things that stood in Rousseau's favour. The first was his literary style. Writing in *De la littérature, considerée dans ses rapports avec les institutions sociales*, for example, Madame de Staël commented that Rousseau was 'the most eloquent of our writers'. No one brought 'more warmth, strength and life' to their work.[10] In a similar, if less uncritical, vein Prosper de Barante was later to remark that no one brought more 'strength, enthusiasm and emotion' to his writings than Rousseau. In his hands, Barante wrote, philosophy rediscovered the qualities of 'eloquence and sentiment'. For all the sordid revelations of Rousseau's *Confessions*, no one better revealed the intricacies of the human heart. In brief, Rousseau was an adornment to French culture.

The second source of attraction was Rousseau's apparent sincerity and his passion for virtue. Madame de Staël – herself a restless and tormented soul – was not the only one of her circle to have been moved by the sense

[6] *Œuvres complètes de Mme La Baronne de Staël* (Paris: Treuttel et Würtz, 1820), I, 1–104.
[7] Ibid., 4. [8] Ibid., 25–26. [9] Ibid., 96–97. [10] De Staël, *Œuvres complètes*, IV, 8.

that Rousseau's opening up of his soul raised him above the status of ordinary mortals and above the imperfections of ordinary existence. Apart from Bossuet, she wrote, Rousseau had no equal 'in the sublime art of stirring the human soul'.[11] From 'the depths of the forests', she continued, Rousseau had summoned up a 'tempest of primitive passions' that had shaken government 'upon its obsolete foundations'.[12] Before the powerful emotions Rousseau unleashed, one felt led on 'as if by a friend, a seducer or a master'.[13] Rousseau, Madame de Staël concluded, 'discovered nothing but he set everything on fire'.[14] Over a century later, Émile Faguet said much the same thing. Rousseau, he wrote, was 'an enchanter whose ideas have upon men the effect that passions generally have'.[15]

The third dimension of Rousseau's writings that appealed is one that has gone largely unnoticed until recently: namely, Rousseau's reflections on religion. Here it is not unimportant to recognise the significant role of Protestants (and of Swiss Protestants in particular) in the formation of French liberal thinking during this period. Recent work by Helena Rosenblatt has shown that, by the late eighteenth century, what passed for a Protestant seminary education was far removed from the ideas of John Calvin and was relatively light on such important theological matters as original sin, salvation, and Christ's divinity. The emphasis fell upon reasonableness, toleration, and the sentiments of the heart.[16] Madame de Staël (like her father, Jacques Necker) was therefore of the view that Protestantism harboured 'no active germ of superstition' and that, in the countries where it was professed, it did not 'retard philosophical inquiry at all'. The Protestant religion, she wrote, 'lends virtue all the support it can extract from sensibility'.[17] In line with this opinion, Madame de Staël could praise Rousseau's *Profession de foi du vicaire savoyard* as a 'masterpiece of eloquence in its sentiments ... and metaphysics'. Rousseau, she wrote, 'was the only man of genius in his age who respected the pious thought of which we have such need; he consulted natural instinct, and thereafter devoted all his reflections to proving the truth of this instinct'. By uniting reason and the heart, she declared, the *Profession de foi du vicaire savoyard* enabled us to avoid the 'errors of fanatics and atheists'.[18]

Perhaps unsurprisingly, a similar line of argument was advanced by Madame de Staël's fellow Swiss Protestant and ardent admirer Benjamin

[11] Ibid., 220. [12] Ibid., 8. [13] Ibid., 8. [14] Ibid., 392.
[15] Faguet, *A Literary History of France* (London: Fisher Unwin, 1907), 502.
[16] Rosenblatt, *Liberal Values: Benjamin Constant and the Politics of Religion* (Cambridge: Cambridge University Press, 2008), 19.
[17] De Staël, *Œuvres complètes*, IV, 268–269. [18] De Staël, *Œuvres complètes*, I, 63–64.

Constant. This was particularly evident in Constant's *De la Religion*, the first volume of which was published in 1824. In essence, Constant drew a distinction between two moral systems. The first assigned personal well-being as our goal and self-interest as our guide. In stark contrast, the second spoke of human perfection and of our motives as those of a sense of self-abnegation and personal sacrifice. In Constant's opinion, the first reduced our behaviour to a form of 'moral arithmetic' whilst the second bore testimony to an inner religious sentiment inherent to all human beings. Everything that was most noble and most beautiful in us, Constant believed, derived from this indefinable and inextinguishable inner sentiment.[19]

These arguments were central to the broader political points that Constant wanted to make about the nature of liberty in the modern age, but in our present context their importance lies in Constant's claim that not only had the *philosophes* failed properly to understand the essence of religion, they had also reduced religion to 'a substitute for criminal law'. In the writings of men such as Voltaire, Constant argued, religion served as 'a kind of police force, guaranteeing their property, protecting their lives, disciplining their children, preserving order in their households'.[20] Three writers, Constant argued, had stood out against this trend: Fénelon, Montesquieu and ... Rousseau. As George Armstrong Kelly wrote over twenty years ago,[21] the general content and tone of the arguments advanced by Constant are sufficient to establish 'a certain literary and moral filiation with Rousseau', but the specific point made here by Constant was that Rousseau's writings bore the imprint of 'a pure, disinterested, religious sentiment, unalloyed by worldly considerations'.[22] The sting in the tail, however, was that in matters of religion, as in politics, Rousseau had put together a set of 'discordant and confused hypotheses'. Like a 'blind architect', he had failed to construct 'a new edifice' and had left behind only chaos and destruction.[23]

The fact that Rousseau was deployed both directly and indirectly by Madame de Staël and Benjamin Constant to distance themselves from the sensationalist epistemology of the likes of Condillac and Helvétius also serves to explain in part why another group of liberal thinkers – Destutt de Tracy and his fellow *idéologues* – felt little or no attraction to him. Writing in *De l'Allemagne*, for example, Madame de Staël made explicit what she saw as the intimate connection between the sensationalist metaphysics of the French eighteenth century and a morality which

[19] Constant, *De la Religion* (Arles: Actes Sud, 1999), 25–34. [20] Ibid., 70.
[21] Kelly, *The Humane Comedy: Constant, Tocqueville and French Liberalism* (Cambridge: Cambridge University Press, 1992), 49.
[22] Constant, *De la Religion*, 71. [23] Ibid.

saw self-interest as our primary motive. Both, she believed, produced equally negative and harmful outcomes. Jacques Necker developed a similar argument in his *De l'Importance des opinions religieuses*, as did Constant throughout his writings. By contrast, the *idéologues* built their entire project of recasting morality upon a sensationalist epistemology and upon the utilitarian maxim that we acted so as to maximise our pleasure and minimise our pain. Although not always citing him by name, they disagreed with Rousseau on almost every issue: the origin of language, how best to structure education, the basis of morality and the nature of society. Society was not, they avowed, the source of all our woes, and the state of nature was far from being an idyllic condition. At best, in their view, Rousseau was a dangerous dreamer. Thus, at the beginning of his *Essai sur les garanties individuelles qui réclame l'État actuel de la société*, Pierre Daunou could announce that 'nowhere will I have resort to abstract principles, to the hypothesis of a social pact, to a discussion of its clauses, or to the anterior or natural rights that it presupposes'.[24] Similarly, when Destutt de Tracy wanted to set out his views on government he turned not to Rousseau but to Montesquieu.[25] Firmly of the view that a non-representative form of democracy could not long survive, he showed no liking for the supposed (republican) virtue of self-renunciation and quite definitely thought that Sparta was not a model to be admired. Men, Destutt de Tracy wrote, 'have need of clothes and not hair shirts'.[26]

Destutt de Tracy and his associates, therefore, produced a decidedly un-Rousseauvian description of the individual self and from this followed their conviction that liberty was to be equated with the satisfaction of our desires. If, in political terms, this generated a support of representative government, it also demanded a society resting upon the solid foundations of private property and a free market. So, for example, despite the fact that Destutt de Tracy shared Rousseau's distaste for luxury, he believed it to be no part of the functions of government to reduce inequality.[27]

This point introduces a further one: namely, that liberal political economists in France – usually referred to as the *laissez-faire ultras* – showed a complete disregard for anything Rousseau had written on economic issues and, if truth be told, an open contempt for Rousseau as both

[24] Daunou, *Essai sur les garanties individuelles qui réclame l'État actuel de la société* (Paris: Foulon, 1819), 6.

[25] Destutt de Tracy, *Commentaire sur L'Esprit des lois de Montesquieu* (Paris: Delaunay, 1819).

[26] Ibid., 33.

[27] Destutt de Tracy, *A Treatise on Political Economy*, trans. Jeremy Jennings (Indianapolis: Liberty Fund, 2011).

a philosopher and man. This is no minor matter, as it was this school that dominated French economic thinking until the final years of the nineteenth century. Typical of the view arrived at was the short entry by Henri Baudrillart published in the *Dictionnaire d'économie politique* of 1853. Rousseau, Baudrillart opined, was not an economist but his influence upon economic thinking had been enormous. In sum, he was 'one of the fathers of modern socialism'.[28] A more overtly polemical attitude was adopted by Frédéric Bastiat. This was how Bastiat summarised the content of the *Discours sur l'origine et les fondements de l'inégalité parmi les hommes*:

> The most frightful fate awaits those who, having the misfortune of being born after us, will add their knowledge to ours. The development of our productive capacities already makes us very unhappy . . . But man's true bliss is to be found living in the woods, alone, naked, without ties, without affections, without language, without religion, without ideas, without family.[29]

Rousseau's opposition between the state of nature and society, Bastiat concluded, 'is as fatal to private morality as it is to public morality'.[30] Moreover, no one, according to Bastiat, had more completely accepted 'the hypothesis of the entire passivity of the human race in the hands of the lawgiver' than Rousseau. He could 'not admit that men, acting on their own initiative, will turn of themselves toward agriculture if the soil is fertile, toward commerce if the coastline is extensive and accessible'.[31] In Rousseau's opinion, Bastiat continued, 'the law should transform persons and should create or not create property'.[32] Yet, Bastiat responded, 'it is clear that the systems which are based on the idea that the right of property is socially instituted all end either in the most concentrated privilege or in complete communism'.[33] It was rather the case, Bastiat believed, that property did not exist because there were laws but there were laws because property existed. 'Imposture for means, slavery for result' was perhaps Bastiat's most succinct summary of what he took to be the import of Rousseau's doctrines.[34] The disciples of Rousseau, for all that they believed themselves to be 'the apostles of human fraternity' and 'very much advanced', were 'twenty centuries behind the times'.[35] In a similar tone, a later dictionary entry by Charles

[28] Charles Coquelin (ed.), *Nouveau Dictionnaire de l'économie politique* (Paris: Guillaumin, 1853), 554.
[29] Frédéric Bastiat, 'Baccalauréat et Socialisme', *Œuvres complètes* (Paris: Guillaumin, 1884), IV, 465.
[30] Ibid., 467. [31] 'La Loi', ibid., 371–372. [32] 'Propriété et Loi', ibid., 276.
[33] Ibid., 284.
[34] Bastiat, 'Harmonies économiques', *Œuvres complètes* (Paris: Guillaumin, 1893), VI, 60.
[35] 'La Loi', ibid., IV, 350.

Royer simply dismissed Rousseau as a 'superficial thinker' and 'hateful philosopher' lacking any scientific understanding. *Du Contrat social* was 'pure rhetoric', lacking all historical and psychological truth. Taking up what had by now become a very familiar theme, Royer concluded by stating that 'Rousseau spent his life preaching virtue but, in truth, lived the life of a lout. He was a moral *déclassé* who could only be a moralist by condemning himself'.[36]

If we return briefly to Madame de Staël, another feature of the liberal response to Rousseau is immediately apparent. She, like almost all the writers of her generation, took *La Nouvelle Héloïse* and *Émile* to be of far greater significance than anything Rousseau had written about politics. Moreover, when – out of a spirit of completeness – she did discuss the writings on politics, she focused almost exclusively upon *Du Contrat social*. This was not something that was to change. Almost without exception, French liberals were to ignore the writings on the proposed constitutional arrangements for Poland and Corsica.[37] So too they paid little attention to the *Lettres écrites de la montagne*. This is worth mentioning because it is there that Rousseau provides a description of the citizens of Geneva that would surely have struck a chord with their own perspectives and preoccupations. To remind ourselves, it is in these *Lettres* that Rousseau boldly announced that 'the ancient peoples are no longer a model for the moderns'. You, he told the Genevans, are 'neither Romans, nor Spartans, you are not even Athenians'. Rather, he continued, 'you are merchants, artisans, bourgeois, always busy with your private interests, with work, with trade, with profit; people for whom liberty is only a means of acquiring without hindrance and of possessing in safety'.[38] Moreover, it is in these letters that Rousseau presents a far more balanced account of the principles of English constitutionalism and English liberty than is to be found in *Du Contrat social*. In brief, had the French liberals looked farther afield they might have produced a more nuanced reading of Rousseau.[39] As this was not the case, the liberal focus fell heavily upon the many dimensions of Rousseau's theory of social

[36] Charles Royer, 'Rousseau', in Léon Say and Joseph Chailley (ed.), *Nouveau dictionnaire d'économie politique* (Guillaumin: Paris, 1892), 758–765.

[37] French liberals, however, were not alone in this. 'Unfortunately', Benjamin Constant wrote, 'only [Rousseau's] absolute principles have been taken up, his Spartan fanaticism, everything which was unworkable and tyrannical in his theories, and in this way, his most enthusiastic supporters . . . have managed to make him of all our writers the most fertile in false notions, in vague principles, and the one most dangerous to freedom.' (Constant, *Principles of Politics Applicable to All Governments*, trans. Dennis O'Keefe (Indianapolis: Liberty Fund, 2003), 513.)

[38] Rousseau, *OC* III, 881. On the complex relationship between Rousseau and the Genevan political reformers, see Richard Whatmore's contribution in this book (Chapter 1).

[39] Thanks to my colleague Robin Douglass for encouraging me to make this point.

contract. In particular, liberal writers came to be troubled by Rousseau's views on sovereignty and representation.

Writing in 1788, however, Madame de Staël was decidedly untroubled by these matters. Speaking of the forthcoming meeting of the Estates-General, called to resolve France's growing financial and constitutional crisis, she announced (with what even for her was an unusually fulsome rhetorical flourish): 'Oh Rousseau! What happiness for you if your eloquence could be heard in this august assembly'. Raised from the ashes, he would inspire the person France had chosen as her 'guardian angel'. This, of course, was none other than her father, Jacques Necker![40]

Unfortunately – some would say predictably – these optimistic hopes for national regeneration were quickly dashed, and, in liberal eyes, France began her descent into chaos. This is not the place to assess whether the liberals were subsequently right to see such a close connection between Rousseau and the traumas of the Revolution of 1789 – in speaking of 'the institutionalized Rousseauism of the Jacobins',[41] Jonathan Israel would seem to suggest that they were right – but it is important for us to acknowledge that, from the moment it was believed that the Revolution was the work of a conspiracy on the part of the *philosophes*, it was widely taken as given, to quote the title of a famous book by Louis-Sébastien Mercier, that Rousseau was 'one of the first authors of the Revolution'.[42] In seeing this connection, therefore, the liberals were no different from Catholic reactionaries such as Joseph de Maistre or from the revolutionaries themselves, all of whom cited Rousseau endlessly, as and when it suited their purposes and as and when they wished to assert their rhetorical superiority over their opponents.[43] The picture here is complicated – how directly, if at all, Rousseau was implicated in the Terror was never agreed upon – but Tocqueville's unpublished remark that, 'At the beginning, it was Montesquieu who was cited and commented on; in the end, they only spoke of Rousseau. He became and he was to remain the sole teacher of the Revolution in its youth' was broadly typical of liberal opinion in these years.[44] Bastiat, for example, was of this view. 'No man', he wrote, 'exerted a greater influence on the French Revolution than Rousseau.'[45] Robespierre, on this account, had copied

[40] De Staël, *Œuvres complètes*, I, 71–72.
[41] Israel, *Democratic Enlightenment: Philosophy, Revolution, and Human Rights 1750–1790* (Oxford: Oxford University Press, 2011), 933.
[42] Mercier, *De J. J. Rousseau considéré comme l'un des premiers auteurs de la Révolution* (Paris: Buisson, 1791), 2 vols.
[43] See Bruno Bernardi (ed.), *Rousseau et la Révolution* (Paris: Gallimard, 2012).
[44] Alexis de Tocqueville, *The Old Regime and the Revolution*, trans. Alan S. Kahan (Chicago: University of Chicago Press, 2001), II, 57.
[45] Bastiat, 'Baccalauréat et Socialisme', 463–464.

'Rousseau literally'.[46] Liberals were further encouraged to take a dim view of Rousseau's work when they saw what they took to be the use of his ideas to justify the authoritarian rule of Napoleon Bonaparte. 'People still speak endlessly', Benjamin Constant wrote, 'of a power without limits residing in the people or its leaders, as a thing beyond doubt; and the author of certain essays on morality and politics' – Constant had Louis-Matthieu Molé in mind – 'has recently reproduced, in support of absolute power, all the arguments of Rousseau on sovereignty.'[47]

To that extent, throughout the first half of the nineteenth century and beyond, it was largely agreed among French liberal opinion that the influence of Rousseau's ideas upon the Revolution of 1789 had produced a catastrophe without precedent, and that the Revolution itself would only be brought to an end if political debate could be purged of Rousseauvian doctrines (whatever they might be).

In the space available, it is not possible to provide more than an overview of how liberal writers contributed to this debate. To begin, it might be useful to remember that writers of a liberal disposition in France tended to favour the idea of a mixed and balanced constitution and that, in line with this, they also, following Montesquieu, tended to be admirers of English parliamentary practices and constitutional principles.[48] As Aurelian Craiutu has shown,[49] Jacques Necker, father of Madame de Staël and a leading light of the Coppet circle, criticised the idea of popular sovereignty as an abstract and unworkable ideal, and as one believed only by a credulous people. In his *Réflexions philosophiques sur l'égalité*, for example, Necker argued that the attempt to apply such a doctrine by those he described as 'political Quakers' had reduced France to 'a mixture of anarchy and tyranny'. Necker was similarly critical of those who believed that some form of 'perfect equality' could be imposed upon a large, complex society composed of diverse and conflicting interests.[50] 'The reign of violence and the reign of equality', he wrote, 'have a direct connection'.[51]

By the late summer of 1789, the leading advocates of a balanced constitution – known as the *monarchiens* – had been defeated and the political initiative had passed over to those, led by the Abbé Sieyès, campaigning for an institutional settlement resting upon the indivisible sovereignty of

[46] Bastiat, 'La Loi', 379.
[47] Constant, *Principles of Politics Applicable to All Governments*, 12.
[48] See, for example, Jacques Necker, 'Du Pouvoir exécutif dans les grands états', *Œuvres complètes* (Paris: Treuttel et Würtz, 1821), VIII, 1–317.
[49] Craiutu, *A Virtue for Courageous Minds: Moderation in French Political thought, 1748–1830* (Princeton: Princeton University Press, 2012), 113–158.
[50] Necker, *Œuvres complètes*, X, 341–502. [51] Ibid., p.399.

(an as yet undefined) nation. From the liberal perspective, therefore, the question that needed an answer was that posed by Jean-Joseph Mounier in 1792: How could the French have allowed themselves 'to be dragged into the harshest slavery under the guise of liberty'?[52]

The answer given by Mounier himself – and subsequently largely accepted by liberals – was that the revolutionaries, given their lack of a political education and their undue haste in wanting to rebuild society from top to bottom, had taken Rousseau's 'absurd dream of democracy' for a reality. 'They announced as the patron of liberty', Mounier wrote, 'he who viewed the representation of the people as a mark of servitude, and they applied principles proposed for a small city to a large country of twenty-five million people.'[53] Not only this, but 'in conformity with the doctrine of J. J. Rousseau', the revolutionaries had asserted that 'the general will was the law and that the nation was sovereign'.[54] By way of reply, Mounier asserted that it was impossible for a nation as a whole to exercise sovereignty and therefore 'to affirm that sovereignty belongs to the people is as absurd as claiming that a general must be subordinated to his soldiers, a magistrate to his inferiors, a father to his children'.[55] Yet Rousseau's 'ridiculous maxims' and 'principles of anarchy' – *Du Contrat social*, Mounier remarked, was 'the worst book ever written on government'[56] – had been applied by 'our modern legislators', with the result that government had been handed over to the ambitious, the corrupt, the envious, and the lazy, and with inevitably disastrous results for the liberty of the people. It is interesting to note, however, that in a slightly later text Mounier conceded that Rousseau would not have approved of the crimes of the Revolution.[57]

Needless to say, resolving these issues became a more pressing and immediate concern after the rise to power of the Jacobins and the mass murder associated with the Terror. For example, if, in his famous lecture comparing the liberty of the ancients to that of the moderns, Constant could speak of Rousseau as a 'sublime genius animated by the purest love of liberty', he qualified this remark by adding that Rousseau had 'nevertheless furnished deadly pretexts for more than one kind of tyranny'.[58] 'It would be easy to show, by countless examples', Constant wrote

[52] Mounier, *Recherches sur les causes qui ont empêché les français de devenir libres et sur les moyens qui leur restent pour acquérir la liberté* (Geneva, 1792), II, 147.
[53] Ibid., 152. [54] Ibid., 155. [55] Ibid., 158. [56] Ibid., 150.
[57] Mounier, *De l'Influence attribuée aux philosophes, aux francs-maçons et aux illuminés sur la Révolution de France* (Tübingen: Gotta, 1801), 126. For twentieth-century views on the links between Rousseau's thought and the Terror, see Christopher Brooke's contribution in this book (Chapter 8).
[58] 'The Liberty of the Ancients Compared to That of the Moderns', in Constant, *Political Writings*, 318.

elsewhere, 'that the greatest sophisms of the most ardent apostles of the Terror ... were only perfectly consistent consequences of Rousseau's principles'.[59]

First, Constant's position on Rousseau was more complicated than this might initially lead us to believe. Where Constant agreed with Rousseau was that political authority was only legitimate if it derived from the general will. 'Short of reviving the doctrine of divine right', Constant argued, all other forms of government were illegitimate as they rested upon force and would lead to either anarchy or despotism. The difficulties associated with this principle arose from problems in recognising or expressing the general will, rather than from the principle itself.[60]

However, in the opening chapter of his *Principles of Politics Applicable to All Governments*, Constant argued that 'all the ills' of the French Revolution arose from the subversion of a second principle: that all political authority should have limits.[61] It was because Rousseau's 'eloquent and absurd theory' had failed to recognise this principle that he had provided a justification of despotism. Rousseau's mistake, and that of his admirers, was wrongly to imagine that 'society may exercise over its members an unlimited authority and that everything the general will ordains is rendered legitimate by that alone'.[62] It was simply not true, Constant asserted, that in handing oneself over to everyone else, one was giving oneself over to no one or that the social body as a whole could not harm either the collectivity or any one of its members individually. Not everyone regained the equivalent of what they had lost. Several chapters of the *Du Contrat social*, Constant wrote, were worthy of the scholastic writers of the fifteenth century: they were full of 'deadly theological sophisms such as give weapons to all tyrannies'.[63] Rousseau, in short, had started from 'an invalid hypothesis' and, as soon as someone had tried to put his 'superfluous subtleties' into practice, it had led inevitably to a loss of liberty and civil strife. In a note to his text, Constant added: 'Jean-Jacques's system and all the reasoning it rests on are forgetful of reality, a terrible, vicious flaw'.[64] As Constant wrote, what Rousseau 'felt so powerfully, he failed to define precisely'.[65]

Rousseau's further error was to seek to distinguish the prerogatives of society from those of government. This, Constant countered, was only possible when government was understood in the most restricted sense. Rousseau, however, defined government in its widest sense, thereby

[59] Constant, *Principles of Politics Applicable to All Governments*, 20. [60] Ibid., 6–7.
[61] Ibid., 5.
[62] Ibid., 13. On this conundrum in Rousseau's *Social Contract*, see Philip Pettit's contribution in this volume (Chapter 10).
[63] Ibid., 26. [64] Ibid., 431. [65] Ibid., 25.

rendering the distinction illusory. Moreover, it was not possible for society to exercise the prerogatives bestowed upon it by Rousseau. Therefore, society was compelled to set up government, and once this was done, men – 'by a swift and easy manoeuvre' – were obliged to submit themselves to those individuals who acted in the name 'of the all-powerful majority, of the sovereign nation'. 'This doctrine', Constant continued, 'creates and then carelessly casts into human arrangements a degree of power which is too great to be manageable, and one which is evil whatever hands you place it in. Entrust it to one person, to several, to all, you will still find it an evil.'[66]

And here, in Constant's opinion, was probably the greatest of all the mistakes committed by Rousseau and his admirers. They had directed their wrath 'against the wielders of power and not power itself. Instead of destroying it, they have dreamed only of relocating it'.[67] Rousseau himself, according to Constant, had been 'terror struck at the immense political power he had just created': hence his declaration that sovereignty could be neither alienated nor represented. 'We cannot refute [Rousseau's theories] strongly enough', Constant concluded, 'because they put insuperable obstacles in the way of any free or moderate government, and they supply a banal pretext for all manner of political outrages.'[68] In essence, as an admirer of the republics of antiquity Rousseau had overlooked the fundamental truth that there is 'a part of human existence which by necessity remains individual and independent, and which is, by right, outside any social competence'.[69]

Versions of this argument continued to be presented by French liberals for some decades to come. We see it, for example, in a series of texts written by François Guizot, one of the great writers of his age as well as the dominant politician of the July monarchy (1830–1848). If, like Constant, Guizot was concerned to undermine claims to an indivisible sovereignty exercised in the name of the people, here the focus fell more specifically upon what Guizot saw as Rousseau's mistakes and confusions on the purpose of representation. 'The fundamental principle of the philosophies which we oppose', Guizot wrote in *The History of the Origins of Representative Government in Europe*, 'is that every man is his own absolute master, that the only legitimate law for him is his individual will.'

Starting from this principle, Guizot continued, 'Rousseau saw, and saw truly, that the will is a purely individual fact, so that all representation of

[66] Ibid., 20. [67] Ibid., 21. [68] Ibid., 26.
[69] 'Principles of Politics Applicable to all Representative Governments', in Constant, *Political Writings*, 177.

the will is impossible.'[70] From this it followed that all forms of representative government were necessarily illegitimate, 'for a man only remains free so long as he obeys no law but that of his own will'. Rousseau's 'only fault', according to Guizot, was that he had not pushed this conclusion far enough. Had he done so, he would have ceased seeking the best form of government and would have affirmed 'the illegitimacy of all law and all power'.[71] As Guizot observed, 'how does it concern me that a law emanated yesterday from my will, if today my will has changed? Yesterday my will was the only source of legitimacy for the law; why then should the law remain legitimate when it is no longer sanctioned by my will? Can I not will more than once? Does my will exhaust its rights by a single act?'[72]

Carried to its logical conclusion, therefore, Rousseau's doctrine would have rendered not only all government, but all morality and all society impossible. 'It imposes upon man', Guizot wrote, 'an absolute and continued isolation, does not allow him to contract any obligations, or to bind himself by any law, and brings an element of dissolution even into the bosom of the individual himself, who can no more bind himself to his own nature than to any other person.'[73] Rousseau, Guizot conceded, was aware of these difficulties and, at times, was doubtful of the application of his principles. His own solution to this problem, according to Guizot, was to pronounce that all large states were illegitimate and that 'it was necessary to divide society into small republics in order that, once at least, the will of each citizen might give its consent to the law'.[74] 'Minds less powerful' and 'far more timid', however, had used Rousseau's theory of representation to conclude incorrectly that laws were legitimate only if they emanated from a power constituted by the people and from this had drawn the dangerous inference that the majority should always have priority over the minority.

At bottom, then, Rousseau's mistake was to have misconceived the purpose of representation. It was not, and could never be, that of representing the individual wills of all citizens, and this was so because it was not true 'that man is absolute master of himself – that his will is the only legitimate law – that no one, at any time, under any circumstances, has any right over him unless he has consented thereto'.[75] In Guizot's opinion, power was only legitimate to the extent that it conformed to reason, and therefore the purpose of representation was 'to collect into one focus, and to realise, public reason and public morality, and to call them to the occupation of power'.[76] And where Guizot differed most obviously and

[70] Guizot, *The History of the Origins of Representative Government in Europe* (Indianapolis: Liberty Fund, 2002), 287.
[71] Ibid., 287–288. [72] Ibid., 288. [73] Ibid., 288. [74] Ibid., 289. [75] Ibid., 291.
[76] Ibid., 295.

markedly from Rousseau was in his belief that these qualities were to be found in the bourgeoisie – in fact, in a small portion of the upper bourgeoisie, *les notables* – and that these were the people who should rule. 'What we call representation', Guizot wrote, 'is nothing else than a means to arrive at this result.'[77]

Unhappily for Guizot, the political supremacy of his ideal of a bourgeois *juste milieu* proved to be short-lived and power swiftly passed into the hands of the supporters of a democratic republic. It is interesting to note, therefore, that in the extensive and detailed constitutional debates that followed the formation of the Second Republic in 1848, the name of Rousseau scarcely figured. Edouard Laboulaye, the man who did most to keep the ideas of Benjamin Constant alive at this time, aptly commented that no longer did people refer to Locke or Rousseau – the ideas of whom, he remarked, had had 'so much influence upon the legislators of the Revolution' – and that no longer did political philosophy start from the assumptions that there had once been a state of nature or that, upon entering the political community, the individual had sacrificed his or her natural rights. The worry now, he commented, was not that 'the philosopher of Geneva' would cause his 'initiates' to return to the woods but that the socialists and communists would turn France into an imitation of the 'sugary despotism of the Jesuits of Paraguay'.[78] Similarly, when, in the next decade, Alexis de Tocqueville set about his examination of the *ancien regime* and the French Revolution, he made only a single passing reference to Rousseau as one of the causes or sources of 1789. Towards the end of the century, Tocqueville commented, the writings of Diderot and Rousseau came to infuse the state's bureaucrats with a 'false sensibility'.[79] Rather, it was Tocqueville's view that it was in the Physiocrats that 'all that is most substantial' in the Revolution was to be found. It was, then, the likes of Quesnay and his followers, and not Rousseau, who here stood accused of not wanting to destroy absolute power but to convert it, and in whom were to be found the roots of 'democratic despotism'.[80]

Certainly, the old stereotypes remained much in evidence. For example, Hippolyte Taine's monumental *Les Origines de la France Contemporaine* did nothing to spare Rousseau from his share of the blame for the 'spontaneous anarchy' that had engulfed and destroyed France at the end of the eighteenth century. If, Taine wrote, 'there was ever a utopia which seemed capable of realisation, or, what is still more to

[77] Ibid., 295.
[78] Laboulaye, *Considérations sur la Constitution* (Paris: Durand, 1848), 28–30.
[79] Tocqueville, *The Old Regime and the Revolution*, I, 139. [80] Ibid., 210–212.

the point, was really applied, it is that of Rousseau in 1789 and during the three following years'.[81] Yet Rousseau's was a doctrine fashioned for 'human abstractions, men of no age and no country, pure entities hatched under the divining rod of metaphysics',[82] for men 'without a past, without a family, without responsibility, without traditions, without customs, like so many mathematical units, all separable and all equivalent'.[83] It was, however, this theory that the people had taken to heart and, as a consequence, they had 'treated magistrates like servants, promulgated laws, conducted themselves like sovereigns, exercised public power, established summarily, arbitrarily, and brutally whatever they thought to be in conformity with natural law'.[84] According to Taine, wilder Rousseauvian follies were proposed under the Jacobins by those he described as hissing parrots.[85] Later still, at the turn of the century, Charles Maurras and his friends in the monarchist movement continued the anti-Rousseau invective. As I have commented elsewhere, it is difficult to do full justice to the venomous and vitriolic scorn heaped upon Rousseau by Maurras.[86] In particular, Maurras, along with those such as Pierre Lasserre,[87] accused Rousseau of undermining the literary and moral glories of French classicism through the introduction of an infantile, sick, and effeminate romanticism. That Rousseau was a Swiss Protestant, and thus the incarnation of a corrosive moral individualism, only confirmed their case against this 'despotic rhetorician'. But, for all that, a more even-handed approach to Rousseau became established among moderate, liberal opinion, and even some of the most ardent republicans came to free themselves from their Rousseauvian rhetorical excesses.

A writer such as Jules Barni was emblematic of these developments. More easily cast as a republican than a liberal, during the Second Empire (1852–1870) Barni played a key role in encouraging his colleagues to make the political compromises required to establish the Republic on a solid foundation.[88] In doing so, he established a picture of Rousseau which many could find congenial.

[81] Taine, *Les Origines de la France Contemporaine*, IV (2): *La Révolution: L'Anarchie* (Paris: Hachette, 1900), 49.
[82] Ibid., IV (1), 217. [83] Ibid., 218. [84] Ibid., 31.
[85] Taine, *Les Origines de la France Contemporaine*, V (1): La Révolution: La Conquête Jacobine (Paris, Hachette, 1901), 125.
[86] Jeremy Jennings, *Revolution and the Republic: A History of Political Thought in France since the Eighteenth Century* (Oxford: Oxford University Press, 2013), 368.
[87] Lasserre, *Le Romanticisme français: essai sur la révolution dans les sentiments et dans les idées au XIXe siècle* (Paris: Mercure de France, 1907), 7–74.
[88] See Jennings, *Revolution and the Republic*, 60–63.

Writing in the mid 1860s,[89] Barni reaffirmed that the influence of Rousseau upon the French Revolution had been immense. 'One can say without exaggeration', Barni wrote, 'that the citizen of Geneva was the soul of this great revolution.'[90] Moreover, unlike Tocqueville, Barni took this to be the case from the summer of 1789 onwards. Thus, according to Barni, the key decision of the Estates-General to abandon voting by Estates had been inspired by Rousseau's ideas. So had the abolition of the feudal order on the night of 6 August 1789. Most of all, the *Declaration of the Rights of Man and the Citizen* had been 'the putting into practice of the principles of the *Social Contract*'. More generally, an admiration for Rousseau amongst the members of the Constituent Assembly had pushed the Revolution in the direction of a republic. But, by the same token, Barni took the all-important step (and one that distanced him from the earlier analysis of Constant) of denying that Rousseau had been 'the theorist of the Terror'. Rousseau, Barni asserted, had not been responsible for the 'politics of the abattoir that had soiled the French Revolution and that had made possible the resurrection of Caesarism in the France of the nineteenth century'.[91]

As for Rousseau's broader political philosophy, it was not without its errors or weaknesses. In particular, Barni was firmly of the view that the liberty of the individual and the rights of the human person were not sufficiently recognised or safeguarded.[92] Having insisted that the liberty of the individual was inalienable, Barni argued, Rousseau immediately 'reduced it to nothing' by 'swallowing it up' into the general will. Moreover, Barni continued, 'the general will, taken not as an ideal but as a reality, is far from being infallible'.[93] As of old, the charge was that Rousseau was too admiring of Lycurgus and Calvin.[94] Barni also took special exception to Rousseau's ideas on the need for a civil religion.[95] In addition, and with an eye to France's future constitutional arrangements, Barni raised serious doubts about the consequences of Rousseau's rigid distinction between the executive power and the sovereign. Under Rousseau's scheme, Barni argued, executive power was deprived of the 'consistency and independence it needed' to function properly. Was it necessary, Barni asked, that the law 'should always be ratified by the people in person'?[96] Followed to the letter, the danger was that Rousseau's theory 'renders all government impossible'.[97]

But these failings, in Barni's opinion, did not diminish the fundamental worth of Rousseau's ideas nor 'the eternal debt' we should feel towards

[89] Barni, *Histoire des idées morales et politiques en France au dix-huitième siècle* (Paris: Baillière, 1867), II.
[90] Ibid., 295. [91] Ibid., 300. [92] Ibid., 232. [93] Ibid., 248. [94] Ibid., 231.
[95] Ibid., 279–290. [96] Ibid., 273–274. [97] Ibid., 263.

him. For all his exaggerations, Rousseau had seen that morality could not be reduced to convention or to a matter of personal interest, that we had been 'strangely disfigured' by the institutions and prejudices in which we lived.[98] This was not the full extent of our debt, however. At bottom, what Rousseau had seen was that 'the holders of executive power are not the masters of the people but the officers of the people',[99] and that political legitimacy derived only from the free consent of the people to the institutions and laws that they themselves had created.[100] More than any of his contemporaries, Rousseau had also seen that men were born equal in rights and that this equality applied not only to civil rights but to political rights.[101] It is, Barni, wrote, 'from universal suffrage that results the general will and it is the general will that constitutes the sovereignty of the people'.[102] It was in this sense, therefore, that Rousseau could be described as 'one of the apostles of modern democracy'.[103]

Of course, to get his readers this far Barni had to dismiss some of the old Rousseauvian myths. It was not true, as he knew Madame de Staël had believed, that there was any evidence proving that Rousseau had either shot or poisoned himself.[104] Despite the glaring contradictions between what Rousseau said and did, he was no moral hypocrite or charlatan. As Barni put it, Rousseau was no 'Tartuffe de morale'.[105] Rather, in Barni's eyes, of far greater importance was that Rousseau had established that all arbitrary and despotic power was irredeemably illegitimate and that only a regime resting upon the sovereignty of the people and the principle of equality could provide the French nation with the liberty it yearned for. Moreover, it was around these maxims that both liberals and republicans were able to unite in the later years of the Second Empire and upon this alliance was a new and enduring political culture built in the early years of the Third Republic after 1870.

In summary, among French liberals – as elsewhere – Rousseau was subject to a complex and often incomplete reading from the late eighteenth century onwards.[106] Madame de Staël's pre-1789 enthusiasm, if not entirely abandoned, was largely replaced by an appreciation that the seemingly contradictory principles enunciated by Rousseau could pose a major threat to the liberty of the individual. This was thought to be especially so when, as had repeatedly been the case, Rousseau's ideas fell into the wrong hands. But, with the passing of time and as memories of the Terror retreated into the distance, Rousseau, like the Revolution of

[98] Ibid., 205. [99] Ibid., 264. [100] Ibid., 223. [101] Ibid., 292–293.
[102] Ibid., 292. [103] Ibid., 294. [104] Ibid., 73–97. [105] Ibid., 99–116.
[106] Roussel, *Rousseau en France après la Révolution*; Masseau, *Ennemis des philosophes*, 373–376. Cf. the similar tensions in nineteenth-century socialist interpretations of Rousseau, as analyzed in this volume by Jean-Fabien Spitz.

1789 itself, was made safe for the bourgeois republic. However, if ever this consensus faltered, there was always the traditional fallback position on which everyone had always agreed: Rousseau was a great writer. As Jules Simon of the *Académie Française* remarked at the inauguration of the statue in Rousseau's honour in Paris during the centenary of the Revolution, whether loved or hated, whether admired as the author of *Émile, La Nouvelle Héloïse*, or *Du Contrat social*, 'the style was the man'.[107]

[107] Jules Simon, *Inauguration de la Statue de Jean-Jacques Rousseau, Le dimanche, 3 fevrier 1889* (Paris: Firmin-Didot, 1889), 7.

# 5 Rousseau and the redistributive republic
## Nineteenth-century French interpretations

*Jean-Fabien Spitz*

### I

There are two different ways to integrate freedom and equality in contemporary political philosophy. Moreover, John Rawls argues that these two values hold a moral attraction for us.[1] In freedom, what appeals to us is the idea that we should be able to choose and revise our own aims without external constraints in the light of all the relevant information we have, and to take full responsibility for our choices. In equality, we are attracted by the idea that all human lives have equal worth and that there is no reason that they should be too different under the impact of arbitrary factors that are wholly exterior to people. Rawls nevertheless thinks that these two values can both be derived from a higher moral ideal – which is the aspiration to live in a society of free, cooperating equals. The principles of this collaborative project would be acceptable to all its participants because they would be able to satisfy optimally the attraction felt by each of us to both of these central values. Ronald Dworkin's proposal, on the other hand, is to define freedom as moral independence, the fact of not being considered as having lesser value, or the fact of being granted equal respect.[2] He shows that having access to equal resources, as he defines this concept, is a requisite of such a moral independence.

Both strategies are based on the idea that being free is not a condition of factual non-interference, but is rather a moral status which implies that those around us have some duty toward us, and that the relations we have with one another have some kind of legitimacy and reciprocity. Rousseau contributed significantly to the development of this theme in Western political philosophy by stressing that freedom is based on reciprocal duties and that, in turn, such reciprocal duties imply equal access to the

[1] John Rawls, *Justice as Fairness: A Restatement*, ed. Erin Kelly (Cambridge, MA: Harvard University Press, 2001), 1–38.

[2] Ronald Dworkin, *Sovereign Virtue: The Theory and Practice of Equality* (Cambridge, MA: Harvard University Press, 2000), 120–123.

means of independence. In the *Social Contract*, Rousseau explicitly claims that freedom and equality are mutually connected:

> If one inquires into precisely what the greatest good of all consists in, which ought to be the end of every system of legislation, one will find that it comes down to these two principal objects, freedom and equality. Freedom, because any individual dependence is that much force taken away from the State; equality, because freedom cannot subsist without it.[3]

Individual interdependence is what Rousseau calls in the *Social Contract* 'personal dependence', the fact of being dependent on the particular will of some other person.[4] Such a personal dependence, which is the negation of freedom, can only be overcome, Rousseau writes, by the impersonal subordination of all to the general will of the state. When Rousseau adds that all personal dependence is 'so much force withdrawn from the state', he means that those who are subjected to some personal dependence can have no kind of obligation toward the law, since such an obligation implies exact and strict reciprocity – and this reciprocity of rights and duties can no longer exist when one is subjected to the particular will of another person. The union of a state's members gives it its force and the reciprocity of the members' conditions brings about their union. We can, therefore, understand that any 'particular dependence' weakens the union and, in turn, the force of the state.

Rousseau then argues that freedom cannot subsist without equality and, in the *Letters Written from the Mountain*, he adds that freedom without justice is a true contradiction.[5] This does not mean that all inequalities are incompatible with freedom, but only that those that are acceptable must be compatible with the requirement of equal independence for all. In any state, even one founded on the social contract, there will be two kinds of conventional inequalities, the term 'conventional' here implying that those inequalities are authorized or established by human consent. One is inequality of authority or power, which means that some men have a right to give orders to others and to be obeyed by them. The other is inequality of wealth.

With regard to inequality of power, Rousseau says that in order to be compatible with freedom it should 'stop short of all violence and never be exercised except by virtue of rank and the laws';[6] no form of command or constraint should be exercised by open force, but rather because the magistrate who exercises it has received explicit authority to act in such

[3] Rousseau, *Social Contract*, II.11, in *OC* III, 391; *SC*, 78.
[4] Ibid., I.7, in *OC* III, 363–4; *SC*, 51–53.
[5] Letter 8 in *Lettres écrites de la montagne*, *OC* III, 842.
[6] Rousseau, *Social Contract*, II.11 in *OC* III, 391; *SC*, 78.

a way – his actions are authorized by the terms of the law. Any unauthorized power would inevitably lead to personal dependence. Therefore, if some have too much power, they acquire power which is not 'under violence'[7]; this does not mean that they actually resort to violence, but that they have various means to coerce other people to abide by their will. This is what we might call domination. Domination is destructive of moral equality; it brings force – actual or potential – into civil relationships and it undermines completely the bases of reciprocal duty. It renders the civil association a merely factual one, without any right or legitimacy. In Rousseau's terms, such an association is a *rassemblement* – a mere gathering, not a civil union.

As to inequality of wealth, Rousseau says that 'no citizen should be so very rich that he can buy another, and none so poor that he is compelled to sell himself'.[8] Here again, we understand that if some citizens are too rich, they may be able to skirt around the laws or buy off those who are in charge of them. The consequence of excessive wealth is thus that some citizens can manage to escape the law and, as soon as some are no longer subject to the law, reciprocity of rights and duties disappears and the social contract itself is broken. Moreover, the excessive wealth of some citizens necessarily goes along with the excessive poverty of others; when some citizens are too poor to live in an independent way, they are ready to sell themselves – which means that they are ready to submit themselves to some particular will to cover their subsistence. The poorest citizens are thus led to consent to some asymmetry of duties, but their consent is not enough to legitimize this absence of the reciprocity of rights and duties. Rousseau constantly stresses that the question is not whether one has consented to some inequality, but whether this inequality is compatible with equal independence.

The way Rousseau integrates freedom with equality thus aims at showing that one can be free only if one lives among peers who have a duty to respect one's actions, and that such a duty can exist only if these others can perform the same actions in an independent way. They should not only have the right to perform such actions but an actual possibility of doing so, a *power* to perform them. This confirms that for Rousseau, strict reciprocity of independence is the basis of all legitimate moral duties toward others. I am free only when those around me have a duty to let

[7] Ibid.: 'Quant à la puissance, qu'elle soit en dessous de toute violence'. Rousseau means that if people have more power than others, this excess of power should never take the physical form of forceful constraint.

[8] *Social Contract*, II.11 (*OC*, III, 391–392; *SC*, 78). Rousseau adds there in a footnote: 'Do you, then, want to give the State stability? bring the extremes as close together as possible; tolerate neither very rich people nor beggars.'

me act as I do, but they can have such a duty only because they have *the right and the power* to act exactly as I do.

The second element in Rousseau's analysis is that, if such limitations of wealth and power are violated, freedom is irretrievably lost. Here is what he says in the *Discourse on Political Economy*:

> What is most needful and perhaps most difficult in government is a strict integrity to render justice to all, and above all to protect the poor against the tyranny of the rich. The greatest evil has already been done where there are poor people to defend and rich people to restrain. The full force of laws is effective only in the middle range; they are equally powerless against the rich man's treasures and the poor man's misery; the first eludes them, and the second escapes them; the one tears the web, the other slips through it.[9]

There are two different reasons why going backward is not possible. The first is that excessive wealth endows those who possess it with the power to evade the laws, while excessive poverty induces its sufferers to try to flatter and please those who can provide them with their subsistence. Rousseau explicitly formulates this fact in the *Project for a Constitution for Corsica*:

> Civil power is exercised in two manners: the one is legitimate from authority; the other abusive through wealth. Everywhere that wealth dominates, power and authority are ordinarily separated, because the means of acquiring wealth and the means of attaining authority, not being the same, are rarely employed by the same people. Then the apparent power is in the hands of the magistrates and the real power is in those of the rich.[10]

Where material conditions are wide apart, the least advantaged section of the citizenry is deprived of the equal protection of the laws, since in such a situation those very laws would be made and operated according to the will and interests of the wealthiest. The rule of law, according to Rousseau, is possible only among those who have moderate wealth (*des fortunes médiocres*).

The second reason why we cannot go back in time to a different condition is also very important. Trying to correct the excessive differences of wealth would be contradictory to the generality and impersonality of the law, since it would imply that certain laws would be specifically designed to extract some wealth from those who have too much and provide additional resources to others who have too little. In this case, Rousseau

[9] *Discourse on Political Economy*, *OC* III, 258; *SC*, 19.

[10] *Constitution for Corsica*, *OC* III, 939; Rousseau, *The Plan for Perpetual Peace, on the Government of Poland, and Other Writings on History and Politics*, trans. Christopher Kelly and Judith Bush (Lebanon, NH: University Press of New England, 2005), 155 (henceforth *Plan*).

implies, the means resorted to in order to return to equality would contradict the very aim of such a redistribution, since the generality of the law is the very substance of equal freedom. Those whose wealth would be redistributed might no longer have any duty toward the state, since they would be treated in an unequal manner and with unequal respect. As Rousseau frequently emphasizes, the law can mention nobody in particular and it should be applied to the entire citizenry without any distinction.

According to Rousseau, one must consequently make a strict distinction between *preventing* excessive differences of wealth from developing themselves, and *correcting* those excessive differences of wealth after they have emerged. The first objective can be pursued through general laws, but the second cannot be realized without impairing the sacred principle according to which laws should always be general and impersonal.

> It is, therefore, one of the most important tasks of government to prevent extreme inequality of fortunes, not by taking their treasures away from those who possess them, but by depriving everyone of the means to accumulate treasures, nor by building poorhouses, but by shielding citizens from becoming poor.[11]

Rousseau makes here a clear-cut distinction between 'those who possess' and 'all the citizens', and between 'the poor' (if there are some) and the 'whole body' of the state. Any law that would bear only on 'those who possess' or on 'the poor' would be a particular law, thus contradicting freedom.

In addition to the break with the generality of law that would be implied by a redistributive state, transfers of wealth in order to re-establish equality of conditions might deprive some citizens of what truly belongs to them, of what they have legitimately acquired by their own work and personal exertion within the context of equal laws. Yet again, such deprivation would be a negation of the very conditions of general freedom. Rousseau argues several times that securing property, which has been acquired in conformity with just principles, is the very basis of the social order.

> No law can despoil any private individual of any portion of his possession. Law can only keep him from acquiring more; then if he breaks the law he deserves punishment and the illegitimately acquired surplus ought to be confiscated.[12]

Rousseau also highlights that the right to property has a sacred character and that, in the absence of such a sacred right, it would make no sense to claim that citizens have any obligation. One can in effect be assured that

[11] *Discourse on Political Economy* in *OC* III, 258; *SC*, 19.
[12] *Constitution for Corsica* in *OC* III, 937; *Plan*, 153.

the citizens will fulfil and respect their commitments only because their property plays the role of a 'security' that can be taken by the state if they do not respect their obligations.

It is certain that the right of property is the most sacred of all the rights of citizens, and more important in some respects than freedom itself; either because it bears more directly on the preservation of life; or because goods being easier to usurp and more difficult to defend than persons, greater respect ought to be accorded to what can more easily be seized; or, finally, because property is the true foundation of civil society, and the true guarantee of the citizens' commitments.[13]

A few pages later in the *Discourse on Political Economy*, Rousseau reminds his readers that property is the true foundation of the social contract. The first condition in this contract is that each citizen 'be maintained in the peaceful enjoyment of what belongs to him'.[14] According to Rousseau, the Romans did not correctly understand this sacred character of property and they took no account of the essential distinction between preventing excessive inequalities from developing and trying to amend them after they have emerged. They understood much too late that, in order to keep liberty alive and maintain the material bases of personal independence for all, property should remain distributed so that no one should be forced to sell himself and no one would be able to buy the freedom of any other citizen. By the time they understood this point, writes Rousseau, the distribution of wealth had already reached a degree of inequality that could not be corrected without committing some injustice:

The Romans saw the necessity of agrarian laws when it was no longer time to establish them, and, for lack of the distinction I have just made, they finally destroyed the Republic by a means that ought to have preserved it: the Gracchi wanted to deprive the patricians of their lands, but better would have been to prevent them from acquiring them in the first place.[15]

Agrarian laws transferring land from the richest to the poorest citizens can thus be seen as forms of despoliation, when those who appear excessively rich did not become so by violating the law and the previously applicable conditions of legitimate acquisition.

Rousseau acknowledges that the art of preventing excessive inequalities of wealth from developing is exceedingly difficult, and that it requires a very robust civic morality. When this morality is weakened, the desire to acquire and to dominate tends to overthrow all institutional and political barriers.

[13] *Discourse on Political Economy*, in *OC* III, 262–263; *SC*, 23.
[14] Ibid., *OC* III, 269–270; *SC*, 29.
[15] *Constitution for Corsica* in *OC* III, 937; *Plan*, 153 (translation modified).

This equality, they say, is a chimera of speculation which cannot exist in practice: But if abuse is inevitable, does it follow that it ought not at least be regulated? It is precisely because the force of things always tends to destroy equality, that the force of legislation ought always tend to maintain it.[16]

The difficulty of maintaining inequality within its proper limits, nevertheless, does not impair the legitimacy of such an aim; the proper object of legislation is not to *correct* inequalities after they have developed but to *prevent* them from developing. A posteriori redistribution seems to be altogether excluded here. One of the upshots of this analysis is also that when Rousseau argues that the right of property is a consequence of social conventions, he certainly does not mean that the government can redistribute property freely according to needs or whatever it deems convenient. The meaning of Rousseau's claim is rather that only the social contract has the power to transform mere factual possession into legitimate property. This grounds the very title of property in the public acknowledgment that what we own is truly ours because it has been rightly acquired, and because it does not interfere with the freedom of others to own what is necessary for their independence.

If Rousseau's intuitions are correct, there is no perspective for real freedom in a deeply non-egalitarian society since any attempt to redistribute wealth and reduce inequalities would necessarily contradict freedom (defined as equal dependence upon an impersonal and general law). Such an idea is widely accepted today, for instance by libertarians. Nevertheless, Rousseau's argument is very different from the libertarian notion. Libertarians claim that redistribution would violate the natural rights each individual has to his own person and to the products of his own activity; Rousseau's claim is that redistribution would impair the substance of freedom by undermining the conventional and institutional structure of common dependence upon an equal and impersonal general law which secures for each citizen the necessary conditions of his non-dependence upon any particular will. On the other hand, one should mention that Rousseau's argument is very similar to the way Friedrich von Hayek tried to show that redistribution and transfer of resources was incompatible with justice in the sense of the rule of impersonal laws, and there is at least one occasion where Hayek praises Rousseau for having understood that impersonal and general laws are the very substance of civil freedom.[17]

[16] *Social Contract,* II.11 in *OC* III, 392; SC, 79.

[17] Friedrich A. Hayek, *Law, Legislation and Liberty,* vol. III: *The Political Order of a Free People* (Chicago: University of Chicago Press, 1979), 102.

## II

When read in this light, therefore, it does not seem that Rousseau's approach could justify a welfare state based on social transfers and various kinds of redistribution. Nevertheless, it is a striking fact that in the nineteenth century many liberal writers claimed that Rousseau could be considered as the spiritual father of a social and redistributive republic. His political philosophy was replete with internal contradictions since it could be used both to justify individual freedom under an impersonal law and to legitimize redistribution from the rich to the poor according to needs.

Among various possible examples, Henri Baudrillart's *Études de philosophie morale et d'économie politique* (1858) argues that Rousseau, as a political writer, philosopher, and moralist, had two distinct masters: Lycurgus and Jesus Christ.[18] Baudrillart adds that Rousseau should have chosen between these two masters in order to prevent the internal contradictions of his genius from giving birth to violent social conflicts. Writing under the impact of the proletarian uprising of June 1848, Baudrillart sees Rousseau as the intellectual father of a whole generation of socialist writers who claimed that the democratic state should equalize the material conditions without which freedom, as an individual right, would remain nothing more than a delusion. When Baudrillart tries to be more precise in his claim that Rousseau is a forerunner and an intellectual father of this mid-nineteenth-century socialism, he points to several elements of his political thought that bear special significance from this vantage point. Firstly, according to Baudrillart, Rousseau thought that the individual should submit himself to the state without any reservation.

> He is the most authoritative master of those principles of political and social pressure that overburden the human person under the tyranny of the State. He is one of the instigators of this levelling system which is condemned by spiritualism and disowned by the partisans of freedom.[19]

Secondly, Rousseau argued more specifically that, after the social contract is concluded, all rights should be considered as purely conventional and literally granted or conceded by the general will. This is supposed to be especially true of the right of property, so that Rousseau is supposed to have said that one can only possess what has been attributed to him by the general will, and to have granted that the state could freely redistribute private property according to want and other social necessities. Thirdly,

[18] Baudrillart, 'J. J. Rousseau et le socialisme modern', in *Etudes de philosophie morale et d'économie politique* (Paris: Guillaumin, 1858), I, 68–69, and 96–101.

[19] Ibid., 89.

Rousseau allegedly denied – still according to Baudrillart – that any natural superiority, any capacity for hard work or superiority of talent, could endow one with any title to any superiority of rank and fortune. For Rousseau, the simple fact of being richer is a privilege without any justification, and he makes no distinction between aristocratic wealth deriving from legal privileges and bourgeois wealth deriving from work, abstinence, and personal exertion or talents. Such charges are frequently voiced by liberal writers who put Rousseau at the fountainhead of a tradition of radical political thinking which runs through Mably, Morelly, and Robespierre, and which, via Babeuf and his 'conspiracy of equals', ends up in the French brand of mid-nineteenth-century socialism – as illustrated, for instance, by Pierre Leroux.[20]

But most striking of all is the fact that this genealogy is also accepted by some socialist writers, who claim that Rousseau's philosophy justifies the project of redistributing private wealth and using the state in order to strengthen, by special laws, the economic condition of the poorest. Louis Blanc is a good example here. Blanc's promotion of free credit for those who have no prior access to work and to the means of production is an appropriate illustration of the claim that it is legitimate for the state to legislate in a specific and partial way so as to allow the proletarians to remedy their personal subordination – while providing them with access to material independence. Blanc praises Rousseau's political thought by stressing that he clearly anticipated the difference between a *formal* or *purely legal right* on the one hand, and an *actual power to act in an independent way* on the other. For Blanc, Rousseau perceived the distinction between individualism – which is blind to the difference between those who possess the means of leading an independent life and those who do not – and fraternity, which takes this essential difference into account and aims at erasing it.

In his *History of the French Revolution*, Louis Blanc claims that three different principles shape the history of the world: authority, individualism, and fraternity.[21] The principle of authority grounds the life of the nations in blindly accepted beliefs, superstitious respect for tradition, and inequality and privilege. Authority resorts to force and constraint as means of government. The second principle, individualism, takes man as being outside society, making the individual the sole judge of all that is around him and of himself while endowing him with the exalted feeling of his rights without teaching him his duties. Individualism resorts to *laissez*

[20] On such interpretations of Rousseau in nineteenth-century French liberal thought, see Jeremy Jennings's essay in this book (Chapter 4).

[21] Blanc, *Histoire de la révolution française* (Paris: Pagnerre, 1857), I, 104.

*faire* as the means of government. The third and final principle is fraternity: this considers all the members of human society as a great family and tends to organize society (the work of man) after the model of the human body (the work of God). As a means of government, it resorts to persuasion and to the voluntary consent of the heart. Blanc argues that the principle of authority generates oppression by suppressing individual personality, that the principle of individualism leads to oppression through competition and anarchy, and that only the principle of fraternity may lead to freedom through harmony.

The reason why individualism cannot generate genuine freedom is that it does not pay any attention to the fact that whole classes of citizens are deprived of any material means and any kind of knowledge or instruction that are required to exercise the formal independence granted to all. Thus, the kind of freedom praised by individualism is a false one, a freedom liberating only those who already have the means for independence from anyone else. This individualism is 'par excellence' the philosophy that suits the class named by Louis Blanc as 'the bourgeoisie', which is made up of those citizens who possess the means of production, who work with the resources they own, and 'who depend on other people only in a partial manner'. But such a philosophy is not suitable for those who have no capital, who are *entirely* dependent on others in order to subsist, and who (due to their subordination) are free only in name.

The 'bourgeoisie', claims Louis Blanc, found its *philosophy of man* in the work of Helvétius and in his praise of personal interest; it found its *political philosophy* in the work of Montesquieu and in the idea that the public authority of the state should be reduced as much as possible without destroying it and without preventing it from protecting the individual and his property. The 'bourgeois' had no difficulty, writes Blanc, in accepting a political theory which, having promised so many new guarantees to the individual, disarmed the state. This theory tended to make every man his own master by freeing him of any social action, supressing any obstacles the strongest could encounter on their way to self-aggrandizement, and simultaneously suppressing any help the weakest could have found in the state to resist what was being realized at their expense. None of the bourgeois thinkers, says Blanc, managed to understand that when public authority refrains from acting and remains content with the protection of the existing situation, it actually does act – behind the mask of impartiality and equal rights – in favour of those who possess the means of an independent life and against those who have no access to such means.

Blanc then binds Rousseau and Robespierre in common praise for having understood that a strong public authority would remain a necessity as long as there were weak people to protect from the oppression of the wealthiest and unhappy ones to be saved from their own helplessness. Both Rousseau and Robespierre understood, according to Blanc, that the absence of the state would allow the strongest – those who have exclusive access to the means of production – to subject the weakest to a kind of new servitude under the guise of equality of rights. In the absence of equality of interests, argues Blanc, individual freedom is a hypocritical despotism, and this is why the individualist philosophy has given us, instead of freedom of thought, a deep moral anarchy; in lieu of political liberty, an oligarchy 'censitaire' where only the propertied minority have the right to vote; and as an alternative to industrial freedom, competition between the rich and the poor to the exclusive advantage of the former.

Rousseau and Robespierre are thus supposed to have perceived that the public authority of the state should rectify this unfair competition (whose results are a foregone conclusion), and that only the democratic state could gather enough might in order to contain the private power generated by monopolistic access to wealth, natural resources, and knowledge. Rousseau, according to Blanc, felt that a regime that merely guaranteed rights was not enough for those who had nothing to be guaranteed – requiring instead a regime of active protection by specifically designed protective laws:

> The towering feature in the Social Contract is the preoccupation with freedom. When Rousseau invokes social unity and when he wants to acknowledge as legitimate only those laws which have their source in the general will, it is because he has in view the possible oppression of the weakest by the strongest, it is because he feels the necessity to oppose the despotism of the few – either in an organized or in an anarchical form – with the regular and organized strength of all, so that in forming this association Rousseau has given the individual the truest guarantees and drawn the only path which can lead all men equally to happiness and freedom.[22]

Of course, Blanc wrote in a context which seems entirely foreign to Rousseau, characterized by the fact that the means to use one's work in a productive way as well as to access natural resources were concentrated in the hands of a minority. In this situation, an equal right to work and to endeavour under an impersonal and general law becomes the right to submit, bound hand and foot, to the conditions imposed by those who possess those means of production. In the absence of any means for independent existence, equal rights expose the propertyless to a kind of dependence which, while much less visible than the direct personal

[22] Ibid., 393.

dependence of the aristocratic past, is nevertheless as substantial and inescapable as was their former kind of servitude.

I cannot work, says the poor, without accepting the conditions which will be offered to me by the owners of the means of work. And if, in virtue of what you call the liberty of contracts, those conditions are exceedingly hard, if I am expected to sell my body and my soul, if nothing does protect me from this unhappy condition, or if – in the worst case – I am useless and those who can offer work just do not need me, what will I become? . . . The right, considered in an abstract manner, is only a delusion apt to maintain the people in hopes which will always be frustrated.[23]

Louis Blanc says that freedom is not the *right* to do something but an actual *power* to do it. More generally, he defines freedom as the actual power one has to develop innate potentialities and faculties. The physically impaired have the right to walk, but such a right is useless for them;[24] the same is true for the poorest members of modern industrial society. The Revolution of 1789 abolished all the juridical bonds that had prevented them from working wherever they wished and in any sort of trade; it provided them with all individual liberties. Yet this right to be free and to choose their own goals is of no use if it cannot ensure that they will have the material means necessary for the realization of their projects. So a man can be said to be free only if nothing prevents him from realizing his faculties or, more precisely, if the means he possesses in order to do so are no less significant than those at the disposal of other members of society. A man is truly free if he is not more hindered than anyone else in achieving his goals by the two main enemies of personal development: poverty and the lack of education.[25] Freedom is not equal where individuals with equal abilities do have access to unequal resources in order to develop themselves. The result of this unequal freedom – if such an expression makes any sense – is that individuals with fewer capacities but more opportunities for their realization become better placed than those with more capacities yet fewer opportunities, and this is fundamentally unjust.[26]

Rousseau and his presumptive heirs (Blanc's list here includes Mably, Morelly, Robespierre, and Babeuf) are supposed to have understood the need for going well beyond this individualism and toward fraternity. For Blanc, the meaning of this word – which would be replaced by

[23] Ibid., 397.
[24] Blanc, 'La liberté', in *Questions d'aujourd'hui et de demain* (Paris: Dentu, 1873–1884), III, 216; 220; 223.
[25] Blanc, *Questions*, II, 23; *Pages d'histoire de la révolution de Février* (Paris: Bureau du Nouveau Monde, 1850), 213.
[26] Blanc, *Questions*, III, 217.

'solidarity' a generation later – is that no one can have rights without acknowledging their corresponding duties. Thus, when equal access to independent means of living does not exist, it may and should be established through the state. This is meant to rectify the unfair results of the competition and contractual relations between owners and non-owners, and to restore the reciprocity of rights and duties which such inequality undermines. 'Rousseau', writes Louis Blanc, 'felt the necessity to oppose the despotism of the few with the organised and regular strength of all.'[27]

When he claims that the regular might of the republic should be used in order to contain the despotism of the few who own the means of production, Blanc entirely bypasses the distinction Rousseau had made between preventing and correcting inequalities of wealth, between resorting to general laws in order to prevent some citizens from amassing a level of wealth incompatible with common freedom and transferring the wealth of those who have too much to the needy. Blanc seems to be entirely blind to the fact that correcting inequalities a posteriori implies that the republic makes *special laws* concerning determinate economic groups and that it breaks dramatically with the principle of justice, which postulates that law should always be general and impersonal.

In fact, Louis Blanc abandoned the idea that freedom should be defined as a common subordination to equal laws or to impersonal general laws. He claims that when property is distributed in a widely unequal manner, equal rights and impersonal laws are only a recipe for the subordination of non-owners and for outright domination by those who possess the means of production. He then puts forth a different idea of freedom based on special legislation meant to limit the power of the strongest, to control the various ways property can be used in order to exert pressure on non-owners, and to provide substitute means of independence to those who lack any access to property – for instance, a *right to work* (by which he means a right to have employment) and access to free credit. A free society, according to Blanc, would permanently assess the material effects of such a special legislation in terms of the actual independence of all, and it would constantly re-elaborate and adjust it in order to promote real autonomy for all and maintain society as a continuum of independent citizens.

## III

This leaves two questions on our agenda. Both Rousseau and Louis Blanc want to argue that freedom is the absence of dependence on the will of

[27] Blanc, *Histoire de la révolution française*, 2nd ed. (Paris: Furne et Pagnerre, 1869), 445.

others and that it should be thought of as non-domination. But Rousseau is looking toward equal law and equal rights in order to secure such a freedom for all, whereas Blanc is looking for unequal or special laws and differentiated rights ('affirmative action', in a way) to correct inequalities and secure freedom. One might say that Rousseau and Blanc share the same notion of freedom but that they have differently conceptualized the way to realize it. The first question, then, is: How can we explain such a difference in conceptions about a shared concept? The second question is as follows: Is Louis Blanc committing an interpretive blunder about Rousseau's thought when he claims to be in agreement with his fundamental principles?

The answer to the first question seems rather obvious. The social context in which Blanc published his theory was entirely different from the context of Rousseau's own thought. Rousseau suggests that equality of rights and impersonal laws could generate common freedom when all citizens have access to a sufficient share of material resources in order to lead an independent life. But as Blanc knew well, in the middle of the nineteenth century, such a condition could no longer be satisfied; he therefore postulates differentiated rights and special legislation in order to generate real freedom for all. Where there is sharp asymmetry of access to the means of production, there can be no real freedom unless the state actively supports and protects the weakest, namely those who have nothing to live on but the cost of their manpower.

Rousseau does not seem to have anticipated that even without violence or usurpation, land and the other means of personal independence might become monopolized by some at the expense of the greatest number. Any dynamic economy is wholly out of his mental universe. He does not envisage either that the rights to acquire property and to work freely might lose all of their relevance once there is no more vacant land to settle on, and where non-owners would have to accept the very severe conditions imposed by property holders in order to gain access to potential work for their subsistence. Nor does Rousseau address the question of those who cultivate more land than they need and who subsequently offer non-owners salaried work for their subsistence. But how could he have denied that such a situation endangered or eliminated the freedom of non-owners, so that the validity of the owner's initial title lost all its strength in the presence of such a negative impact on the freedom of others? He does not foresee that, under the impact of equal rights, on the one hand, and relative scarcity of land on the other, the opposition between what Blanc calls the bourgeoisie (the independent class, having access to natural resources and means of production) and what he calls the 'proletariat' (the dependent class) is bound to appear. In other words,

Rousseau does not address the question of how freedom as personal independence can survive in a society where access to the material means of production has become impossible for some. Nor does he address the problem of how legitimate prior private appropriation is when there is no more vacant land to occupy (a question which did bother Locke a great deal).[28] These questions were to become burning issues in the nineteenth century, when two opposing answers appeared.

On the one hand, the classical liberal solution is that private appropriation is legitimate even when some individuals are deprived of any opportunity to appropriate parts of nature or do not have independent access to means of production. For the classical liberal, there can be no usurpation, no theft, in private appropriation since the land itself is valueless. Appropriating it does not deprive anyone from what is his, since the land has no value: all value comes from work. Those who have no property cannot complain, since they have not been robbed of anything and their position under the impact of past private appropriations is better than their initial condition before such appropriations occurred. Thus no rights have been violated by those who are now the owners of natural resources, nothing is due by them to non-owners, and no redistribution will ever be legitimate. One can find such an answer, for instance, in a booklet on the right to private property written by Pierre Louis Roederer in 1801, or in classic presentations of the liberal right to property such as R. Troplong's *De la propriété d'après le code civil* or Thiers's *De la propriété*, both tellingly published in 1848.[29]

The leftist or 'fraternalist' solution is also clear. According to Blanc, the private appropriation of natural resources and the monopolization of the means of production by some to the exclusion of others are outright violations of the right of non-owners to independence. Natural resources are common property and those who exclusively appropriate them should thus pay a rent to society, so as to compensate those who are concretely deprived of access to what is theirs. This was the argument put forth by Thomas Skidmore in the United States and by John Thelwell in Britain;[30] in France, François Huet contributed to this kind of left libertarianism *avant la lettre* in a book published in 1853, *Le règne social du christianisme*.[31]

[28] Ch. 5, §27 in John Locke, *Two Treatises of Government*, ed. Peter Laslett (Cambridge: Cambridge University Press, 2003), 287–288.

[29] Pierre Louis Roederer, *Discours sur le droit de propriété lus au Lycée les 9 décembre 1800 et 18 janvier 1801* (Paris: Firmin Didot, 1839); A. Thiers, *Traité de la propriété* (Paris: Paulin et Lheureux, 1848).

[30] Thomas Skidmore, *The Rights of Man to Property* (New York: Alexander Ming, 1829); John Thelwall, *The Rights of Nature against the Usurpations of Establishments* (London: Symonds), 1796.

[31] François Huet, *Le règne social du christianisme* (Paris, Firmin-Didot, 1853).

The outcome of such a view is that, under one form or another, redistribution is wholly legitimate. It is also important to stress that in such a 'fraternalist' or 'solidarist' approach the origin of the title to property is not important. Even if property has been acquired through personal work, it can be deemed illegitimate once it is not essential for the owner's independent way of life and if, on the other hand, some other individuals have an urgent need of it in order to lead an independent life. Therefore, the legitimacy of private property cannot be established in a historical way or by reference to its origin; it has to be established structurally by assessing the availability of an independent life to all members of the political community. If someone may be said to own X legitimately, it is not because he worked personally to produce it, but because X is for him a precondition of his personal freedom as non-domination, and because its appropriation does not hinder the independence of others. Louis Blanc is thus part of an intellectual conversion to a theory of freedom that is no longer based on natural rights but on consequentialist considerations.

As to the second problem, we might argue that Louis Blanc is not entirely wrong in claiming that Rousseau's thought could be seen as hinting at this direction. If Rousseau did not address those questions in an explicit manner, he nevertheless gave two series of very important indications concerning them. The first bears on the conditions which must be satisfied for private appropriation to be legitimate. The second concerns the consequences of equal rights and impersonal laws in a context where inequalities of wealth reached a point where a minority had concentrated the means of production in its hands while the majority would be propertyless. On the first point, Rousseau is clearly in favour of the Lockean proviso that the legitimacy of any private appropriation is conditioned on the fact that what is left unoccupied is enough, in quantity as in quality, for all others to be able to make an equivalent appropriation.[32] This is explicit in the chapter of Book I of the *Social Contract* on property (*Du domaine réel*). The right of the first occupier, says Rousseau, is legitimate if it satisfies three conditions: the land should be truly vacant and unoccupied; the appropriator must take only what he needs for his own subsistence; and the occupation should be realized not only through mere words but by work and actual cultivation of the land which is, Rousseau says, 'the only sign of property which others ought to respect in the absence of legal titles'.[33] Having enumerated these three conditions, Rousseau adds:

[32] Locke, *Two Treatises*, ch. 5, §27. [33] *SC*, I.9, in *OC* III, 366; *SC*, 55.

Indeed, does not granting the right of the first occupant to need and to labor extend it as far as it can go? Can this right be left unbounded? Shall it suffice to set foot on a piece of common land forthwith to claim to be its master? Shall having the force to drive other men off it for a moment suffice to deprive them of right ever to return? How can a man or a people seize an immense territory and deprive all mankind of it except by a punishable usurpation, since it deprives the rest of mankind of a place to live and of foods which nature gives to all in common?[34]

Rousseau could not be more explicit in calling 'robbers' those who take what others need for independent subsistence when they do not themselves require it for their own subsistence. Of course, Rousseau does not consider here the case of an appropriator who would work and cultivate more land than he needs for his subsistence and who would, afterwards, offer a salary to non-owners in exchange for the necessities of their subsistence. But his logic leads to the idea that such a behaviour would endanger the freedom of non-owners and that, consequently, the validity of the initial title would lose its former strength due to exerting such a negative impact on the freedom of others.

Rousseau is also well aware that, when inequality has reached a point where some members of the community are forced to sell themselves for subsistence, the impersonal rule securing for each what he has acquired becomes a recipe for oppression and servitude. In a footnote to the last chapter of Book I of the *Social Contract*, Rousseau thus makes clear that some degrees of inequality of wealth are incompatible with moral equality and that they render equality before the law a mere sham.

Under bad governments this equality is only apparent and illusory; it serves only to maintain the poor in his misery and the rich in his usurpation. In fact the laws are always useful to those who possess something and injurious to those who have nothing: Whence it follows that the social state is advantageous for men only insofar as all have something and none has too much of anything.[35]

Therefore, if some do have too much, they acquire power which is not 'under violence'; not actually resorting to violence, they have various means to coerce other people to abide by their will. And this is what we might call domination. This domination is destructive of moral equality: it brings force – actual or potential – into civil relationships and undermines completely the sources of reciprocal duty.

In *Emile*, Rousseau has an even clearer statement of the way inequality of wealth is destructive of moral equality.

In the state of nature there is a de facto equality that is real and indestructible, because it is impossible in that state for the difference between man and man by

[34] Ibid. [35] Ibid.: *OC* III, 367; *SC*, 56.

itself to be great enough to make one dependent on another. In the civil state there is a de jure equality that is chimerical and vain, because the means designed to maintain it themselves serve to destroy it, and because the public power, added to that of the stronger to oppress the weak, breaks the sort of equilibrium Nature had placed between them.[36]

It appears then that individuals can have the same rights without being morally equal and without being morally united with one another, and this happens when equality of rights is married to great inequality in degrees of wealth and power. The question for Rousseau is therefore not whether public action to close the gap between widely different degrees of wealth might destroy equality of rights; where inequality of wealth reaches a certain point, it is accompanied by a kind of inequality of power which in itself is destructive of equality of rights. In this case, equality of rights and the generality of law no longer exist. If equality of rights disappears under excessive social differentiation, no public action to halt or reduce this inequality of wealth can destroy an equality of rights that does no longer exist. Equality of rights, if genuine, is moral equality requiring comparable degrees of wealth and power.

If we pay attention to what Rousseau actually says, we see that he goes even further than that: in a condition of substantial inequality of wealth, equal rights are not only void of content but they become instruments of oppression since they add public force to the power of the oppressors, imposing on those who have nothing a duty to respect the property of the wealthy. Equal rights conferred on unequal persons amount to a system of secret oppression. In the *Discourse on Inequality*, when Rousseau describes the false social contract proposed by the richest after a process of differentiation has taken place, he says that the rich man did at that point conceive 'the most well-considered project ever to enter the human mind'. His plan was 'to use even his attackers' forces in his favour, to make his adversaries his defenders, to instil in them other maxims and to give them different institutions, as favourable to himself as natural Right was contrary to him'.[37] In Rousseau's eyes an equal right to property, in a situation where only some already have property, is not a right: it is a device by which those who possess impose on those who do not an apparent moral duty not to attack the very means by which they are dominated. Thus it is a way to ask those without property to consent to their own servitude. Many individuals, according to Rousseau, have actually consented to be slaves, but this cannot mean that they have an

[36] Book IV in *Emile*, ed. Christopher Kelly and Allan Bloom (Hanover: University Press of New England, 2010), 390; *OC* IV, 524.
[37] *Discourse on Inequality, OC* III, 177; *DI,* 172–173.

actual duty to abide by this consent and to remain slaves. In the *Social Contract* (Book I, chapter 4) Rousseau explains very clearly why it is impossible to have a duty toward someone who has no duty of his own toward us.

The general orientation of Rousseau's thought is thus clear: inequality of wealth induces inequality of power, and those two inequalities taken together make equality of rights void and a matter of appearance only. In his *Constitution for Corsica*, as we have observed above, Rousseau has an elaborate formulation of this idea.[38]

Where material conditions are so wide apart that the poorest do not have enough for life in an independent manner, the least advantaged section of the citizenry is deprived of the equal protection of the laws. In such a situation, these very laws would be made and operated according to the will and interests of the wealthiest citizens. The upshot is that the rule of law, according to Rousseau, is possible only among those who have *des fortunes médiocres*, medium-range wealth.

This means that equality of rights and an impersonal general law generate common freedom only if all have the kind of property necessary to secure their personal independence. When this is not the case – when the means of personal independence of the greatest number are in the hands of a minority – the equality of rights generates a kind of servitude that is radically opposed to freedom.

## IV

Let us now go back to where we started. Rousseau was convinced that it was impossible to restore the conditions of freedom once inequality has gone beyond a critical point. One of his reasons is that it would be impossible to correct this kind of excessive inequality without breaking with the impartiality and generality of the law – without depriving some citizens of what belongs to them and thus committing a sort of injustice. But there are at least two arguments, the foundations of which could be found in Rousseau's own thought, that allow us to argue that any sort of excessive property is necessarily illegitimate – and may in this sense be taken away and redistributed to restore the conditions of independence for all without committing any injustice. If this is true, the dominant interpretation of Rousseau's thought among both liberal and socialist writers in the mid nineteenth century was perhaps not so incorrect after all.

[38] *Constitution for Corsica, OC* III, 939; *Plan*, 155.

The first argument is that if the acquisition of private property consequently subjects individuals to personal dependence, this is enough to make it illegitimate – even if it has not been accumulated through violence and usurpation and when it is the result of work and cultivation. The mode of acquisition (work or violence) is less important than its consequences (dependence or independence) for the determination of legitimacy. The reason is that property is only legitimate and part of freedom as far as it is acknowledged as such by the people around us, who are under a duty to respect it as sacred and inviolable. But, as Rousseau hinted on many occasions, it would be contradictory to argue you have a duty to respect, at the hands of another man, the very means this man uses to reduce you to personal dependence. Such a duty would be exactly equivalent to the pact of submission which Rousseau considers as incapable of producing any right. Thus there is a sort of instability in Rousseau's thought concerning private property, because one of the criteria he proposes for grounding its legitimacy (appropriation should be realized through work and cultivation) could be annulled or contradicted by another (private appropriation should not hinder the possibility of independence for all). If this is true, Rousseau's conception could validate public action by a redistributive state, which would legitimately take away acquired property and transfer it to those who need it in order to lead an independent life.

The second argument that might justify the nineteenth-century reading of Rousseau is an extended version of the Lockean proviso; indeed, this is frequently used by left libertarians. Since natural resources are scarce by definition, any private appropriation of them violates the rights of those who (today or tomorrow) are deprived of any potential to make a similar appropriation. This infringement of the rights of others implies that, under one form or another, the appropriator is under an obligation to give back part of what he has taken from the community or pay a rent for what he occupies. In turn, this obligation might justify various kinds of social transfers and redistribution, and consequently the transfers of the welfare state do not violate equality of rights but aim at rectifying some of its past violations. The first break with equal rights takes place when the initial appropriator withdraws for his exclusive use part of the goods which belong to the community.

If this is the case, equality of rights and the generality of the law can no longer be considered as the heart and substance of common freedom, at least as far as property is concerned. In an industrial and modern society, where the means of production and natural resources are concentrated in a few hands, an equal right to work and acquire private wealth – as well as general laws protecting the product of our work – cannot secure equal freedom for all. On the contrary, maximizing freedom requires that the state attempt to correct the detrimental consequences of such a concentration of wealth, and in particular the fact that some members of the community are forced to lead a dependent life under domination (because they have to accept very severe conditions in order to attain their subsistence). Maximizing freedom thus requires that the state establish specific means to protect the weakest and reduce the power of concentrated wealth. This is a strategy of intelligent affirmative action which conceives a society of free human beings no longer as one where the law is the same for all, but rather as a community collectively trying to amend the results of impersonal laws in order to constitute itself as a collaboration among free and equal persons.

Therefore, under the impact of unequal wealth and the resulting asymmetry of conditions, freedom as generated by equal law simply vanishes. It would be quite consistent to conclude that special laws, in this context, cannot contradict either justice or freedom since neither justice nor freedom are available under such unequal conditions. If there is no rule of law where inequalities are too crucial, correcting inequalities in such a situation cannot possibly go against the rule of law nor imperil or deny a freedom that simply does not exist.

There is at least one author who read Rousseau in precisely this key in 1789. His name is Aubert de Vitry, and his pamphlet features Rousseau emerging from his grave and addressing the National Assembly. Here is what Aubert makes him say:

> Private property that goes beyond what is needed for the subsistence of the family is a crime against the state, a crime against humankind, a crime against other properties, a theft committed against all citizens and against each of them in particular, since when a family has something in excess, there is another family that lacks the necessities of life. Punishing such a crime is not a violation of justice, but an homage to justice; forcing a thief to give back what he has stolen is not taking away from him anything which is his.[39]

[39] François-Jean-Philibert Aubert de Vitry, *Rousseau à l'assemblée nationale* (Paris: Rue du Hurepois, 1789), 252–253.

# 6 Echoes of the *Social Contract* in Central and Eastern Europe, 1770–1825

*Monika Baár*

Rousseau's *Social Contract* left an indelible impression on political thought in the lands of the Habsburg Monarchy and also exerted a more modest impact throughout the Russian Empire. In addition to its thought-provoking content, the key to its success lay in the multiplicity of meanings that its readers and interpreters could derive from it. That some tenets of Rousseau's argument were not entirely clear and transparent undoubtedly contributed to these multifarious and often contradictory interpretations. However, only relatively rarely did readers have a genuine interest in seeking a full and accurate understanding of Rousseau's arguments. Instead, the *Social Contract* was exploited to provide justification for a wide spectrum of ideological orientations: defenders of the status quo appropriated its arguments just as eagerly as proponents of reform or even revolution. Readers also readily applied Rousseau's abstract ruminations to their own particular circumstances; in that context the *Social Contract* provided inspiration for numerous (albeit unrealized) constitutional projects. Moreover, it became common practice to assess national history in the light of Rousseau's work, for example by (re-)interpreting various historical pacts and agreements in terms of a social contract and subsequently confirming or challenging their validity with respect to contemporary circumstances. The myriad ways in which the *Social Contract* penetrated local discourses ranged from translations to cursory references and from political appeals to fictional writing and poetry. In some cases the authors' familiarity with the original work was evident, while in others appropriations were based on only a vague acquaintance with the original. It was not uncommon to learn about the fundamental concepts of Rousseau's work through an intermediary account.[1]

This article discusses some of the paradigmatic ways in which scholars and political thinkers interpreted the *Social Contract* throughout the

[1] One such medium was Abbé Raynal's *Philosophical and Political History of the Settlements and Trade of the Europeans in the East and West Indies* (1770), which contained the tenets of the *Social Contract* in a diluted version.

Habsburg territories, where the most intensive engagement with this work took place in the last quarter of the eighteenth century. In addition, it also provides an insight into the arguably weaker responses that the *Social Contract* generated in the Russian Empire. Variations in the pattern of reception principally arose from the differences in the legal-political traditions and societal structures within these two realms. Whereas in the Habsburg lands the *Social Contract* was arguably Rousseau's most widely received work, in Russian political theory the *Discourse on Political Economy* and *Considerations on the Government of Poland* had a stronger resonance. For the Habsburg Monarchy, natural law and contract theory, although not yet in the form espoused by Rousseau, constituted an essential part of Enlightened Absolutist legal theory in the second half of the eighteenth century. This was also the case in Russia, but initially to a much lesser extent; there the influence of Byzantine political thought, which imbued the monarch with divine right, exerted formidable influence well into the eighteenth century.

Throughout the Habsburg territories, contract theory was employed by legal scholars to legitimate Joseph II's Enlightened Absolutist rule and this created a framework for the subsequent reception of Rousseau's thought. In his former guise as the reformist Grand Duke of Tuscany (1765–1790), Joseph's brother and successor to the throne, Leopold II, bolstered constitutional plans for his realm with specific references to Rousseau's *Social Contract*. Subsequently, during Leopold's two-year term as Habsburg emperor, the *Social Contract* came to enjoy 'celebrity status' both in the arguments advanced by the feudal nobility and in those of the reformists who sought the abolition of feudal structures. As shall be shown, depending on the context and the political climate, anti-feudal initiatives could range from cautious to radical-revolutionary. In addition, the *Social Contract* could be commandeered for the purposes of national emancipation, as will be revealed in reference to the document submitted by the representatives of the Transylvanian Romanians to Emperor Leopold II. Moreover, compelling proof of Rousseau's permeation of the intellectual landscape of the region can be found in the allusion to the *Social Contract* in a fictional piece called *The Gypsy Epic*, an allegorical epic poem by a Transylvanian scholar, Ion Budai-Deleanu.

Although relatively few people were sufficiently educated or literate to read the work in French or buy it in translation, in Russia the *Social Contract* exerted influence on constitutional projects and revolutionary thought because it articulated the right of citizens to assess the legitimacy of their government against an ideal and to withdraw their support or seek redress if it was found lacking. It also fostered an emotional attachment among the citizens to their fatherland in both its ideal and applied forms.

As shall become clear, a summary of the main tenets of the *Social Contract* appeared in a compendium as early as 1768, but this was not followed by similar instances. The *Social Contract* also drew attention to various ways in which imperial Russia violated the rights of its foreign population and of humanity in general. When the Baltic German scholar Garlieb Merkel embarked on translations of David Hume's *Essay on the Original Contract* and Rousseau's *Social Contract*, to which he also added his own contribution on the history of serfdom in Livonia (then part of the Russian Empire), he was motivated by a desire to raise awareness among the European learned public of the unlawful and deplorable conditions under which the Livonian serfs lived.

Rousseau's encounters with Poland were extraordinary. The anti-Russian Polish republican nobility asked Rousseau to provide them with a draft constitution designed to protect them against royal absolutism, which resulted in *Considerations on the Government of Poland*. This work gave some insight into how Rousseau envisaged the abstract principles of right and justice set out in the *Social Contract* would operate in practice, conditioned by accidents of time and space.[2] Because of this intensive exchange of ideas, the impact of Rousseau's oeuvre, including that of the *Social Contract*, followed a unique trajectory in Poland, which has been relatively well-documented in earlier literature.[3] This chapter is primarily concerned with hitherto lesser-known instances and will therefore not discuss the idiosyncrasies of the Polish reception specifically.

Before scrutinizing these patterns of reception, it is worth assessing the context and the intellectual landscape in which the reception of Rousseau's ideas was rendered relevant. In particular, it is vital to take into account the paradox that despite its huge and sustained impact, the *Social Contract* was never actually legalized by the authorities. In fact, official attitudes to Rousseau's works at different stages of the late eighteenth century provide us with a litmus test of the contemporary political situation. For example, in the Habsburg Monarchy, Rousseau's oeuvre was banned under Maria Theresa's reign (1740–1780), but was subsequently tolerated under Joseph II (1780–1790) and, as we shall see, although not officially permitted, it evolved into an ideological weapon under the short reign of Leopold II (1790–1792). However, it was proscribed once again when Francis II acceded to the throne in 1792.

[2] In this context it has been frequently observed that despite the high value which Rousseau placed on equal liberty for all, he proposed only gradual liberation of the serfs in Poland: see Nicholas Dent, *Rousseau* (London: Routledge, 2005), 23.

[3] Marian Szyjowski, *Myśl Jana Jakuba Rousseau w Polsce XVIII wieku* (Cracow, 1913), Jerzy Michalski, *Rousseau i sarmacki republicanizm* (Warsaw, 1977), Ewa Rzadowska (ed.), *Voltaire et Rousseau en France et en Pologne* (Warsaw, 1982).

Unsurprisingly, though, these prohibitions had a negligible effect on the popularity of the *Social Contract*, and the whims of the censors could even be counterproductive as they sometimes served to arouse interest in the work among people who otherwise might have been indifferent to it. Moreover, private libraries, shielded from public scrutiny, could easily elude the authorities and hold illegal literature. In this context, the Bohemian aristocrat and patriot Kaspar Sternberg's account of how he gained access to the *Social Contract* is particularly illuminating. Sternberg's father, as a law-abiding, loyal subject in a conservative household, refused to allow banned books in his home library. This was in stark contrast to his mother, who possessed her own private book collection and did not feel similarly bound by such regulations.[4] Another strategy favoured by some translators included tampering with the original text so as to make it appear more palatable to the authorities. In Hungary, for instance, the Latin translation of the *Social Contract* was presented to the *Consilium locumtenentiale* in 1792 to request permission for printing, and when permission was refused despite the support of several members of the *Consilium*, the translator claimed – albeit unsuccessfully – that Rousseau's text was rendered much less radical in Latin than in its original form.[5]

Nevertheless, at times of escalating political repression, such as during the reign of Emperor Francis (1792–1835), evidence of familiarity with the *Social Contract* constituted proof of illegal or even treasonable activity. During the trial of the Hungarian Jacobin conspirators (described in more detail below), one accusation levelled against Ferenc Szentirmay was that the police had found a nearly completed Hungarian translation of the *Social Contract* at his home.[6] In his defence, Szentirmay offered the following words:

> It is true that I embarked on translating the *Social Contract* into Hungarian. My motivation was merely to test to what extent the Hungarian language is suitable for rendering such a complicated text. Should the censor not have granted permission for the publication of the text, I would have suppressed it. I am not

[4] Rita Krüger, *Czech, German and Noble: Status and National Identity in Habsburg Bohemia* (Oxford: Oxford University Press, 2009), 49.

[5] Comparing the first sentence of the Latin text with the original version confirms that it was indeed a watered-down version: '*Olim omnis homo natus est liber; nunc omnes abique inter vincula gemunt, et, qui se cetercrum Dominum arbitratur, servus est, et ipse. Unde haec revolutio? equidem nescio. Quid est, quad eam justam legitimamque queat efficere? Confido me huic questioni satisfacturum* ...'. See Margaret C. Ives, *Enlightenment and National Revival: Patterns of Interplay and Paradox in Late-Eighteenth Century Hungary* (Ann Arbor: University Microfilms International, 1979), 76.

[6] *Vertrauliche Akten*, Secr. 11/A, (No. 51), Hungarian National Archives, published in Kálmán Benda, *A magyar jakobinusok iratai* (Budapest: Akadémiai, 1957), Vol. I, 744.

aware of a secret publishing house in Hungary and it would never have been my intention to publish it illegally.[7]

Unsurprisingly, this line of defence failed to convince the authorities and the translator paid with his life for his part in the conspiracy. The argument advanced by one of his fellow conspirators proved equally unconvincing, but testified to the widespread popularity of the *Social Contract*: he admitted to familiarity with the work, but claimed that it was so well-known among the Hungarian public that the official prohibition had long become redundant.

In Russia, too, the authorities' stance on Rousseau served as a reliable indicator of the contemporary political climate. Although the early years of Catherine II's reign (1762–1796) were characterized by an unprecedented degree of freedom of expression, the French edition of Rousseau's *Emile* remained banned, along with a handful of other texts. The *Social Contract* was initially forbidden but subsequently became tolerated under the reign of Tsar Paul I. In 1799, a member of the Censorial Committee of the Council of the State demanded its prohibition on the grounds that the text was at least partially responsible for the 'false equality' of the French Revolution. Ultimately, however, the Committee agreed to grant permission for the book to be published legally, because it was already available in many libraries and enjoyed widespread circulation. The young poet Vasili V. Popugaev interpreted this as a landmark decision, and it inspired him to compose a joyful poem entitled: *Ode on the Occasion of the Approval Granted by the Council, of the Release of the Social Contract, a work of the Famed Genevan Philosopher Rousseau, which had been presented by the Censorship for Examination.*

O Russians, no longer are you forbidden
The works of geniuses to read
No bounds set down for your unbidden
In their courageous path to tread
Enlightenment's open road now beckons,
That once Great Peter paved,
Amphictyon's bondage does not threaten
The judgment of free minds if saved.[8]

However, Popugaev turned out to be overly optimistic because the initial decision was overruled by an edict from the monarch, and even the poem itself remained in manuscript. Nonetheless, these obstacles still could not

[7] Ibid., 744.
[8] Thomas Barran, *Russia Reads Rousseau, 1762–1825* (Evanston, IL: Northwestern University Press, 2002), 262.

prevent the *Social Contract* from permeating Russian soil; its later influence on the Decembrists was clearly visible.

In the lands of Habsburg Monarchy, natural rights and contractual theory provided the cornerstone of political and legal thinking during the Josephinist period. Two legal theorists in particular, Karl Anton von Martini and Joseph von Sonnenfels, made significant contributions to the formulation of Josephinian state philosophy. Their legal textbooks, commonly used throughout the Monarchy until the mid nineteenth century, prepared the ground for the popularization of social contract theory. Joseph II, himself a student of Martini, subscribed to contract theory and professed that his rule was based on the general will and the consent of the citizens. He justified the abolition of the feudal estate system by claiming that it impeded the direct relationship between the ruler and his subjects.[9]

Rousseau's *Social Contract* also influenced the thinking of Joseph II's brother, Leopold, who from 1765 ruled as Grand Duke of Tuscany and, following his brother's death in 1790, became heir to the Habsburg crown and Holy Roman Emperor. Contrary to the tenets of classical Enlightened Absolutism, Leopold's reformist tendencies in Tuscany included – albeit only in theoretical form – the stated belief that the populace should play a role in government. A project particularly close to Leopold's heart was the creation of a constitution for his duchy. Although this never materialized, Leopold's personal observations on political theory, such as his sympathetic assessment of the first Pennsylvania constitution, provide one of the most fascinating manifestations of Rousseau's influence on an enlightened ruler. Leopold's text, 'Observations sur les Constitutions de la Republique de Pensylvanie', was probably written between 1779 and 1782, and remained incomplete.[10] In all likelihood, it was written for his own purposes and for further reference, and was based on the French translation of the 1776 Pennsylvania Constitution, being mainly concerned with the preamble and the declaration of rights. Leopold began his commentary by citing Rousseau's *Social Contract*:

> If one inquires, says Rousseau [Leopold's words], into precisely what the greatest good of all consists in, which ought to be the end of every system of legislation, one will find that it comes down to these two provincial objects, *freedom* and *equality*. Freedom, because any individual dependence is that much force taken away from the State; equality, because freedom cannot subsist without it.[11]

[9] George Bárány, 'Hoping against Hope: The Enlightened Age in Hungary', *American Historical Review* 76:2 (1971), 327.

[10] Gerald H. Davis, 'Observations of Leopold of Habsburg on the Pennsylvania Constitution of 1776', *Pennsylvania History*, 29:4 (1962), 376.

[11] Leopold stated in his notes that this passage came from chapter 2 of the *Social Contract*. This is, however, incorrect; it can be found in Book II, chapter 11 (*SC* 78; *OC* III, 391).

Leopold then goes on to explain how he understands freedom and equality, identifying the connections between these two concepts in a way that follows Rousseau's line of argument. These references to the *Social Contract* introduced the following observation by Leopold:

> What I ask is that in order to construct a viable code in all states, even in monarchies, one must begin with the principle posited by the Americans, the principle of equality. They extend it to politics: I want it only to apply to civil society. That all citizens be *politically* equal is essential to the democratic order of government. But in a monarchy, they should be equal in a *civic* sense, that is to say, that all must be equally subject to the law, and that no exception should be made for anyone.[12]

Leopold's engagements with constitutional plans and contractual theory further intensified when, following his brother Joseph II's death in 1790, he ascended to the Habsburg throne, simultaneously becoming Holy Roman Emperor. The two short years of his reign, brought to an abrupt end with his untimely death in 1792, were informed by a significant upsurge in political initiatives and led to an unprecedented boom in the acquisition of Rousseau's *Social Contract*. On the one hand, the demands of the noble estates were fuelled by their dissatisfaction with the absolutist centralism of the recently deceased Joseph II. On the other hand, the former supporters of the Josephinist project of social and religious emancipation – now inspired to some extent by events in France – became disheartened by the crisis of Enlightened Absolutist rule. Tension came to a head when the cumulative frustrations of these two groups met in a common agenda for reform at the newly convoked provincial diets.[13]

The appeals, which acted as a vehicle for the formulation of these groups' demands, abounded in references to Rousseau's *Social Contract*. Representatives of the privileged nobility sought to establish their relationship with the ruler on a new footing and in this context envisaged the 'social contract' between themselves – the noble *natio* – and the ruler. The Bohemian estates addressed their demands to Emperor Leopold II in 1792 with the following justification:

> Because the happiness of a state can only be sustained in every measure if its constitution and the fundamental laws, on which it is based, are strong and unshakeable, because its essence contains the basic law of the state, that is to say *a contract*, a bond between the sovereign and the nation which came into being

[12] Davis, 'Observations of Leopold of Habsburg on the Pennsylvania Constitution of 1776', 377. Emphases in the original.

[13] Gerda Lettner, *Der Rückzugsgefecht der Aufklärung in Wien, 1790–92* (Frankfurt: Campus Verlag, 1988).

by the mutual consent of both parties and which cannot be altered without the consent of those two.[14]

If the Bohemian estates were eager to appropriate social contract theory, it is perhaps unsurprising that their Hungarian counterparts, for whom legal reasoning constituted almost the basis of their national existence, seized upon it with even greater zeal. One peculiarity which accounted for this exceptional response was that the ancient Hungarian political tradition, the nobility's privilege of the *ius resistendi*, had been written into Hungarian constitutional documents since the thirteenth century. This privilege afforded the nobility the right to resist the king if he should violate the law or fail in fulfilling the duties entrusted to him. This ancient tradition contained the seeds of the notion of a contract and thus seemed tailor-made for modern formulations of the *Social Contract*. The restitution of rights was one of the nobility's demands at the diet of 1790; they professed that, by refusing to take the coronation oath, Joseph II had broken the terms of his contract with the 'nation', and that the nobility was therefore entitled to withdraw their allegiance and elect a new ruler. Consequently, they demanded a new contract between Joseph II's successor and the 'Hungarian nation', and a draft document even delineated the parameters of that new arrangement: it attempted to limit the ruler's authority in every possible way. Following the example of the national convention, the representatives of the feudal estates made frequent references to popular sovereignty and 'the people'. However, this category only extended to the privileged classes and they explicitly declared that burghers and peasants were excluded from the contract.

Some contemporaries had already observed that this 'feudal' interpretation directly contradicted Rousseau's original intention. In addition, they alleged that the feudal estates were selfishly trying to 'safeguard' their appropriation of the *Social Contract* by refusing to allow the translation of Rousseau's work into either Latin or the vernacular in the hope that this would prevent its circulation among the common people. Although they justified their own position by frequent reference to Rousseau, they did not want those outside of the privileged elite to gain access to his work because they feared the consequences: 'it is common knowledge that the *Social Contract* powerfully evoked the French Revolution, and what is more, the revolution rested on Rousseau's philosophical ideas'.[15]

[14] Anna M. Drabek, 'Die Desiderien der Böhmischen Stände von 1791', in Ferdinand Seibt (ed.), *Die böhmischen Länder zwischen Ost und West, Festschrift für Karl Bosl zum 75. Geburtstag* (Münich: Oldenburg, 1983), 136; my emphasis.

[15] Kálmán Benda, 'Rousseau és Magyarország', in Benda, *Emberbarát vagy hazafi? Tanulmányok a felvilágosodás korának magyarországi történetéből* (Budapest: Gondolat, 1978), 353.

A reformist member of the lower clergy astutely observed that the nobility considered only their own, privileged classes as 'human beings' and criticized their resistance to measures designed to improve the conditions of burghers and peasants on the grounds of hypocrisy: they namely claimed that these strata had no desire for change because the laws already favoured them.[16] As he expressed it: 'There is no similarity between our nobility's system and that of the French democrats, and the latter one is surely much more mature than our own. It is true that the French annulled the royal prerogative, but they replaced it solely with the guiding principle of natural law according to which every man is equal.' In a similar vein, the history professor Alajos Hoffmann pointed out that

> The Hungarian noblemen who like to imitate Mirabeau and play the French national convention do not want to recognize the immense difference between the two countries: in France the common people oppose the nobility and aristocracy, here the nobility opposes both the ruler and the common people. There, the people destroyed the Bastille, the symbol of aristocratic tyranny. Here, the nobility wants to erect a new Bastille.[17]

These critiques of the feudal interpretation, issued mainly by the lesser nobility and members of the intelligentsia, sought democratic transformation by extending constitutional liberties to all social strata which had previously been excluded from those privileges. József Hajnóczy offered a similarly democratic interpretation of the *Social Contract* which made recourse to Rousseau's arguments in explaining the unjust nature of feudal privileges. He professed that the inequitable distribution of tax burdens was in conflict with the *raison d'être* which organized people into society and that it violated personal security and the right to property, to which everyone was entitled by the law of nature. Hajnóczy doubted whether the Hungarian constitution, which only made provision for the rights of the nobility, could be equated with the ancient contract which 'people relinquishing their natural rights concluded when they joined to form a human society'. He rejected the position of the nobility which held that the ancestors of the unprivileged classes had once voluntarily relinquished their rights. Hajnóczy argued that even if this were true, it would no longer be valid with reference to the present situation because no one has the right to enslave his successors. He thus concluded that 'just as our ancestors cannot force us to give up our natural rights, the state cannot deprive its citizens of those rights which they were entitled to by nature'. He suggested rectifying this unlawful situation by creating an entirely new

[16] Kajetán Sauer's letter to the English ambassador in Vienna, written in French, ibid., 354.
[17] Ibid., 354.

social contract which would embrace the entire 'nation' rather than just the privileged estates.[18]

Leopold died unexpectedly and was succeeded, at a time when the revolutionary Terror in France was striking fear into the hearts of rulers everywhere, by his conservatively inclined son, Francis. Some members of the intelligentsia were already thinking along radical lines, and the proclamations of the French national assembly the previous autumn had precipitated a revival in agitation against the monarchy. Francis acted swiftly and decisively; in 1794 the discovery of a 'Jacobin club' in Vienna along with another branch in Hungary prompted a wave of highly repressive measures. One of the key texts of the Hungarian Jacobin movement, *Catéchisme de l'homme et du citoyen*, was authored by its leader, the abbot Ignác Martinovics (1755–1795). It contained direct echoes of the French Revolution in its assertion of the principle of popular sovereignty and the right to dissolve the monarchy if the ruler became tyrannical. In response to the question, 'May the slave be said to have forfeited his rights?' Martinovics declared: 'By no means. The rights of man cannot be annulled in any way. As long as man lives, he has the right to preserve and protect his life, freedom, property and individuality.'[19] Moreover, he defined revolution as 'nothing more than the rising of a nation's strength against a tyrant, it is the end of slavery and the dawn of freedom', arguing that the harnessing of physical strength and skills were vital to the likely success of such a rebellion. He believed that citizens should then immediately elect representatives to attend the National Constitutional Assembly, whose job it was to punish the tyrants and abolish their administration. Kings, the nobility, and the priesthood were portrayed as the three scourges of mankind. Martinovics made his position clear in response to the question, 'What must be done with tyrants and those who betray the nation?', stating unequivocally: 'They must die for the sake of the free people.'[20] He argued that revolution should be the means of creating a democratic republic, the only form of government which he believed could restore the natural rights of man.

The profound influence of Rousseau's *Social Contract*, as well as the *Declaration of the Rights of Man and the Citizen*, can be clearly seen in Martinovics's demands for the abolition of class privileges. His attack on the noble estates drew extensively on these works; according to Martinovics's interpretation, the contract had been created between the

[18] József Hajnóczy, *De diversis subsidiis publicis dissertatio* (Leipzig, 1792), republished in Andor Csizmadia (ed.), *Hajnóczy József közjogi-politikai munkái* (Budapest: Akadémiai, 1958).

[19] Ignác Martinovics, *Catéchisme de l'homme et du citoyen*; the translation is based on the excerpt in Ives, *Enlightenment and National Revival*, 248–249.

[20] Ibid., 249.

ruler and the common people, while the nobility and the clergy were usurping the law and concealing from them the principles of the social contract: 'How grievously are the laws of humanity and liberty denied by those who consider it dangerous for the community to be led from the darkness of ignorance into the light . . . and to be allowed to learn the simple truths of the *Social Contract*, which unite and harmonize the society of the citizenry.'[21] Moreover, in a similar vein to Hajnóczy's argument, Martinovics claimed that the nobility's assertion that the common people, in their ignorant state, had voluntarily relinquished their freedom could not be valid. Even if this was the case, future generations could not be forced to bear the consequences of their predecessors' actions. Therefore he insisted that in order to pave the way for the revolution, the lower classes should be familiarized with the concept of the social contract so that they could gain a permanent awareness of their rights.[22]

The opportunities which the 'Leopoldian moment' offered for the expression of political demands were also seized upon by the representatives of the Romanians in Transylvania, who discovered the *Social Contract*'s potential for the purposes of political-national emancipation. The Romanian masses had been excluded from participation in Transylvanian political life since 1437, when the leaders of the so-called *nationes* – the Hungarian nobility, the Szeklers and the Saxon burghers – formed a political union to protect their privileges if they were faced by a revolt of the peasantry. In 1791, a group of leading intellectuals submitted a petition entitled *Supplex Libellus Vallachorum* to the emperor, in which they called for the same political rights that the other three 'received nations' enjoyed in Transylvania and also demanded a share in the Transylvanian diet proportional to the size of the Romanian population. They argued that this extension of rights would contribute to the stability of the Empire and that in fact it would not be a novel development, but a return to the *status quo ante*.

For this reason, the Romanian nation, which lives in the Great Principality of Transylvania, by way of this *Supplex* falls publicly at the throne of Your Majesty, and prays with all its power *to have its old rights returned*, rights which are connected by the very nature of things to all citizens, and of which, in the last century, she was deprived of, as it will be shown in the following, without any right, but only by reason of the unfavourable times.[23]

[21] Hajnóczy, *De diversis subsidiis*, chapter VII, quoted in Sándor Eckhardt, *A francia forradalom eszméi Magyarországon* (Budapest: Franklin, 1924), 51.

[22] Ibid., 49.

[23] The translation of the text is based on the excerpt in B. Trencsényi and M. Kopeček, *Discourses of Collective Identity in Central and Southeastern Europe* (Budapest: CEU Press, 2006), Vol. I, 279.

The *Supplex* constituted the most important political act on the part of the Transylvanian Romanians during the Enlightenment era. Although it met with an unfavourable response from the Habsburg authorities, the document played a crucial role in proclaiming the Romanians' right to national existence. The precise identity of its authors remains unknown, but it was probably a collective effort by members of the Greek Catholic (Uniate) clergy, who had benefited educationally from the ecclesiastical union of the Transylvanian Greek Catholic Church with Rome (1699–1700). This union accommodated them with the Roman Catholic educational system and enabled them to study in Rome. This gave them an awareness of the similarities between the Latin language and their own tongue, contributing to the development of the theory of the antiquity and continuity of the Romanian nation, which held that the Romanians were the oldest of all the nationalities in Transylvania. While these historical precedents constituted an important justification for the *Supplex*, the authors also evoked natural law, the rights of man, and the theory of the social contract in their demands for political rights and social privileges to be restored to the Romanians. They explained that Romanians constituted the majority in Transylvania, comprising around 60 percent of the total population, and that they bore the most onerous burdens. They sought proportional representation within the region's administrative structures and asserted the necessity of organizing a 'national congress' composed of nobles and clergy under the common leadership of the Uniate and Orthodox bishops to discuss the demands of the Romanian population. However, this raises the question of precisely what they meant by the 'restoration' of original rights. The following passage from the *Supplex*, which drew on the account of a medieval Hungarian chronicler, is illuminating in this respect:

> Both the history of the Homeland and Roman history prove that the Romanians had undoubtedly been living in Transylvania for many centuries before the Hungarians arrived and when their Duke Gelu lost a battle, they ended their animosity towards the Hungarians. Of their own free will, holding out their right hand, they chose the Hungarian duke Tuhutum to be their ruler too and by doing so they permitted the Hungarians to cohabit with them, to enjoy equal citizenship and common civic rights. The Hungarians welcomed this free and spontaneous action by the Romanians and both nations found in equal citizenship and community of rights a happiness which they were unwilling to jeopardize in a subsequent war whose uncertain outcome both feared. This sets out clearly the *compacts* concluded between both nations.[24]

[24] The translation is based on, but is not identical to, the version in David Prodan, *Supplex Libellus Vallachorum* (Bucharest: Academy of Sciences Press), 459.

Thus, according to the *Supplex*, the Romanians and the Hungarians lived in Transylvania on the basis of a 'compact' which they negotiated after the Romanians had been defeated in battle by the Hungarians and which guaranteed equal citizenship. Therefore, the contract constituted a mutual arrangement and was not wrought by military force, as the Hungarians would argue. The *Supplex* thus located the original arrangement between the Hungarians and the Romanians in the 'social contract' (*pactum conventum*). The word 'contract' itself appears nine times altogether in the document, and on one occasion it even refers directly to Rousseau's text: 'The clauses of this contract are so completely determined by the nature of the act that the slightest modification would render them null and void.'[25] What is remarkable, however, is the shift that it underwent from the *social* to the *national* arena. It was no longer understood as a contract between members of a nation to create a sovereign, but between two groups of people: the Hungarian and the Romanian nations.

It is worth noting that a similar 'national' understanding of the social contract informed the Croatian delegates' appeal at the diet of 1790, when they launched a protest against the intention to introduce Hungarian as an official language in the Hungarian part of the Monarchy. Like their Romanian counterparts, they justified their argument for the preservation of the Latin language with reference to a medieval chronicle, according to which a *pacta conventa* was concluded between the king of Hungary and the Croatians in the thirteenth century. Interpreting this act with reference to Rousseau's *Social Contract*, they argued that the Croatian estates were equal partners of the Hungarian nobility, and therefore changes in matters which also affected them could not be introduced without their prior consent.[26]

Another instance of the 'nationalization' and the 'internalization' of Rousseau's arguments, including those expounded in the *Social Contract* and also in the *Discourse on Inequality*, can be observed in a fictional work, *The Gypsy Epic* (*Ţiganiada*). This allegorical poem was written by one of the authors of the aforementioned *Supplex Libellus Vallachorum*, Ion Budai-Deleanu. Despite being a member of the Greek Catholic clergy, Budai-Deleanu was influenced more by the radical views of the French Enlightenment than by the Enlightened Absolutism prevalent in the Habsburg lands. *The Gypsy Epic* remained unpublished in his lifetime as its anti-clerical message, rejecting fanaticism and clearly recalling

[25] Prodan, *Supplex Libellus Vallachorum*, 434, 'Les clauses de ce contrat sont tellement . . . .': *SC*, 50; *OC* III, 360.

[26] Deér József, *A magyar-horvát államközösség kezdetei* (Budapest: Royal University Press, 1931), 97–131.

Diderot's and d'Alembert's *Encyclopédie*, meant that it would never pass the stringent censorship criteria.

As has been hinted above, rather than engaging with Rousseau directly, this work contains implicit allusions to some of the main tenets of his thought. Therefore, to attempt to extrapolate 'political philosophy' from *The Gypsy Epic* would take literature beyond its boundaries and might prove misleading. However, this piece expresses Rousseau's message on a different level, one which is punctuated with parody, humour, and irony. Moreover, in the absence of more intensive and visible engagements with the *Social Contract* in addition to the *Supplex*, it provides evidence of the reception of Rousseau's thought by a handful of scholars in this region.

Rousseau's hypothetical reconstruction of the past owed little to any chronicle of factual events; his state of nature is constructed as a fictitious world. While Budai-Deleanu's world is likewise fictitious, the plot of his poem is well-defined: it takes place in his native Transylvania and tells of the members of a Gypsy clan who are asked to help fight the Turkish enemy during the rule of Vlad the Impaler (better known as Dracula) in the fifteenth century. It is perhaps unsurprising that in contemplating the nature of human society, the author invoked the Gypsies and thereby the trope of the noble savage: they provided him with a perfect vehicle through which to portray spontaneous voluntary society.[27] The Gypsies' spontaneous coexistence does not compare to the republican vigour and the political sophistication of Rousseau's version of the social contract. Instead, it is informed by its implicit variant: they can assemble freely and equally in voluntary association without a formal pact, and each has the choice to leave if and when he sees fit. While in the *Social Contract* Rousseau's citizens intentionally relinquish their natural freedom to the larger body of the state (arguably receiving it back in the form of civil freedom), the Gypsies automatically enjoy the kind of liberty that Rousseau wanted to restore in his political treatise.[28]

As the poem continues, however, the Gypsies choose not to fight the Turks but instead hide in the thick forests. In a surprising move, they plan to organize themselves into a functional society. The attempt to decide

[27] A comparable work is Alexander Pushkin's narrative poem, *The Gypsies* (*Tsygany*, 1824). Pushkin's poem has been described 'as a terse anti-Rosseauian drama built on Rousseauian premises' (Alexander Pushkin, *Collected Narrative and Lyrical Poetry*, translated in the prosodic forms of the original by Walter Arndt (Ann Arbour: Ardis, 1984), 267). The poem certainly abounds in Rousseauvian vocabulary. It recounts the tragedy of Aleko, who leaves urban civilization hoping to escape human law and 'enlightened corruption', and settles in a simple environment among the Gypsies.

[28] On the tensions inherent in Rousseau's depiction of the self-ruling community, see Philip Pettit's contribution in this volume (Chapter 10).

what form this society should take, which involves various clan members promoting their own favoured version, ends in chaos; they therefore decide to convene a general assembly to decide the most appropriate form of government, to which each clan should send a delegate. (This new legislative body clearly recalls the French National Convention, and a reference to the 'Mountain' indicates its Jacobin wing.)

> Here we can see together
> The best and brightest minds,
> Building a new citadel,
> Exactly as today in Paris those from the Mountain;
> At those high and learned thoughts
> Many nations marvel.[29]

Thereafter the delegates embark on a 'constitutional debate', alluding to Book III, chapter 3 of the *Social Contract* in which Rousseau considers the best form of government. In *The Gypsy Epic*, the protagonists of the 'constitutional debate' include Baroreu (Latin *baro* + *reu*, 'bad' in Romanian) who advocates monarchy, Slobozan (*slobod* means 'free') who is the defender of the republic, and Janalău din Roşava,[30] who favours constitutional monarchy. The case for the monarchy is expressed via an examination of the history of human evolution, which resonates with Rousseau's analysis.[31] Next, Slobozan, defender of a republic founded on natural law, enters the stage and leads an onslaught against the monarchy which resonated with contemporary Jacobin speeches in the Convention. Finally, Janalău puts forward his case for a constitutional monarchy in which the nation is governed by laws rather than men, and representatives hold office for a limited time. Which of these options proves most suitable for the Gypsy deputies? After careful consideration, they decide on a 'demo-aristo-monarchy' as their unique form of government – that is, a combination of all three options.[32] This decision may be a playful reference to Rousseau's argument that that there is no point in looking for the best form of government, since conditions differ everywhere. Nevertheless, the decision is never implemented, as it is challenged by other groups of Gypsies. In the final scene of the poem, the

[29] Ion Budai-Deleanu, *Ţiganiada* (Bucharest: Cugetarea, 1944), 272. In the description of *The Gypsy Epic*'s narrative I relied on Titus G. Sfirlea's unpublished MA thesis 'The Transylvanian School: Enlightened Instrument of Romantic Nationalism', (North Carolina State University, 2005). The translation of this passage is also taken from this work and can be found on page 57 of the thesis.

[30] A name which might have been an allusion to Jean-Jacques Rousseau.

[31] Budai-Deleanu, *Ţiganiada* 279–283, cited in Sfirlea, 59.

[32] Ibid., 314, cited in Sfirlea, 71.

Gypsy camp dissolves into violence and chaos once again, and its members disperse throughout the country.

As has been alluded to above, in Russia Byzantine political theory continued to play a key role throughout the eighteenth century and contributed to the sacralization of the tsar. Nevertheless, during the reign of Catherine II, the influence of Western political thought was increasing: theories of natural law, such as those advanced by Pufendorf, Hobbes, and Grotius (maintaining that political authority derived from an original social pact) came to rival the assumption that kings were appointed by God. Catherine herself was influenced by Enlightenment thought. For example, when her *Instruction to the Legislative Commission* (*Nakaz*) was published in 1767, it clearly reflected the influence of Montesquieu and Beccaria on the Empress's ideas.[33] Overall, the impact of Rousseau's philosophy on Russian politics has been compared to the effect of the Protestant Revolution on religion in the sense that it gave the individual personal authority to judge the legitimacy of the government according to his or her own conscience.[34]

The only exposition of the *Social Contract* in eighteenth-century Russia can be found in a compendium of enlightened philosophical ideas entitled *Philosophical Propositions*, which was compiled by Yakov Kozelsky and published in 1768. This work, which was the first systematic exposition of philosophical ideas by a Russian author, contained summaries of works by Voltaire, Helvétius, and Montesquieu, together with Rousseau's *Discourse on the Arts and Sciences* and *Discourse on Inequality*, as well as the *Social Contract*. Kozelsky did not intend to promote a reform agenda with his work. His aim was merely to spread knowledge that he believed would improve the conditions of human life and inform individuals who were unable to read the original works themselves.[35] He did not aspire to critically analyse the texts, but the process of 'summarizing' by its very nature meant that he chose to emphasize particular parts of the arguments. As a result, during the course of his engagement with the texts, simplification occurred and certain subtleties were lost. This effect was exacerbated because he did not attempt to offer a full summary of Rousseau's texts, but instead included sections relating to writings by other theorists such as Montesquieu and Helvetius.[36] This selective treatment made it impossible to accurately convey Rousseau's key concepts, with the consequence that Rousseau's theory appeared to be more

[33] Andrzej Walicki, *A History of Russian Thought: From the Enlightenment to Marxism* (Stanford: Stanford University Press, 1979), 8.

[34] Barran, *Russia Reads Rousseau*, 253.

[35] Yakov Kozelsky, *Filosoficheskia Predlozenia* (St Petersburg, 1768), 411.

[36] Barran, *Russia Reads Rousseau*, 55.

closely aligned with the ideas of his contemporaries than was actually the case. One such simplification was that Kozelsky implied that Rousseau preferred aristocratic to democratic rule, while overlooking the fundamental concept of Rousseau's politics: the separation of sovereignty from administrative government. He thus failed to take into account that for Rousseau, once the condition of popular sovereignty was met, no form of government was intrinsically advantageous or detrimental.[37]

Overall, Kozelsky offered a relatively favourable reading of Rousseau, with no accompanying revolutionary agenda: in fact, it provided a counterbalance to the democratization of Rousseau, a trend which was beginning to gain momentum at this time. Even much later, during the nineteenth century – unlike elsewhere in Western Europe – Rousseau did not provide a template for revolutionary activities. Although Russian constitutionalists were aware of the implications behind the ideas conveyed in the *Social Contract*, it was more the tone of Rousseau's work – particularly his mastery of neo-Stoic rhetoric and his appreciation of the civic virtue of Sparta and the Roman Republic – which they assimilated.[38] The Decembrist uprising of 1825 represented the first attempt to impose a set of permanent constitutional laws on the Russian state by military force. The Decembrists, a group of mainly aristocratic intellectuals, had studied political theory prior to the rebellion. Rousseau's political writings played a role in their rationale, although ultimately not in the actual form of the uprising.

As we have seen above, the *Social Contract*, along with Rousseau's other works, was frequently used to draw attention to the plight of particular social and ethnic groups. The writings of the Baltic German scholar Garlieb Merkel (1776–1850) were informed by a similar motivation when he called upon the Russian imperial government to intervene in order to ameliorate the deplorable conditions of the Latvian and Livonian serfs who suffered severe mistreatment under their Baltic German landlords. Merkel viewed the French Revolution as an uprising by an entire population against a false constitution (*Staatsverfassung*), and hence he warned the Baltic landlords that the oppressed Latvian peasants might be driven to a similar course of action if fundamental agrarian reform was not forthcoming. Additionally, Merkel engaged with Rousseau in a rather curious way: he wrote fictional stories and novellas featuring the French philosopher as the protagonist.

Merkel's indebtedness to the *Social Contract* was significantly more tangible and intense than the other instances discussed in this chapter so far, because he actually attempted to translate Rousseau's text. He

[37] Ibid., 55. [38] Ibid., 254.

published it alongside a translation of David Hume's *Essay on the Original Contract* and a self-penned essay on the history of serfdom in Livonia (then part of the Russian Empire), which he hoped would capture the attention of the Livonian landlords and the Russian and European reading public. Merkel explained that his purpose was more extensive than merely to render Hume's and Rousseau's words into German. He also sought to correct certain prevailing prejudices which were causing unnecessary suffering in his country.[39] Moreover, his opus magnum, *The Latvians*, also drew upon the theory of the social contract as an explanatory tool.[40]

The main target of Merkel's criticism was the institution of serfdom (*Leibeigenheit*) which he defined as 'a relationship, more precisely an abuse of a relationship between one stratum and another' whereby the serfs become crushed and debilitated by the nobility. 'It is a form of plague which differentiates itself from actual plague and starvation only in that it wreaks havoc continuously for half a millennium and does not even kill its victims.'[41] Merkel also believed that it constituted a grave error to consider slavery and serfdom interchangeable: both are terrifying cruelties, but the former is comparable to slaughtering the enemy on the battlefield whereas the second amounts to pre-arranged fratricide.[42] He made recourse to Rousseau' *Social Contract* when explaining the source of serfdom: 'it is a generally accepted truth that under every civil constitution there is a tacit contract'. He implied that an unwritten contract of this kind existed between the German nobility and the Baltic serfs, dating back to the time of the German conquest. However, this contract had been violated by the gradual erosion of the rights of the serfs, which occurred through the arbitrary increase of the burden of their obligations over several centuries.

Johann Gottfried Herder's influence was apparent in Merkel's historical and ethnographical emphasis, as well as in the formulation of his critique of the oppression of the Latvian population. Herder himself published an approving review of Merkel's essay in which he characterized serfdom 'as a stigma of a barbarian time which, in an enlightened epoch, makes an impression like a cancerous tumour on a beautiful face,

[39] Garlieb Merkel, *Hume's und Rousseau's Abhandlungen über den Urvertrag, nebst einem Versuch über Leibeigenschaft den Liefländischen Erbherren gewidmet* (Leipzig: Heinrich Graeff, 1797), XII–XII.

[40] Garlieb Merkel, *Die Letten, vorzüglich in Liefland am Ende des philosophischen Jahrhunderts. Ein Beytrag zur Völker- und Menschenkunde* (Leipzig, 1796); reprint (Wedemark: Hirschheydt, 1998).

[41] Jürgen Heeg, *Garlieb Merkel als Kritiker der livländischer Ständegesellschaft* (Frankfurt am Main: Peter Lang, 1996), 116.

[42] Merkel, *Die Letten*, reprint, 467.

like a pyre of the Inquisition in the midst of a flourishing field'.[43] In a similar vein to the authors of the *Supplex Libellus Vallachorum*, Merkel's discourse elevated nationality and ethnicity as the chief determinants of social status. He reshaped traditional agrarian and social reform discourses and his work represents a milestone in the formation of Latvian national identity. Accordingly, he elucidated the social divide and feudal relationship between the German landholding aristocracy and the local peasantry by recasting the established concepts of *Deutsch* and *Undeutsch* as 'Germans' and 'Latvians/Estonians', as well as transforming the nature of relations between them from reciprocal into parasitic.[44]

All in all, the *Social Contract* was a key text for scholars in Central and Eastern Europe in the late eighteenth and early nineteenth centuries. Although it continued to exert an influence throughout the rest of the nineteenth century in the region, it no longer provided a paradigmatic ideological framework for political thought. A chronological divide was marked in the Habsburg realm in the late eighteenth century and in the Russian Empire by the Decembrist rebellion of 1825: thereafter those who sought models of political and social change no longer looked to the French Enlightenment and the Revolution, but found new ideals in other emerging ideological constellations.

[43] Johann Gottfried Herder, *Sämtliche Werke zur Philosophie und Geschichte,* vol. XIII (Tübingen: J.G. Gottaschen, 1817), 337–339.

[44] Andrew Blumbergs, *The Nationalization of Latvians and the Issue of Serfdom: The Baltic Literary Contribution in the 1780s and 1790s* (Amherst, NY: Cambria Press, 2008), 175.

# 7 Reading Rousseau in Spanish America during the wars of independence (1808–1826)

*Nicola Miller*

Rousseau was cited widely, if sometimes anonymously, throughout Spanish America during the wars of independence, in proclamations, political pamphlets, manifestos, newly founded periodicals and even in draft constitutions. The *Social Contract* was probably the most important single theoretical statement in Spanish America during the 1810s, a touchstone text for the key questions of the age. Yet few of Rousseau's ideas featured in the actual founding documents of the new republican order.[1] At the close of long, destructive wars, with the threat of persistent lawlessness looming, the majority of Spanish American constitutionalists opted for delegated sovereignty, representative government, and separation of the three powers, a model associated more with Montesquieu.[2] Nor, with rare exceptions, did Spanish Americans accept Rousseau's views on freedom of belief, let alone his ideal of a civic religion: nearly all of the documents from the independence era, even the most Jacobin, proclaimed allegiance to the Catholic faith, which duly became the established Church in all of the new states.[3] Although Spanish American

[1] Spanish American constitutionalists drew on a wide range of sources from political philosophy, but the resulting documents were mainly based upon the existing modern republican constitutions of France, usually the 1791 version; Spain (Cádiz), 1812; and the United States, 1787. An important source on the United States was the collection of translations by Manuel García de la Sena: *La independencia de la Costa Firme justificada por T. Paine treinta años há* (Philadelphia: no publisher stated, 1811), which included extracts from Thomas Paine, the Declaration of Independence, the Articles of Confederation, plus the 1787 Constitution and the constitutions of various states.

[2] Rousseau's essay *Considerations on the Government of Poland* (written 1770–1771, published 1782), which contained much material of direct relevance to cautious republicans, was apparently not translated into Spanish at this time. It is a matter of dispute whether Rousseau rejected representative government (as is implied by the small scale of the ideal republic envisaged in *SC*) or delegated sovereignty. The former view was promoted by his Spanish translator, José Marchena.

[3] A striking example is the constitution agreed at Apatzingán, Mexico, in 1814, which was full of Rousseauvian terminology (as discussed below) but proclaimed loyalty to Catholicism in its first article. 'Decreto constitucional para la libertad de la América Mexicana, sancionado en Apatzingán (22 de octubre de 1814)', in Ernesto de la Torre Villar, *La Constitución de Apatzingán y los creadores del estado mexicano* (Mexico City: UNAM, 1964), 380–382. Two significant exceptions were Bernardo O'Higgins in

nation-builders agreed with him that public education was central to building a modern republic, in most of the independent states Rousseau's idealistic vision of autonomous personal development was set aside in favour of elementary schools and prosaic Lancastrian teaching methods as the most likely to be effective given prevailing shortages of teachers, buildings, books and equipment.[4] Even the most famous myth about Rousseau and Spanish America is just that: the appealing image of the great liberator, Simón Bolívar, as a Spanish American Émile, steered towards authentic self-expression in bucolic encounters with his tutor Simón Rodríguez, sadly does not stand up to scrutiny.[5]

So the question arises: if Rousseau's political theories were not implemented in Spanish America, how and why did his ideas matter there? How are we to understand the ubiquity of his presence in political discourse and his equally striking absence from political outcomes in Spanish America? His unhesitating denunciations of enforced rule evidently lent coherence and, even more importantly, moral weight to the cause of independence, which took several years to gather sustained momentum and critical mass. But was there anything beyond the fact that the rhetorical brilliance of his writing compelled many individuals to express certain widely shared ideas, above all passion for liberty and loathing of tyranny, in his memorable words?

I think that there was: namely, that Rousseau was interpreted as expressing – for good or ill – the possibility of fundamental transformation, not only of institutions and structures, but also of social relations, cultural practices and individual ways of being.[6] No other thinker (with the possible exception of Thomas Paine) went so far in developing a voluntaristic conception of a new social order. As I will illustrate below, the presence of a distinctively Rousseauvian vision of transformation, persuasively articulated by certain key figures in the independence movements, had significant consequences at certain crucial moments during the early stages of the independence movements (*c*. 1810–1813). It also contributed, I will argue, to a legacy of radical political projects,

Chile and José Artigas in what is now Uruguay, both of whom advocated freedom of worship.

[4] There are elements of Rousseau's theories in Spanish American curricula throughout the nineteenth century, for example physical education (part of the ancient Greek conception of citizen virtue), but that would be true of virtually any country with a public education policy.

[5] Jesús Andrés-Lasheras, *Simón Rodríguez: Maestro Ilustrado y Político Socialista* (Universidad Nacional Experimental Simón Rodríguez/Ediciones Rectorado: Caracas, 2004), 103–105.

[6] Transformation is one among several factors identified as accounting for Rousseau's prominence in Latin America in Boleslao Lewin's study, *Rousseau en la independencia de Latinoamérica* (Buenos Aires: Ediciones Depalma, 1980), 5.

which, despite failing themselves, helped to inspire later, more successful initiatives. I will go on to suggest two other, related ways in which readings of Rousseau stimulated Spanish American thinkers to develop ideas and practices that had lasting effects: the prospect of the Americas as a force for world-historical regeneration and the embedding of a particular archetype of the intellectual based on the writer as an agent of social transformation.

The question of how Rousseau was interpreted in Spanish America is germane both to empirical debates about the role of Enlightenment ideas in the history of the Spanish American wars of independence and to methodological debates in intellectual history. Historians of ideas have long debated the role of Rousseau in the French Revolution, but have paid far less attention to analysing how he was read in the area of the world where republicanism next took root. Historians of the Spanish American independence wars tend to concur – perhaps too readily – that the political ideas of the Enlightenment played no causative role in events that are mainly attributable to a political crisis in Europe, although such ideas are usually deemed to have provided a framework for the articulation of a new political order. There is a widespread, related assumption that those who were familiar with Enlightenment thinking were supporters of independence, and that those who were not were loyalists. The evidence on the reception of Rousseau, however, casts doubt on all of these arguments.

It was not only supporters of independence who cited Rousseau in defence of their cause, but also its opponents. For example, Manuel de Vidaurre (1773–1841) was known as 'the Peruvian Rousseau', yet he continued to advocate Spanish rule until the very last stages of the lengthy Peruvian war of independence, contending – as had Rousseau with respect to ideal republics – that it would be impossible to establish a democratic republic given the stark inequalities in his country.[7] Moreover, some critics of Rousseau were in favour of independence, such as the Mexican friar Servando Teresa de Mier, who came to see a break with Spain as inevitable but feared an alien egalitarianism he thought could only be implemented by force, and sought to preserve the institutions of creole society (especially the Church) as bulwarks against lawlessness.[8] The Catholic clergy, like almost everybody else, was divided over Rousseau: some clerics, especially among the more senior,

[7] Manuel de Vidaurre, *Cartas americanas, políticas y morales* (Philadelphia: Juan F. Hurtel, 2 vols., 1823).

[8] Servando Teresa de Mier, *Historia de la revolución de la Nueva España*, 1813, extract in José Luis Romero and Luis Alberto Romero, eds., *Pensamiento político de la emancipación*, 2 vols. (Caracas: Biblioteca Ayacucho, 1977), vol. II, 46–52, 50.

denounced him, but many of his staunchest advocates were priests or friars. It is testimony to his prominence in the public debates of the era that even people who were profoundly out of sympathy with him felt compelled to cite him or at least borrow his language to authorise their own arguments, either because they were engaged in a polemic with one of his advocates or simply because his name carried such weight.[9] Even the explicitly anti-Jacobin Agustín de Iturbide, briefly emperor of Mexico (1822–1823), publicly justified his actions with reference to 'the general will'. In short, Rousseau was invoked by some surprising people in support of some surprising arguments, and it is not possible to map reference to his ideas onto political and/or religious divides in Spanish America in any predictable way. Instead, there were ardent champions and engaged critics, wary opponents and virulent detractors, for all of whom Rousseau was an inescapable cultural reference point. This suggests that there was overall no simple equivalence between Enlightened Independentistas and reactionary loyalists.

The modern debate about whether advocates of independence drew mainly on European Enlightenment thinkers or on scholastics such as Francisco Suárez misses the main features of Spanish American intellectual life at the time,[10] namely its sheer diversity and changeability. The thought of the *philosophes* was by no means the only source of ideas and inspiration for Spanish Americans as they sought to negotiate the unprecedented situations created by Napoleon's deposition of Fernando VII from the Spanish throne. Works of scholasticism – itself a far more varied tradition than is usually acknowledged – were still read, alongside accounts of modern scientific developments, treatises on natural law and elaborations of creole patriotism, all of which, plus the various French and US Constitutions and related commentaries, contributed to the political repertoire of Spanish American independence. Moreover, different sources were drawn upon – and combined and re-combined with one another – as seemed most appropriate to a rapidly changing political situation.

In a context in which a great variety of sources was drawn upon, it is always potentially misleading to focus upon a single thinker. It is not always easy to distinguish what was specifically derived from Rousseau

[9] For example, Chilean cleric Tadeo Silva oversimplified a passage from *Émile*, changing its sense, in support of his argument that fanaticism was less of an evil than irreligion, in the course of a polemic against the Rousseauvian priest, Camilo Henríquez, about reform of the religious orders. Tadeo Silva, *El Observador Eclesiástico de Chile* (Córdoba: Imprenta de la Universidad, 1824), no. 8, 9 Aug. 1823, 100; cf *Émile*, book IV, 84.

[10] For a summary of these debates, see José Carlos Chiaramonte, *La Ilustración en el Río de la Plata* (Buenos Aires: Editorial Sudamericana, 2007), 46–48.

in the wider field of 'Enlightenment thought' that featured prominently in public discourse after 1808 and became the requisite cultural capital of any educated Spanish American. Rousseau was often invoked as one of a troika of 'moderns', usually with Montesquieu, often with Voltaire, sometimes with Locke, Raynal or Filangieri. A good many of the ideas that have been attributed to 'Rousseau's influence' – liberty as the foundation of good government, the social contract, republicanism, virtuous citizenship – could be found in many of the European works circulating in Spanish America during the independence era. Several of the texts that have been claimed as Rousseauvian turn out, on closer scrutiny, to be precisely examples of how the ideas of various philosophers were combined, often with local sources, to respond to the particular circumstances in which they were written. A full account of how Rousseau was read in Spanish America during the early nineteenth century would require analysis of how various other thinkers were read, above all Montesquieu. In the early stages of the independence struggles, Rousseau's arguments about liberty as a natural right and his denunciations of colonial rule were combined with Montesquieu's case that laws should be based on the customs and practices of a particular society. Neither argument worked in isolation: it was only together that they justified the break from Spain. Advocates of independence needed *both* Rousseau *and* Montesquieu.

These textual collages provide a clue about how to explore what happened when ideas travelled. The history of movement of ideas from Europe to Spanish America, with its distinctive mix of European, indigenous and African cultures, highlights a range of questions that may well need to be addressed even when ideas moved between more closely comparable societies. In thinking about the cultural context into which the ideas were moving, we need to ask not only about other texts available but also about a far broader range of values, assumptions, and practices that may have shaped how they were interpreted. The history of dissemination is of course crucial, but so too is the reputation of the author. Rousseau in Spanish America provides a telling example of this point: his public image in the region before 1808 is a significant factor in explaining the role of his ideas subsequently.

## A whiff of embers: Rousseau's reputation in Spanish America

Rousseau's works were proscribed in Spanish America before 1808 by an Inquisition ban dating back to 1764. Nonetheless, copies of most of them arrived in the region shortly after their publication in Europe.[11] They were smuggled in by French émigrés, diplomats, intellectually curious clerics, and other members of the educated minority who read French, visited Europe, and regarded European culture as their own. Societies that had long lived with censorship had correspondingly well-established mechanisms for evading it: underground circulation of handwritten copies, extracts slipped into other volumes, books that glossed or summarised the ideas of banned authors without naming them. In any case, the Bourbon monarchy was itself committed to reform of the Spanish state, including the reduction of the political power of the Catholic Church and the courts of the Inquisition. It is clear that there was significant local variation in the extent, coherence and effectiveness of their initiatives, which were felt strongly in New Spain or Peru, far less so in New Granada or Chile. Even so, overall there is little doubt that the Declaration of Free Trade in 1778 opened up new opportunities for the movement of people and goods, including books, between the old world and the new; more liberal viceroys turned a blind eye to – or even encouraged – the discussion of modern scientific ideas in institutions of learning; and the Sociedades Económicas de los Amigos del País were founded to encourage the adoption of modern political economy.[12] Until the 1790s, then, Rousseau was one among many Enlightenment thinkers banned by the Inquisition but tacitly sanctioned for discussion among the illustrious minority in Spanish America by the modernising Bourbons. The few responses that have been identified consisted of refutations of his early argument that science and the arts had corrupted morality and that urban life was degenerate.[13] He was probably of less interest to most creole readers in the 1780s than Adam Smith.

Rousseau acquired a distinctive and radical profile after the Revolutions in France and then – even more significantly for Spanish America – in Saint Domingue, where a victorious slave uprising in 1791, in which some 4,000 whites were killed, resulted eventually in the founding of the Republic of Haiti in 1804. The ramifications of these events were felt in a wave of slave revolts, especially in the River Plate (1795 and 1803) and in Venezuela (1795 and 1798), and a radical republican tradition among free peoples of

[11] Jefferson Rea Spell, *Rousseau in the Spanish World before 1833* (Austin: University of Texas Press, 1938), 129–139.

[12] Gabriel B. Paquette, *Enlightenment, Governance, and Reform in Spain and Its Empire, 1759–1808* (Basingstoke: Palgrave Macmillan, 2008).

[13] There was no complete translation into Spanish of the *Discourse on the Arts and the Sciences* until 1910, although its arguments were known through refutations, such as Cristóbal Mariano Coriche's *Oración vindicativa del honor de las letras y de los literatos* (1763).

colour.[14] Many creoles were therefore receptive to denunciations of Rousseau, such as the Mexican friar Servando Teresa de Mier's famous New Year sermon of 1791 attacking him for having inspired the Declaration of the Rights of Man.[15] As often happens, Rousseau's detractors were some of his most important disseminators. For the generation born during the 1760s and 1770s, whose formative years spanned the course of the French Revolution, the reassertion of peninsular power in the colonies became increasingly unacceptable. For a radical minority of them, the Inquisition's edicts against Rousseau and other French authors only served to enhance their appeal. Certain centres became notorious for their discussion of the ideas of the *philosophes*, notably Caracas, Buenos Aires and the University of Charcas in Upper Peru. Moreover, Rea Spell has illustrated the extent of interest in Rousseau's ideas in late-eighteenth-century Spain. It was in this context that the Spanish intellectual José Marchena embarked upon translations into Spanish of most of Rousseau's works, starting with the *Social Contract* in 1799.[16] A Spanish translation of the *Discourse on the Origins of Inequality* was also published in Charleston in 1803, stimulating the Inquisition to impose a specific ban on Rousseau's works, first in 1803 and again in 1808. Therefore, Rousseau was widely perceived as the most dangerous of all. His works travelled clandestinely through the Americas 'accompanied by a whiff of embers', an association which lent them 'huge subversive potential'; his very name became 'a message in itself, a virtual propaganda slogan against the old regime'.[17] This was not only the case in the august private salons where restless young creoles excitedly discussed revolution under the ardent eye of 'Juan Jacobo',[18] but also, far more dangerously, among other individuals from outside the elites. Inquisition documents from Mexico record that towards the end of the eighteenth century there was an increase in persecutions of 'minor officials, artisans, [and] soldiers'.[19] Recent research has

[14] David P. Geggus, ed., *The Impact of the Haitian Revolution in the Atlantic World* (University of South Carolina Press: Columbia, 2001); Aline Helg, *Liberty and Equality in Caribbean Colombia, 1770–1835* (University of North Carolina Press: Chapel Hill, 2004).

[15] Adolfo Sánchez Vásquez, 'La filosofía de Rousseau y su influencia en México', in *Presencia de Rousseau* (Mexico City: UNAM, 1962), 39–87, 74.

[16] His versions were published as *Emilio*, 1817; *Julia, o, la Nueva Heloysa*, 1820; and *Discurso sobre el origen y los fundamentos de la desigualdad de condiciones entre los hombres*, 1820. For an extensive bibliography of Spanish translations of Rousseau, see Rea Spell, *Rousseau*, 275–296.

[17] Juan Francisco Fuentes, *José Marchena: Biografía política e intelectual* (Barcelona: Editorial Crítica, 1989), 33 and 37–38.

[18] Eduardo Ruiz, *La librería de Nariño y Los Derechos del Hombre* (Bogotá: Editorial Planeta, 1990), 141.

[19] Monelisa L. Pérez-Marchand, *Dos etapas ideológicas del siglo XVIII en México a través de los papeles de la Inquisición*, El Colegio de México, Mexico City, 1945, 89.

uncovered clandestine networks of urban discussion groups, based in shops, which covered a wide range of philosophy and political theory.[20] And sermons were intended to be heard – and talked about – by a wide range of people. By 1808, the accumulated historical experiences of revolution and reaction, especially in France and Haiti, offered multiple models and possibilities for interpretation. In this mêlée, Rousseau's reputation, as created by both detractors and disciples – had already made him a touchstone of radicalism.

Once revolution had broken out in 1809, an interest in ideologies shifted abruptly to an urgent need for ideas to help negotiate the new unforeseen and fast-moving situations.[21] New means of dissemination developed rapidly. Spanish America became a markedly transnational arena during these years, as the course of the independence struggle in any particular part of the region inevitably had implications for political decisions elsewhere. Many independence leaders spent time in exile, mostly in London or the United States, comparing developments, debating European responses to events throughout the Americas and exchanging information and experiences, ideas and texts. Within the territories, a new periodical press reached a far wider range of people than did books: the pioneering *Aurora de Chile*, for example, was widely sold on the streets and also read aloud.[22] It is likely that popular theatre was also an important medium for transmitting images and ideas of Rousseau, at least in the River Plate and Chile, where most research has been done on the topic. Rousseau's own plays seem to have been rarely, if ever, staged in Spanish America – whereas Voltaire's works were a standard part of the repertoire – but there were dramatisations of 'Juan Santiago'.[23] We also know that there were prominent actors and theatre directors who were interested in Rousseau and may have contributed to publicising his ideas.[24]

[20] François-Xavier Guerra, Annick Lempérière et al., *Los espacios públicos en Iberoamérica* (Fondo de Cultura Económica: Mexico, 1999).

[21] Romero, 'Prólogo', xxii.

[22] Miguel Luis Amunátegui, *Camilo Henríquez* (Santiago: Imprenta Nacional, 2 vols., 1889), I: 53–54.

[23] Raúl H. Castagnino, *Esquema de la literatura dramática argentina (1717–1949)* (Buenos Aires: Instituto de Historia del Teatro Americano, 1950); Eugenio Pereira Salas, *Historia del Teatro en Chile desde sus orígenes hasta la muerte de Juan Casacuberta 1849* (Santiago: Ediciones de la Universidad de Chile, 1974). Neither of these works mentioned any performances of Rousseau's dramas, although it is at least possible that there was interest in his *La découverte du nouveau monde*. *Pygmalion* (1771) was probably the first of Rousseau's works to be translated into Spanish, from an Italian version, in 1783. There was a hostile play performed in the 1820s entitled *Proceso de Juan Santiago en Sudamérica*, by a cleric, Francisco de Paula Castañeda.

[24] For example, in the River Plate and Chile, the actor-director Luis Ambrosio Morante and the actor Juan Casacuberta.

The extent of popular dissemination itself was part of the context of how members of the elites responded to Rousseau's ideas.

## A radical social contract

The provisional governments declared after Napoleon had deposed the Spanish monarch justified their existence on the principle of reversion of sovereignty to the people in times when the monarch was unable to govern, which had a long tradition in Spanish thought dating back to the thirteenth century. While Fernando VII still lived, the principle of reversion allowed for no permanent change in the relationship between Spain and its American lands. Creoles had a long list of grievances against colonial rule that were compellingly articulated in various statements of 1809–1811, but none of them necessarily entailed seeking political independence; they were compatible with restoration of monarchy and/or with liberal reform in Spain. The moderately liberal Cádiz Constitution of March 1812, which representatives from the Americas played a major role in drafting, addressed at least some of the creole demands, notably for free trade and for greater, albeit not equal, representation in the Cortes. As a result, many creoles showed signs of holding out for continued colonial rule from a reformed Spain over the uncertainties of independence.

In this context, which affected the whole region despite the specificities of the political dynamics in different places, Rousseau's arguments about the need for a newly constituted political order to achieve liberty and allow for the expression of natural rights became crucial to the case of several key figures who advocated full independence. They had other sources of inspiration for the case against absolutism, or even colonialism. But it was only in Rousseau that they found the legitimating principles for moving from a critique of the old order to the foundation of a new one.[25] The fervour for constitutionalism that characterised the independence struggles, especially during the early years, itself found inspiration in the Rousseauvian principle that the right laws would create a virtuous society (rather than Montesquieu's converse argument that laws should be shaped by existing custom and practice). Other thinkers had written about the social contract but only Rousseau conceptualised it as the basis for social transformation. For him, popular sovereignty was not just an abstract political concept but one with social and economic

[25] Raúl Cardiel Reyes, *Los filósofos modernos en la independencia Latinoamericana* (Mexico City: UNAM, 1964), 121; Mario Dotta, *El artiguismo y la revolución francesa* (Montevideo: Fundación de la Cultura Universitaria, 1989), 78.

content, which could only function effectively in a political community with shared history and values. Such a conception of popular sovereignty was actually very different from that of the Spanish tradition, although advocates of independence strategically tended to take advantage of the potential for taking them both to refer to the same thing. The Spanish version assumed that 'el pueblo' would be constituted from local political bodies ('los cuerpos'), such as the municipal councils, in which there was democratic debate, but only by a select group of some social standing within the community.[26] Rousseau's 'pueblo', in contrast, conceptualised all individuals as citizens, equal before the law and equally bound to obey the law. It was no coincidence that creole politicians who were at least thinking ahead to the possibility of independence began to publish openly their own versions and accounts of Rousseau at this time. Versions appeared in Caracas, translated by José Vargas Vila, in 1809, and in Havana (one of the few places where the independence movement failed) in 1813.

The most important of these new publications was the edition of the *Social Contract* published in 1810 by Mariano Moreno (1778–1811), a key figure in the provisional government established after the Revolución de Mayo in Buenos Aires that same year.[27] Moreno, who hoped for independence, declared the *Social Contract* to be the most important of the works of political theory that constituted 'the catechism of free peoples', arguing that anyone who read it 'would not easily be robbed of their rights'. In the prologue to his edition, he stated that he wanted everyone to read Rousseau so that they would understand their rights – and their obligations – as citizens of a republic.[28] He ordered 200 copies for distribution in Buenos Aires schools, although soon after he was sent into exile the following year the Cabildo de Buenos Aires hastily sent them back to the printer and instead adopted a text by a monarchist priest.[29] 'Revolutions among men without enlightenment' could only end in 'disorderly horrors', Moreno argued, an example of which was provided by Spain, which – despite a fine display of heroism and sacrifice – had been unable to form a government that commanded legitimacy or

[26] Luis Villoro, 'Rousseau en la Independencia mexicana', 1981, *Tiempo Cariátide*, 55–61, 58, accessed October 2014 at www.uam.mx/difusion/casadeltiempo/80_sep_2005/55_61.pdf.

[27] *Del Contrato social o principios del derecho político* (Buenos Aires: Real Imprenta de Niños Expósitos, 1810).

[28] Mariano Moreno, 'Prólogo a la traducción del Contrato social' [1810], in his *Escritos políticos y económicos*, ed. Norberto Piñero (Buenos Aires: L. J. Rosso y Cía, 1915), 265–268.

[29] Ricardo Zorraquín Bécu, 'El Contrato Social y la Revolución de Mayo', in *Catálogo de la exposición bibliográfica argentina de derecho y ciencias sociales* (Universidad de Buenos Aires, Facultad de Derecho y Ciencias Sociales, 1960), 17–26, 21.

a constitution to end anarchy, because 'the people were ignorant'. He emphasised the importance of 'each citizen' understanding 'the advantages of a constitution' that 'would restore to the people their rights' and protect them against 'new usurpations' of their sovereignty. He wanted 'each citizen' to regard 'the defence' of such a constitution 'as his own, personal good'. Notoriously, Moreno omitted from his edition Book IV, chapter 8 – on civil religion – arguing in the preface that Rousseau 'talked utter nonsense about matters of religion'.[30] There has been some debate about Moreno's own views on religion, but whatever his personal creed, he would not have wished to provoke the Catholic authorities and thereby distract attention from what he saw as salutary in the rest of the text. As in other initiatives, such as the founding of a public library and a periodical, Moreno sought to prepare the people of Buenos Aires for liberty based on a modern concept of popular sovereignty. In an article in his *Gaceta de Buenos Aires*, he stated explicitly that: 'The bonds that unite the people to the king are different from those that unite men among themselves: a people is a people before it gives itself to a King [*sic*]'.[31]

Creole patriotism had existed for several decades as a cultural phenomenon without any significant political agenda.[32] It was when the two were brought together that a compelling case for independence could be made, as can be seen in the early documents of Chilean independence, particularly the writings of the priest Camilo Henríquez (1769–1825). He was the first person to proclaim the need for independence, in January 1811, less than four months after a provisional government had been founded in Santiago on the principle of reversion. He did so by invoking both patriotism and philosophy. Seeking to move the arguments on from the claims of the natural law theorists, Henriquez argued that there was no natural law obliging provinces ruled by Spain in Europe and America to stay together; indeed, 'nature itself has formed them to live separately'.[33] It was 'a geographical truth' that Chile was capable of independent existence both economically and culturally, he argued, given that it had both mineral resources and agricultural capacity, 'strong men' to work the land and navigate the sea, plus 'solid, profound and perceptive' minds who were 'capable of all the sciences and arts of genius'. Given the country's geography, with its natural borders of the Andes, the desert and the Pacific Ocean, did it not go against the very order of nature, he

[30] Moreno, 'Prólogo', 268.
[31] Mariano Moreno, *La Gaceta de Buenos Aires*, 13 November 1810, 599–600.
[32] A lot of work has now been done on creole patriotism; the pioneer was David Brading, *The First America* (Cambridge: Cambridge University Press, 1991).
[33] Camilo Henríquez, 'Proclama' (2 January 1811), in Romero, *Pensamiento politico*, vol. I, 220–224, 221.

demanded, to be governed from overseas?[34] Henríquez then built up his case by drawing upon philosophy, claiming that only the philosophers had 'dared to tell the people that they had rights and that they could only be governed ... under the conditions of a social pact'.[35] In an audacious act of intellectual appropriation that was characteristic of many such documents from the independence era, Henríquez claimed Aristotle for his cause. The human race would have been a great deal happier, he stated, had ecclesiastical scholars 'read in [Aristotle] the rights of man and the need to separate the three powers ... in order to conserve the liberty of the peoples', instead of wasting time over irrelevant obscurities.[36] Here Henríquez may have been deliberately reminding his audience of a passage on Aristotle in the *Social Contract*, with which he could have assumed at least some of them were familiar. Rousseau argued that Aristotle had mistaken 'the effect for the cause' in saying that some men were born for slavery and others for domination. For Rousseau, slaves were created by acts of oppression, which then changed their nature so that they were unable to resist their servitude: 'Slaves lose everything in their chains, even the desire to be rid of them; ... Force made the first slaves, their cowardice perpetuated them'.[37] It is a reasonable deduction that Henriquez, who was cautiously urging his compatriots to have the courage to claim their liberty, preferred to allow the practical consequences of his arguments to be concluded by allusion. Henriquez had been imprisoned by the Inquisition in 1809, so he had good reason to be cautious about naming Rousseau openly, but he did mention 'Reynal'. In a conclusion ringing with Rousseauvian terms, he urged that 'patriotic virtue should unite with enlightened understanding' to 'break the chains of slavery' and fulfil 'the right of the peoples [and] the general will'.[38]

Both Father Miguel de Hidalgo (1753–1811), who launched an uprising in New Spain in 1810, and his successor and pupil, José María Morelos (1765–1815), were well-versed in French political thought. There is some debate in the historiography about whether Hidalgo, who was executed in July 1811, sought full independence for Mexico. What his public documents show is that, whether out of conviction or for tactical reasons, he represented popular sovereignty as God-given to the king and only reverting to the people because Fernando had been dethroned. For example, in his Manifesto of 1811, he declared that the national congress he sought to convene would consist of 'representatives

[34] Ibid., 221–222. [35] Ibid., 221 and 223.

[36] Ibid., 223. Henríquez also discussed Aristotle in Rousseauvian terms in his 'Nociones fundamentales sobre los derechos de los pueblos', *Aurora de Chile* (Santiago), no. 1, 13 February 1812; also in Romero, *Pensamiento politico*, vol. I, 228–232.

[37] *SC*, 43; *OC* III, 353. [38] Henríquez, 'Proclama', 223–224.

of all the cities, towns and places of this kingdom'.[39] This was still the position that prevailed in late 1813: the Act of Independence declared at Chilpancingo stated that the Congress of Anáhuac there convened had 'recovered the exercise of the sovereignty usurped' because of 'the present circumstances in Europe'.[40] By the time of the Constitution of Apatzingán, approved in October 1814, the restoration of Fernando and his rejection of the new political rights for Spanish Americans stipulated in the Constitution of Cádiz (1812), combined with other factors, had led to the radicalisation of the independence movement. In these altered circumstances, Morelos, who played an important part in drafting the Constitution, deployed a Rousseauvian ideal of sovereignty in order to further his aims. The revised conception was said to derive from 'all the citizens, voluntarily united in society', to reside 'originally in the people' and to be 'imprescriptible, inalienable and indivisible'. Rousseau's absolute concept is, however, diluted by a distinction between the origin of sovereignty in the people and 'its exercise in national representation' in a body of deputies elected by the citizens, in an attempt to negotiate the difficulties of reconciling principles of sovereignty with practicalities of government.[41] Even so, the idea of the inalienable sovereignty of the people has been traced through a series of Mexican constitutions to the document of 1917, which remains in place today.[42] By contrast, in most of the new republics, for example Argentina and Chile, sovereignty was invested in the nation, not the people.[43]

There is a good deal of evidence that in the first few years after 1808, the dominant understanding of sovereignty in Spanish America was drawn from a combination of the Spanish principle of reversion (which could be traced back to the Siete Partidas of Alfonso el Sabio through the works of Francisco Suárez) and theories of natural law theorists (drawn from Grotius and Pufendorf, sometimes through the lens of Jesuit

[39] 'Manifiesto en respuesta a la Inquisición', in J. E. Hernández y Dávalos, ed., *Colección de documentos para la historia de la guerra de independencia de México de 1808 a 1821* (Impresor José María Sandoval: Mexico, 6 vols., 1877–82), vol. I, document 51.

[40] 'Acta de independencia de 6 de Noviembre de 1813', in Hernández y Dávalos, *Colección de documentos*, vol. 5, document no. 91.

[41] 'Decreto Constitucional para la Libertad de la América Mexicana sancionado en Apatzingan á 22 de Octubre de 1814', in Hernández y Dávalos, *Colección de documentos*, vol. 5, document no. 183, quotations from 'Capítulo II: De la Soberanía', 704.

[42] Antonio Colomer Viadel, 'La revolución francesa, la independencia y el constitucionalismo en Iberoamérica', in Leopoldo Zea, ed., *América Latina ante la Revolución francesa* (Mexico City: UNAM, 1993), 181–193, 185–187.

[43] For example, Chile: 'Sovereignty resides essentially in the Nation' (1822 and 1833); Colombia: 'Sovereignty resides radically in the Nation' (1830). In Argentina, there was no clause on sovereignty, but the preamble, echoing that of the United States, made an important change: 'We, the representatives of the people of the Argentine Nation', instead of 'We the people of the United States'.

interpreters).[44] Most of the provisional governments were declared on that basis. However, it is less plausible to account for the subsequent moves towards founding independent republics without acknowledging that certain highly influential figures knew their Rousseau.

## Equality: A radical legacy

The independence wars were both a struggle against colonial rule and a series of local competitions for power, resources and legitimacy, some of which developed into struggles to liberate the dispossessed from elite oppression. There were 'rival visions of the future', with respect not only to economic development but also political institutions and the kind of society that was possible.[45] Those who wanted to pursue a more radical vision of what the new republics would look like found ideas, arguments, concepts and a language for articulating it in the work of Rousseau. A significant minority of the leaders of the early independence movements also agreed with him that liberty entailed equality. Thus Mariano Moreno, in late 1810, in a decree abolishing the privileges attached to certain official roles in colonial society, stated:

> In vain would this government publish liberal principles to enable the peoples to enjoy the invaluable gift of their freedom, if we were to permit the continuation of those privileges, which to the shame of humanity tyrants invented in order to suffocate natural feelings ... If we wish the peoples to be free, let us religiously observe the sacred dogma of equality.[46]

In Mexico, the radical priest Morelos declared that the propertied classes were to pay for their complicity with colonial rule with all their wealth, which was to be confiscated and redistributed half to the poor, half to fund the military campaign.[47] José Artigas (1764–1850) of Uruguay, a *caudillo* (military boss) who led the resistance against both the centralising claims of Buenos Aires and control by the Empire of Brazil, promoted

[44] Chiaramonte, *La Ilustración*; Villoro, 'Rousseau'.

[45] For an overview of the historiography of independence, see Jeremy Adelman, 'Independence in Latin America', *The Oxford Handbook of Latin American History*, ed. José Moya (New York: Oxford University Press, 2011), 153–180, quotation at 159.

[46] Junta Provisional [written by Mariano Moreno], 'Decreto sobre supresión de honores (6 December 1810), in Romero, *Pensamiento politico*, 285–289, 285, and 287. Noemí Goldman has rightly noted that there were limits to the egalitarianism envisaged by Moreno: Article 12 of the same decree stated that nothing should 'prevent the free entry to any public function' of 'respectable citizens' (*los ciudadanos decentes*). See her chapter 'Morenismo y los derechos naturales en el Río de la Plata', in Zea, *América Latina ante la Revolución francesa*, 151–167.

[47] J. M. Morelos, 'Plan Político: Medidas políticas que deben tomar los jefes para lograr sus fines por medios llanos y seguros, evitando la efusión de sangre de una y otra parte', Nov. 1813, in Romero, *Pensamiento politico*, II:56–57.

the sovereignty of all the members of his Federal League, including the indigenous peoples. He maintained that they should not be kept separate in reservations but should play a full part in the government.[48] His public speeches displayed familiarity with the ideas of popular sovereignty and the general will; they showed that by 1813 he had developed a coherent version of democratic republicanism to present to his constituency.[49] Whether or not he read the *Social Contract* himself – and he did have the education to do so – 'he had friends and advisers who could discuss [it] with him', and he evidently deemed the Rousseauvian language to be appropriate for attracting support.[50] He later implemented a land reform, decreeing that land was to be redistributed on the principle that 'the most unhappy will be the most privileged',[51] although the initiative was short lived because of the exigencies of war.

Some of the proclaimed egalitarianism was symbolic (which is of course not without its own significance) but a good deal of it took tangible form in the suppression of privileges, the ending of tribute and the abolition of slavery in most of the new republics during the 1820s (although it is argued that implementation of such policies was uneven).[52] Some of the early advocates of independence, fearful that any concession to their opponents would result in defeat, went far further in promoting equality than Rousseau's texts entail. Their fears proved to be justified: the radical, Rousseau-inspired voices that rang out clearly above the confusion of the early stages of the independence struggles were drowned out – or extinguished – as the practicalities of trying to found states while fighting the Spanish enabled anyone threatened by an inclusive social contract to defend their own interests. Most of the creole politicians who oversaw the eventual victories of the independence movements were distinctly reluctant to extend Rousseau's uncompromising stance on liberty beyond a rejection of colonial rule: they regarded the rest of the populations, including most other creoles, as distinctly unfit even for negative freedoms, let alone Rousseau's positive ones. As is well known, liberals across Spanish America then spent many decades fighting against the resistance, both active and passive, of those who sought to preserve local versions of Spanish institutions, especially the Catholic Church; liberalism only

[48] Dotta, *El artiguismo*, 95.
[49] José Artigas, 'Oración de Abril', 5 April 1813, in Romero, *Pensamiento político*, II:12–14.
[50] John Street, *Artigas and the Emancipation of Uruguay* (Cambridge: Cambridge University Press, 1959), 177–178.
[51] José Artigas, 'Reglamento provisorio de tierras', 1815, in Romero, *Pensamiento político*, vol. II, 24–26.
[52] Slavery was legally abolished in Greater Colombia, 1821; Chile, 1823; Central America, 1824; Mexico, 1829; Uruguay, 1830; and Bolivia, 1831. In Argentina, it was 1853; Venezuela and Peru, 1854; Spanish colonial Cuba, 1886; and the Empire of Brazil, 1888.

achieved sustained power, during the last few decades of the nineteenth century, at the expense of compromise with conservatism. The early independence leaders were severely criticised, especially by the nation-builders of the 1830s and 1840s, for trying to implement absolute principles in disregard of the actual conditions in which they were operating.

Yet the founding commitment to Rousseau's concept of the state as the manifestation and guarantor of liberty and equality before the law, that embedding of principles of equality within the body politic, had far-reaching consequences, the cumulative effects of which can be seen in the revised constitutions adopted across the region from the 1920s to the 1940s, nearly all of which included stipulations expressly committing the state to defending equality.

## The Americas as a source of regeneration

The Spanish American reception of Rousseau's arguments about people in a state of nature has to be understood in the context of the long history of debates about indigenous peoples in the Americas, in which European commentary was only one part of a complex picture.[53] As Peter Gay has noted, the term 'noble savage' cannot actually be found in Rousseau's work,[54] nor does it seem to feature in Spanish American debate during the independence wars, although there were images close in spirit. Mostly, however, the debates took a different turn. Some opponents of independence represented the *Discourse on the Origins of Inequality* as promoting primitivism in order to reject Rousseau's alleged elevation of natural man, arguing that only through reason could people attain virtue. At the same time, they quoted him out of context to support their contention that the pro-independence uprising presaged a return to a barbaric state of nature.[55] Advocates of independence, on the other hand, avoided what Arthur Lovejoy characterised as the 'persistent historical error' that Rousseau was promoting primitivism in that text.[56] Rousseau's schema of humans as naturally good but corrupted by civilisation was read as an explanation for what some creoles saw as the corrupted state of the indigenous peoples – deprived of their natural liberty and thereby brought to ruin by the

[53] Jorge Cañizares Esguerra, *How to Write the History of the New World* (Palo Alto: Stanford Univ. Press, 2006).

[54] Peter Gay, 'Breeding Is Fundamental: Jenny Davidson Reflects on Enlightenment Ideas about Human Perfectibility', *Book Forum*, April/May 2009, www.bookforum.com/inprint/016_1/3519, accessed August 2013.

[55] Sánchez Vásquez, 'La filosofía', 79.

[56] Arthur Lovejoy, 'The Supposed Primitivism of Rousseau's *Discourse on Inequality*', *Modern Philology* (Chicago), 21.2, November 1923, 165–186, quotation at 165.

European conquerors.[57] But what particularly attracted the attention of many independence supporters was Rousseau's idea of perfectibility. This, too, played out in several ways. In some cases, creoles appropriated to themselves the virtues of living without artifice or convention, comparing themselves favourably with their colonial masters. They could easily reconcile this with Christianity – living the simple life, like Jesus. Independence leaders, who were acutely aware of the need to persuade potential supporters that fighting the Spanish was not a crime against Catholicism, adroitly blended Rousseau's arguments against monarchy with those attributed to God in the Book of Samuel, or lent the aura of Rousseau to their visions of Christian community liberated from the corrupting influence of Spain, by selectively citing his discussions of the simple life.[58]

Other Spanish American republicans identified their own conditions with those that Rousseau saw as necessary to successful legislation of the general will but so rarely found: 'simplicity of nature linked with the needs of society'.[59] These creoles felt that they had a great deal to learn from Europe in philosophy, literature and science, but not in politics, the despotism of which they believed themselves destined to replace with liberty and justice. The question of equality between Europe and the Americas was debated – both in Spain and in Spanish America – in political terms in the aftermath of the usurpation of Fernando VII; later, as independence movements attracted increasing support, it acquired a quasi-ideological dimension. A long history of Europe's projection of utopianism onto the Americas began to be refracted back in politicised form, in a version of *americanismo* that contrasted the uncorrupted state of nature in the Americas with the corruption of European society. At the Congress of Panama, in 1826, as Spanish Americans discussed a possible confederation of American states, the Peruvian delegate Manuel de Vidaurre echoed Rousseau's axioms on the state of nature in order to support claims that the peoples of the Americas were destined to realise the dream of human perfectibility. 'The inhabitants of those parts of the Americas that were Spanish', he declared, 'restored to the state of nature, free and independent, in perfect possession of all their rights . . . are more perfect than in the days after creation'. To the advantage of naturalness they could now add experience: 'Today, in complete control of all their faculties, they can distinguish the just from the unjust, the useful and

[57] Cardiel Reyes, *Los filósofos modernos*, 121.

[58] José Amor de la Patria, *Catecismo político Cristiano (selección)*, 1811, in Romero, *Pensamiento politico*, 212–219.

[59] *SC*, 78; *OC* III, 392. For Rousseau, such conditions actually existed only in Corsica (ibid.) and possibly in Poland.

agreeable from the pernicious and the annoying, the safe from the dangerous'.[60] The Spanish American republics were ready, in short, to assume their world-historical role of regenerating civilisation: as beacons of liberty, toleration and equality at home – where the former 'oppressed African' would 'start to become rational in the realisation that nothing distinguished him from other men' – they would promote peace and open exchange abroad.[61]

One compelling example can be seen in a play by Camilo Henríquez: *La Camila, o la Patriota de Sud-América* (1817), which was performed in Buenos Aires (although not, apparently, in Chile).[62] The action takes place a few months after the defeat by Bonapartists of the first declaration of independence from Spain, made in Quito in August 1809. The author included a foreword in which he briefly described a documented incident when loyalist troops from Lima went on the rampage in Quito, killing about 500 people, in revenge for the murder of one of their own captains.[63] The play is set in a village in the Ecuadorian jungle, which is represented as a utopian space where the true nature of the humans who enter it is revealed. In this setting, the Spanish are referred to (there are no Spanish characters) as cruel and superstitious, their way of life 'in contradiction with nature' (324). The Omagua are portrayed as cultured people who combine the virtues of civility, some of which they have acquired from the creoles, with the compassion of people living in harmony with nature (cf. Rousseau's *pitié*). The chief's house is 'decorated to English taste' (334) and he has studied modern political thought in the United States, which Henríquez, here and elsewhere, represented in utopian terms. The creoles are tainted by their support for the misdeeds of the Spaniards, but those that have encountered modern Enlightenment ideas have the possibility of redemption through contact with these indigenous Americans who know how to reconcile nature and culture. The main character, Camila, a young creole woman, and her parents have fled the royalist atrocities in Quito, in which they fear her husband has been killed. They are brought before the chief of the Omagua people, who are referred to throughout as 'Americans'. He feigns lack of sympathy, telling them that there is no reason for him not to hand them over to the Spanish, and

[60] Manuel L. de Vidaurre, 'Discurso en el Congreso Americano de Panamá', 22 June 1826, in Germán A. de la Reza, ed., *Documentos sobre el Congreso Anfictiónico de Panamá* (Caracas: Fundación Biblioteca Ayacucho, 2012), 184–190, quotations at 184.

[61] Ibid., 186–187.

[62] María de la Luz Hurtado, *Teatro chileno y modernidad: Identidad y crisis social* (Irvine, CA: Ediciones de GESTOS, 1997), 47; Castagnino, *Esquema*, 29.

[63] Camilo Henríquez, 'La Camila, o, La patriota de Sud-América', in Amunátegui, *Camilo Henríquez,* II:309-352, 311. Page references to the subsequent quotations in this paragraph are given in brackets.

reminds the creole family of their forebears' complicity in Spanish repression, not least in the failure to protest against the murder of Túpac Amaru. His words provoke deep repentance in Camila and prompt her to declare that 'if America ... did not adopt more liberal principles, it would never escape from the sphere of Spain overseas, [which was] impoverished and ignorant like European Spain' (346). When she reappears dressed in indigenous clothing to symbolise her newfound distance from the Spanish, the chief proclaims her a 'heroine of the new world' (351). Reunited with her husband, who has also found safe haven with the Omagua, she is reassured: 'here there are no tyrants, no persecutors. You are in the sanctuary of liberty, among the people of reason and of nature ... here we are building the foundations of a new Philadelphia' (350). Thus Rousseau's conception of the relationship between nature and culture was adapted by Henríquez to dramatise the potential to realise a modern utopia in the Americas.

## Archetype of an intellectual: The writer as agent of social transformation

Mariano Moreno wrote an *Apotheosis of Rousseau*, which encapsulated the appeal of Rousseau's practice as an author: fierce intelligence complemented by a highly developed sensibility, a vivid and brilliant imagination, a commitment to truth, a vast range of knowledge and moral courage. This portrait contrasted starkly with his *Apotheosis of Voltaire*, which was a far more prosaic piece that merely reported his entry into the Panthéon.[64] Rousseau's self-description as an ancient in modern dress was often cited approvingly in Spanish America, where the claim to be the modern inheritors of ancient greatness was given political expression in republicanism long before it acquired a cultural dimension in *Latinidad*. Rousseau's arguments about the poverty of philosophy lent a modern edge to views already held by many Spanish American thinkers: that reason alone was not sufficient for virtue; that emotion had to be part of the exemplary life; and that truth had an ethical as well as logical dimension. There has been enduring interest in Spanish America in Rousseau's life as exemplary of the struggle between reason and emotion.[65]

[64] Mariano Moreno, *Artículos que la 'Gazeta' no llegó a publicar*, ed. Eduardo Durnhofer (Buenos Aires: Casa Pardo, 1975), 65–70 and 43–50 on Rousseau and Voltaire, respectively. Moreno published a summary of this account of Rousseau's life as exemplary in his 'Prólogo al *Contrato social*', 1810, 267–268.

[65] *Del contrato social*, ed. Mariano Ruiz-Funes (Mexico City: Biblioteca Enciclopedia Popular, 1945).

During the independence wars, particularly during the early stages when everyone in public life seemed to be drafting proclamations and prescriptions for the new political order, there was particular interest in Rousseau's strategies for successful authorship, which meant that his books could function not only as political statements but also as political acts. His literary style – clear, vigorous, passionate and accessible – was widely admired, even by those who spurned his ideas. Style has had a particularly important place in Spanish American cultural history and most commentary on Rousseau's works in Spanish America has celebrated the brilliance of his writing and his knack for creating unforgettable images. But Spanish American publicists were also intrigued by Rousseau's skill in creating a persona, cultivating his own celebrity and managing his reputation.[66] So far as we know, *The Confessions* was not translated into Spanish until 1869, so biographical information about Rousseau must have been disseminated, at least initially, by educated Spanish Americans who read French. Tales of his persecution were certainly well known. One Chilean supporter of independence recalls that they all felt compelled to learn by heart the 'Profession of Faith of a Savoyard Vicar',[67] particularly after a Spanish translation of *Émile* came out in 1817.[68] As a new public stage opened up during the wars of independence, Rousseau provided a model of how to act upon it.

Over the last two centuries, Rousseau has often been invoked in Spanish America, particularly by revolutionaries, as an exemplary intellectual: politically engaged, passionate in the pursuit of truth, upholding the public responsibility of the writer by refusing to publish anonymously. In Spanish America, then, there was a more politicised version of the European reading of him as theorist of individual authenticity: not only did the philosopher's claims have to be founded in personal authenticity, but also the politician's. Famously, Che Guevara carried the *Social Contract* on his campaigns. Slavoj Žižek has a short section entitled 'Guevara as a Reader of Rousseau' in his *Living in the End Times*, in which he cites a passage from Guevara's *Man and Socialism in Cuba* that he sees as echoing what Che took from Rousseau: 'the revolutionary leaders must have a large dose of humanity, a large dose of a sense of justice and truth in order to avoid falling into dogmatic extremes, into

[66] Antoine Lilti has argued that Rousseau's specificity was to claim that the value of his philosophy relied on his own authenticity, a claim that is borne out by Spanish American responses. More on this point in Lilti's article 'The Writing of Paranoia: Jean-Jacques Rousseau and the Paradoxes of Celebrity', *Representations* 103 (2008), 53–83.

[67] José Zapiola, *Recuerdos de treinta años: 1810–1840* (Santiago: Imprenta de El Independiente, 1872–1874), ch. III.

[68] *Emilio, ó De la educación*, trans. J. Marchena (Burdeos: Imprenta de Pedro Beaume, 1817).

cold scholasticism, into isolation from the masses'.[69] Images of Rousseau created during the wars of independence had a lasting impact on Spanish American ideas about what being an intellectual entailed, not least the conviction that cultural practice could be a route to political freedom.

## Conclusion

Rousseau's ideas had consequences in Spanish America, despite – or perhaps because of – being taken out of context, reinterpreted and reconfigured to meet the urgent challenges of anti-colonial wars. No other thinker offered such a compelling justification to the provisional juntas for making the leap from being caretakers of monarchical sovereignty to defenders of popular sovereignty. After the first declarations of independence, a strong dose of voluntarism was required to keep the republican ideal alive, and for a significant number of prominent figures, that voluntarism drew inspiration from Rousseau. There were also far more lasting consequences. Because Rousseau was available as a source of ideas and inspiration, principles of equality were embedded in the political cultures of the new republics, Americanismo acquired a political charge, and a particular ideal type of intellectual took hold. Thus his significance lay less in the areas of constitutionalism or public policy than in a more diffuse but nonetheless powerful impulse towards a particular conception of the relationships between state and society and between politics and culture. That the enlightenment of the citizenry was a public responsibility, that culture could be liberating, that intellectuals could change the world, were all ideas embedded in the mainstream political discourse of Spanish America throughout the nineteenth and most of the twentieth centuries. When later reformers and revolutionaries looked back to the early leaders of independence to find inspiration and legitimation for their own plans to bring about more equal societies, they found a powerful legacy of republican projects based on a radical social contract. José Martí, for example, leader of the Cuban independence at the end of the nineteenth century, elaborated a radical liberalism based on the idea of authentic natural man linked to self-affirmation and self-government for the whole of Latin America. Rousseau is by no means the only reason, but the ubiquity of his presence in the public debates of the founding era of these republics is one significant factor in the explanation.

[69] Slavoj Žižek, *Living in the End Times* (London: Verso, 2010), 108; Ernesto Che Guevara, *Man and Socialism in Cuba*, trans. Margarita Zimmermann (Havana: Book Institute, 1967), 44.

It has only been possible to highlight here a few of the many different ways in which Rousseau was read in early nineteenth-century Spanish America. Nonetheless, these examples are a telling illustration of what can happen when ideas travel from one context to another, radically different one, especially perhaps the ideas of a writer with as much political baggage as Rousseau had acquired by 1808. The context for understanding how Rousseau was interpreted in Spanish America goes beyond the other texts alongside which he was read; beyond the means by which his ideas were disseminated; and beyond even the institutions where they were debated, important although each of these three elements is, to include the political and social dynamics of the independence wars. The initial success of independence leaders in translating Rousseau's principles of natural liberty and equality into laws (even if they were superseded or, at best, patchily implemented) upped the stakes of the wars for all creoles. In these charged circumstances, many parties to the arguments about a possible new political order appropriated Rousseau for their own purposes, often to define their position in relation to opponents. In doing so, they were only doing what many of Rousseau's European commentators did, not to mention Rousseau himself: instrumentally plucking out historically rooted examples to test out general principles, combining an aspect of one problem with that of another, arguing or citing against the grain and, sometimes, simply making things up.[70] This does not mean that there was a limitless variation on the meanings of Rousseau's texts: the principles he articulated were attractive not least because they seemed unchanging and universal. It does mean, however, that Rousseau's place in Spanish American intellectual history cannot be understood in terms of his 'influence', which is shorthand for assuming that his ideas travelled and remained intact. Instead, we have to think in terms of the interaction between the ideas and their new contexts, which can include social and political practices as well as other texts. As historians, we too need both Rousseau and Montesquieu.

[70] Valentina Arena, for example, notes that many of Rousseau's statistics about the Roman Republic were fictional, and that his account of the political institutions was highly idiosyncratic given the historical sources he used (Arena, 'The Roman Republic of Jean-Jacques Rousseau', *History of Political Thought*, forthcoming).

# 8 'The porch to a collectivism as absolute as the mind of man has ever conceived'

## Rousseau scholarship in Britain from the Great War to the Cold War

*Christopher Brooke*

This chapter will consider an identifiable generation of scholars in Britain who had things to say about Rousseau, with a particular focus on seven men, all born between 1901 and 1915: Alfred Cobban (1901–1968), Michael Oakeshott (1901–1990), Isaiah Berlin (1909–1997), John Stephenson Spink (1909–1985), John Plamenatz (1912–1975), R. A. Leigh (1915–1987), and Ronald Grimsley (1915–2003).[1] An eighth scholar, Maurice Cranston (1920–1993), stands slightly apart from this group: not only was he born after the First World War, he only turned to sustained work on Rousseau fairly late in life – the first volume of his biographical study was published in 1982 – and so there is a sense in which he belongs to the successor scholarly generation of John Charvet, Robert Wokler, Nicholas Dent, and the rest. The chapter will also consider the tradition of scholarship on Rousseau's political ideas in twentieth-century Britain in particular as a series of critical responses to the long introduction that C. E. Vaughan (1854–1922) attached to his meticulously compiled two-volume edition of Rousseau's *Political Writings*, first published in 1915, with its famous and controversial identification of Rousseau as a philosopher of collectivism. 'The doctrine of Contract was a commonplace among the philosophers of the seventeenth and eighteenth centuries', Vaughan wrote.

> But Rousseau, like Hobbes before him, gave it an entirely fresh turn. To his predecessors, with one exception, it had served as the cornerstone of individualism. To him – as, in an utterly different way, to Hobbes – it forms the porch to a collectivism as absolute as the mind of man has ever conceived.[2]

[1] For their comments on an earlier version of this chapter, I am grateful to Avi Lifschitz, Gavin Jacobson, Paul Sagar, and Jared Holley.

[2] C. E. Vaughan, ed., *The Political Writings of Jean Jacques Rousseau*, 2 vols. (Cambridge: Cambridge University Press, 1915), vol. 1, p. 39.

Over the decades that followed, scholars continued to engage with Vaughan's argument. At thirty-year intervals, for example, we find significant contributions from Alfred Cobban in 1934, J. H. Burns in 1964, and Robert Wokler in 1994.[3]

Vaughan was a cousin of the idealist philosopher T. H. Green – not the nephew, as has been stated[4] – who had died in 1882, and whose posthumous *Lectures on the Principles of Political Obligation* included what Cobban in 1934 called 'still by far the best discussion of the general will'[5] – and his argument clearly belonged to the twilight of the heroic period of British idealism. In an epilogue to his edition Vaughan remarked that, 'The present war has flashed a fierce light upon many problems of political philosophy', and he offered a sketch of a defence of Rousseau against Fichte's theory of the 'absolute State', which he associated with the real world of German politics.[6] But more influential on subsequent theoretical developments would be the book that L. T. Hobhouse was chewing over during the war, on and against what he called 'the metaphysical theory of the state', which criticised a much broader swathe of idealist political philosophy.[7] For Harold Laski, summarising the argument against idealism in a pamphlet for the Fabian Society, its failure 'lay in its inability to differentiate between state and government . . . with the result that it confused the temporary acts of the latter with the permanent purpose of the former', and it 'confounded the actual motives of social agents with the ideal purpose by which they ought to have been informed', so that 'it detected the existence of benevolent progress where none in fact existed'.[8]

It would not, however, be quite right to say that the turn away from idealism in the aftermath of the war was also straightforwardly a turn away

[3] Alfred Cobban, *Rousseau and the Modern State* (London: G. Allen & Unwin, 1934); J. H. Burns, 'Du côté de chez Vaughan: Rousseau revisited', *Political Studies* 12 (1964), 229–234; Robert Wokler, 'Rousseau's Pufendorf: Natural Law and the Foundations of Commercial Society', *History of Political Thought* 5.3 (1994), 373–402.

[4] Ibid., 375. Vaughan and Green were first cousins, sharing one grandparent, Edward Thomas Vaughan, who died in 1829. The elder Vaughan married twice. Green was the son of his daughter Anna Barbara by his first marriage, to Elizabeth Anne Hill; Charles Edwyn Vaughan the son of one of his sons – also Edward Thomas – by his second, to Agnes Pares. There are some further elucidations of Vaughan's family connections in his posthumous collection, *Studies in the History of Political Philosophy before and after Rousseau* (Manchester: Manchester University Press, 1925), ix.

[5] T. H. Green, *Lectures on the Principles of Political Obligation* (London: Longmans, 1895), esp. 80–120. Cobban, *Rousseau and the Modern State* (1934 ed.), 11–12.

[6] Vaughan, vol. 2, 517.

[7] L. T. Hobhouse, *The Metaphysical Theory of the State: A Criticism* (London: G. Allen & Unwin, 1918).

[8] Harold J. Laski, *Fabian Tract #200*: 'The State in the New Social Order' (London: Fabian Society, 1922), 7–8.

from Rousseau. Among the pluralists, for example, although Laski's own project on the theory of sovereignty was decidedly anti-Rousseauist,[9] G. D. H. Cole had a more protracted and constructive engagement with Rousseau. He not only edited and translated the 1913 Everyman edition of the *Social Contract and Discourses* that is still widely used today,[10] but also, as Peter Lamb has demonstrated, developed an argument that something like Rousseau's voluntarism was an essential component of a morally desirable socialist political theory – although whereas Rousseau had maintained that the existence of 'partial associations' posed a problem for the formation of a general will, however, Cole by contrast considered that such a will could in fact be expressed precisely through an array of what he called 'functional associations'.[11]

One should not, in any case, exaggerate the extent to which idealism was in fact dead and buried in the interwar period, and not just because of the career of R. G. Collingwood. Hobhouse's book, for example, can perhaps best be understood as an assault on right-wing idealism from the pen of a left-leaning idealist, rather than as a full-throated rejection of idealist political theory as a whole. (His subsequent books, after all, included both *The Rational Good* and *The Elements of Social Justice*.)[12] And the idealist tradition found a new exponent, if in various ways an idiosyncratic one, in the young Michael Oakeshott, who began his career teaching in the Cambridge History faculty. Oakeshott clearly judged that Rousseau was a major political philosopher, rather than a mere 'crib-writer' like Machiavelli or Locke;[13] in a very early lecture, for example, he mentioned 'those rare and splendid moments' when political philosophy 'has achieved real concreteness', as he believed was the case in 'Plato's *Republic*, in Aristotle's *Ethics*, in Spinoza's *Tractatus theologico-politicus*, in Rousseau's *Contrat social*, and in Hegel's *Philosophie des Rechts*'.[14]

The first members of the generation with which I am chiefly concerned here that made their mark in Rousseau scholarship, however, were those who worked in a more historically rather than philosophically minded vein. After graduating from Leeds in 1930, John Spink worked

[9] Laski, *Studies in the Problem of Sovereignty* (New Haven: Yale University Press, 1917); *A Grammar of Politics* (London: G. Allen & Unwin, 1925), ch. 2.

[10] Jean-Jacques Rousseau, *The Social Contract and Discourses*, G. D. H. Cole, trans. (London: J. M. Dent, 1913).

[11] Peter Lamb, 'G. D. H. Cole on the General Will: A Socialist Reflects on Rousseau', *European Journal of Political Theory* 4.3 (July 2005), 283–300.

[12] Hobhouse, *The Rational Good: A Study in the Logic of Practice* (London: G. Allen & Unwin, 1921); *The Elements of Social Justice* (London: G. Allen & Unwin, 1922).

[13] Michael Oakeshott, 'Rationalism in Politics', in *Rationalism in Politics and Other Essays* (Indianapolis: Liberty Fund, 1991), 30.

[14] Oakeshott, 'Philosophy Again', *Early Political Writings, 1925–30* (Exeter: Imprint, 2010), 225.

as an *assistant* at the Lycée Henri IV and as *lecteur* at the Sorbonne.[15] His master's research on the early manuscript draft of the *Lettres écrites de la montagne* was published in two instalments in the *Annales de la Société Jean-Jacques Rousseau*,[16] and his doctorate was published in 1934 as *Jean-Jacques Rousseau et Genève*.[17] In this work, Spink argued against those like Gaspard Vallette who offered interpretations of the *Social Contract* centred on the Genevan experience.[18] By contrast, he insisted that Rousseau's knowledge of Genevan politics in the 1740s and 1750s was very poor, and that the *Social Contract* was a work of 'pure speculation'.[19]

Alfred Cobban likewise made an early start to his publishing career. *Burke and the Revolt against the Eighteenth Century* came out in 1929,[20] and this was followed by *Rousseau and the Modern State*, which first appeared in 1934. If Spink's book of the same year had focused on Geneva, and engaged with the francophone scholarship of the time, Cobban's book concentrated more on France, and presented itself in significant part as a response to Vaughan.[21] In contrast to Vaughan's collectivist Rousseau, while based to a considerable extent on a careful reading of the texts Vaughan had so usefully assembled in the *Political Writings* edition, Cobban argued that Rousseau was primarily a 'moralist' whose chief concern was with the 'individual'. Insofar as Rousseau's state had priority over the individual, Cobban noted, 'this priority is justifiable only in so far as the state does actively develop the individual's moral personality and secure his liberty'.[22] The closest he came to 'subordinating the individual to the community', Cobban thought, was with his 'fairly comprehensive idea of the national state'.[23] But,

> On the other hand his economic ideals represent a stalwart championship of the individual, all the more interesting because at the same time he feels it necessary, to call in the state and endow it with extensive power for the purpose of securing the individual's economic independence.[24]

[15] Obituary notice, *French Studies* 39.4 (October 1985), 504.

[16] John S. Spink, 'La première rédaction des Lettres écrites de la Montagne, publiée d'après le manuscrit autographe', *Annales de la Société Jean-Jacques Rousseau*, first part, vol. 20 (1931), 7–216; second part, vol. 21 (1932), 7–156.

[17] Spink, *Jean-Jacques Rousseau et Genève* (Paris: Boivin, 1934).

[18] Gaspard Vallette, *Jean-Jacques Rousseau, Genevois*, 2nd ed. (Paris: Plon-Nourrit, 1911).

[19] Helena Rosenblatt, *Rousseau and Geneva: From the First Discourse to the Social Contract, 1749–1762* (Cambridge: Cambridge University Press, 1997), 3–4.

[20] Alfred Cobban, *Burke and the Revolt against the Eighteenth Century* (London: G. Allen & Unwin, 1929).

[21] Cobban, *Rousseau and the Modern State*, 6–8, 26–27, 43–44, 119–120, 200, and, especially, 239–253.

[22] Ibid., 7. [23] Ibid., 9–10. [24] Ibid., 10.

To strengthen this view of Rousseau's economic thought – to the present day a somewhat neglected topic in the literature – he reminded his readers that with only 'one or two exceptions such as Louis Blanc, the Saint-Simoniens and the early socialists were consistently hostile to Rousseau'.[25]

A measure of the rapid impact studies like these had can be gauged by a note that David Thomson published in *Philosophy* in 1939, commenting on the posthumous reissue of another two-volume work of Vaughan's, his *Studies in the History of Political Philosophy before and after Rousseau.*[26] Only fourteen years had passed since the first edition of 1925, yet Thomson judged Vaughan's approach to be a strikingly dated one. He offered three reasons for this view. First, Vaughan had given Giuseppe Mazzini a critical place in the way he organised the history of political thought, but those who came after him did not share that high valuation of his contribution. Second, studies such as those of 'Dr. Strauss on Hobbes and of Dr. Cobban on Burke and Rousseau' had 'further illumined the significance of these great men'.[27] Third, writing in the later thirties, Thomson noted that 'the fashion in writing histories of political theory has changed' – scholars no longer 'concentrate only on the paladins of politics':

> It is no longer regarded as adequate to leap from peak to peak, living all the time in the rarefied atmosphere of the greatest philosophical heights. It has become customary to spend more time exploring the inter-mediate hillocks, and even to descend into the plains and valleys where ordinary mortals live, in the hope that not only may new treasures be discovered, but also that new truths about even the towering giants themselves may be learnt from lower levels. Indeed, the emphasis has changed from Political Theory to Political Thought; and even from Political Thought to Political Science.

Vaughan's scholarship 'does little', Thomson said, 'to relate these philosophical ideas to the particular circumstances and the historical context out of which they grew'.[28]

The year 1939 also saw the outbreak of renewed hostilities, and the generation of scholars with which I am concerned mostly went off to the war. Oakeshott was a captain in the GHQ Liaison artillery reconnaissance regiment, better known as Phantom; Grimsley was in the Royal Artillery and Intelligence Corps; Plamenatz served in an anti-aircraft battery and joined

[25] Ibid., 38. The complex intellectual relationship between Rousseau and Louis Blanc is examined in Jean-Fabien Spitz's contribution to this volume (Chapter 5).

[26] Vaughan, *Studies in the History of Political Philosophy before and after Rousseau*, 2nd ed., 2 vols. (Manchester: Manchester University Press, 1939) (first ed., 1925).

[27] The references are to Leo Strauss, *The Political Philosophy of Hobbes: Its Basis and Genesis* (Oxford: Clarendon Press, 1936), as well as to Cobban's 1929 and 1934 volumes.

[28] David Thomson, review of Vaughan in *Philosophy* 14.56 (October 1939), 491–492.

the war cabinet of the Yugoslav government-in-exile; Leigh rose to be a major in the Royal Army Service Corps; and Berlin worked for much of the war in New York and Washington DC. (The young Maurice Cranston, finally, was a conscientious objector, and served in civil defence in London.)[29]

Turning then to the postwar period, I shall concentrate my attention in what follows on the tradition of writing about Rousseau's political thought, but it is worth noting before I do so the contribution to Rousseau studies made by scholars of French literature. Grimsley published a pair of volumes in the 1960s: *Rousseau: A Study in Self-Awareness*, written when he was still teaching at the University of Wales, Bangor, and *Rousseau and the Religious Quest*, published after his migration to the chair at Bristol,[30] and there was also a handy little book from J. H. Broome at Keele in 1963, which pushed back against those who denied Rousseau's consistency across his various works. The major contributions from the literature scholars, however, were editorial jobs. Spink was involved in the production of the fourth volume of the Pléiade edition of Rousseau's *Oeuvres complètes – Émile – Éducation – Morale – Botanique* – which was published in 1969.[31] But the jewel in the crown of postwar Rousseau scholarship, of course, was R. A. Leigh's mammoth edition of his correspondence, which began to appear in 1965 and was eventually completed in 1998, eleven years after its editor's death, with the publication of the fifty-second volume.[32] These writers and editors did not ignore politics altogether. Grimsley, for example, also edited the *Social Contract*, and there was a significant contribution from Leigh on Rousseau and the question of toleration.[33] But it is fair to say that politics was not their primary concern, and that it was scholars like these who were taking texts

[29] Spink's wife, Dorothy Knowles, who died aged 104 in November 2010, 'visited military bases in Great Britain where she provided entertainment with her solo dance show, and valuable insights into French life and culture. Such information', her obituarist noted, 'was particularly useful to young pilots who faced the possibility of being stranded in France.' Liz Gardner, obituary for Dorothy Knowles, *The Independent*, 10 December 2010, 'Viewspaper', 8. For an account of a wartime meeting between Cobban and Raymond Aron, see Aron, *Thinking Politically: A Liberal in the Age of Ideology* (London: Transaction, 1997), 67. (Thanks to Gavin Jacobson for this reference.)

[30] Ronald Grimsley, *Rousseau: A Study in Self-Awareness* (Cardiff: University of Wales Press, 1961); *Rousseau and the Religious Quest* (Oxford: Clarendon Press, 1968).

[31] Rousseau, *OC* IV: *Émile – Éducation – Morale – Botanique* (Paris: Gallimard, 1969).

[32] R. A. Leigh, ed., *Correspondance complète de Jean Jacques Rousseau*, 52 vols. (Genève: Institut et Musée Voltaire, 1965–1998).

[33] Rousseau, *Du contrat social*, ed. Ronald Grimsley (Oxford: Clarendon Press, 1972). Leigh, 'Rousseau and the Problem of Tolerance in the Eighteenth Century: A Lecture Delivered in the Taylor Institute, Oxford, on 26 October 1978' (Oxford: Clarendon Press, 1979).

like *Julie* and the autobiographical writings seriously, at a time when the more overtly political writers were not.

The two most significant writers on political philosophy in the immediate postwar decades were Oakeshott and Berlin. It is striking, however, that neither made a substantial contribution to Rousseau scholarship. I have already mentioned Oakeshott's prewar estimation of Rousseau's significance, when he placed him alongside Plato, Aristotle, Spinoza, and Hegel, but when he reworked the same material for his celebrated Harvard lectures in 1958, Rousseau fell off that list;[34] and, more generally, comments about Rousseau, although perceptive, are few and far between in his various writings.[35] Efraim Podoksik has recently remarked that, 'Perhaps Oakeshott could not make up his mind about what to do with Rousseau'.[36]

Isaiah Berlin, on the other hand, knew just what he wanted to do with Rousseau. Rousseau was obviously some kind of presence in his famous 1957 inaugural lecture, 'Two Concepts of Liberty', but it is when we review the unpublished manuscript from a few years earlier on *Political Ideas in the Romantic Age*, which was a major source for the argument of the inaugural, that we see just how central an argument about Rousseau was to Berlin's theorisation – and denunciation – of so-called 'positive' liberty. Another document from the same period is the transcript of a BBC Third Programme radio talk in 1952, which presented Rousseau as an 'enemy of human liberty'.[37] Again and again in these texts, Berlin's rhetorical tactic with respect to Rousseau was to reach for the language of mental illness. This was not a psychoanalytic language. For an American critic like Lester G. Crocker, who published the two volumes of his psychobiography in 1969 and 1973, Rousseau was (among many other things) obsessive, submissive, narcissistic, neurotic, occasionally a mild manic-depressive, later a paranoid psychotic, a latent homosexual, a sadist, a masochist (both physical and moral), a hypochondriac, a voyeur, and an exhibitionist, as well as being someone who found sexual pleasure only in frustration, humiliation, and fantasy.[38] Berlin, by contrast, preferred

[34] Oakeshott, *Morality and Politics in Modern Europe: The Harvard Lectures*, ed. Shirley Robin Letwin (New Haven: Yale University Press, 1993), 14.

[35] See, e.g., ibid., 26; also *The Concept of a Philosophical Jurisprudence* (Exeter: Imprint, 2007), 52; *What Is History? and Other Essays* (Exeter: Imprint, 2004), 62.

[36] Efraim Podoksik, 'Anti-totalitarian Ambiguities: Jacob Talmon and Michael Oakeshott', *History of European Ideas* 34.2 (2008), 216.

[37] Isaiah Berlin, 'Two Concepts of Liberty', in *Four Essays on Liberty* (Oxford University Press, 1969), 118–172; *Political Ideas in the Romantic Age* (Princeton: Princeton University Press, 2006); *Freedom and its Betrayal: Six Enemies of Human Liberty* (Princeton: Princeton University Press, 2003), 27–49.

[38] For these verdicts, see Lester G. Crocker, *Jean-Jacques Rousseau* (New York: Macmillan), vol. 1 (1969), 10, 13, 14, 15, 24, 33, 34, 61, 68, 109, 148, 181, and 309, and vol. 2 (1973), 158, 269, 301, and 347.

a more old-fashioned vocabulary. In the radio address, Rousseau's tone, he tells us, is 'exactly that ... of a maniac ... like a mad mathematician' whose 'answer has ... a kind of lunacy'.[39] In the unpublished manuscript, Rousseau 'preaches' his argument about the general will 'with the almost lunatic intensity of a somewhat crack-brained visionary'; Rousseau looks for a way of squaring total liberty with total conformity, Berlin says, 'with the fanatical cunning of a maniac'; and – my favourite example of the genre – 'His polemic against the babel of voices all claiming to speak for nature is acute, entertaining and convincing', Berlin writes, 'until one realises that he is like the lunatic who rejects the claims of other inmates of his asylum to be Napoleon because he himself is Napoleon.'[40]

If there is not much of real substance to be had from Berlin and Oakeshott, the early 1950s were significant for the appearance of two other influential foreign studies, both of which had a connection to Rousseau scholarship in Britain. J. L. Talmon spent the bulk of his academic career at the Hebrew University of Jerusalem, but he had studied at the LSE during the war, where he wrote a dissertation on 'The doctrine of poverty' in the middle ages.[41] The acknowledgments to his 1952 book, *The Origins of Totalitarian Democracy*, which thank among others Berlin, Cobban, Laski, Ralph Miliband, and R. H. Tawney, indicate that some of the roots of this work, too, lie in Talmon's period in England.[42] Talmon was by no means the first to explore a perceived connection between Rousseau and totalitarianism. The American conservative scholar Robert C. Nisbet, for example, had published an article in 1943 on exactly the same theme,[43] and Bertrand Russell notoriously remarked in the first edition of his *History of Western Philosophy*, published in 1945, that, 'At the present time Hitler is an outcome of Rousseau';[44] but Talmon's book became the canonical presentation of the case, and it clearly belongs to that same intellectual early Cold War moment as Berlin's ruminations in *Political Ideas in the Romantic Age*, being published in the same year as the radio talk on Rousseau as an enemy of human liberty.

39 Berlin, *Freedom and Its Betrayal*, 37.

40 Berlin, *Political Ideas in the Romantic Age*: 'Crack-Brained Visionary', 116; 'Cunning of a Maniac', 112; 'Napoleon', 46–47.

41 J. L. Talmon (writing as J. L. Flajszer), 'The Doctrine of Poverty in Its Religious, Social and Political Aspects as Illustrated by Some XII-XIII Century Movements', unpublished PhD (London School of Economics, 1943).

42 Talmon, *The Origins of Totalitarian Democracy* (London: Secker & Warburg, 1952).

43 Robert C. Nisbet, 'Rousseau and Totalitarianism', *The Journal of Politics* 5.2 (May 1943), 93–114.

44 Bertrand Russell, *A History of Western Philosophy* (New York: Simon & Schuster, 1945), 685.

The other foreign study was Robert Derathé's book on *Jean-Jacques Rousseau et la science politique de son temps*, which first appeared in 1950.[45] The book's connection to British Rousseau scholarship is that it is by far the most sustained single response to Vaughan – whose lengthy entry in the index is rivalled only by names such as 'Hobbes, Thomas', and 'Locke, John' – and it received a warm reception in British Rousseau circles. In a sense, the British scholars had been waiting for a book like this for a long time, with its argument about the continuities between Rousseau's political theory and the broader tradition of modern natural law. Ernest Barker, reviewing Cobban's 1934 book for the *English Historical Review*, for example, had commented that

> Dr. Cobban has not delved deeply enough into either of the antinomies which he seeks to reconcile. He might, on the one hand, have gone more fully into the Natural-Law philosophies on which Rousseau drew so largely for his ideas and even for his terminology. One can hardly explain Rousseau's theory of the State as a *personne morale*, and his theory of the general will which is the will of this 'moral person', without some reference to the large literature of Natural Law, from Pufendorf to Burlamaqui and Vattel ... Dr. Cobban confines his study of the Natural-Law philosophers to Locke; and even here ... he might have carried his study farther.[46]

It is perhaps in Cobban's own response to these works by Talmon and Derathé that we see both the strengths and the limitations of the historical sensibility of that era. Reviewing Derathé in 1951, Cobban warmly endorsed his scholarship:

> It is the great value of M. Derathé's studies that they demonstrate, in my opinion conclusively, that in spite of everything Rousseau's political theory belongs to the rationalist, individualist, liberal and utilitarian eighteenth century. By his careful and penetrating analysis of the relations between Rousseau and the school of Natural Law, he has provided an important clue to the recovery of Rousseau's own ideas, and at the same time revealed the significance of some of the later theorists of Natural Law, like Barbeyrac and Burlamaqui, who had become mere names in the history of political thought. His subject, like theirs, was *les principes du droit politique*, or *allgemeines Staatsrecht*. Their books, and not the constitutional law of the Genevan Republic, which he left so early and knew so little, provided the intellectual climate in which his ideas grew.[47]

[45] Robert Derathé, *Jean-Jacques Rousseau et la science politique de son temps* (Paris: Presses universitaires de France, 1950).

[46] Ernest Barker, review of Cobban, *Rousseau and the Modern State,* in *English Historical Review* 50.200 (October 1935), 724–727.

[47] Cobban, 'New Light on the Political Thought of Rousseau', *Political Science Quarterly* 66.2 (June 1951), 273. For more on the British reception of Derathé, see Burns, 'Du côté de chez Vaughan', esp. 231–232.

A footnote here referred approvingly to Spink's earlier study of Geneva on just this point.[48] When *Rousseau and the Modern State* was reissued in a revised edition in 1964, furthermore, Cobban incorporated some of Derathé's findings, and also pushed back against Talmon's argument, observing that 'when Professor Talmon tries to show that totalitarianism is what the general will meant for Rousseau, he can only do so by ignoring all Rousseau's practical qualifications of his theoretical discussion and even changing the sense of what he says'.[49] It is not of course eccentric these days to suggest that Talmon's argument reveals more about the immediate postwar period than it does about the eighteenth century. But it is worth raising the question as to whether the revised edition of *Rousseau and the Modern State* was in fact superior to its predecessor of three decades earlier. In a review of an edition of Gierke that appeared in the same year as the first edition of Cobban's book, Oakeshott had remarked as follows:

> It is all very well to say that Hobbes or Rousseau cannot be understood apart from the background of Natural Law theorists in which they appear to take their place; but it is no less important to hold on to the fact that, while a writer like Hobbes may reach conclusions which place him along with others in a 'school,' his reasons and arguments may be so unlike those of writers who appear to be of a similar persuasion that to think of him as a member of this 'school' may be seriously misleading.[50]

Oakeshott's one-time student Robert Wokler developed the same thought in his 1994 essay on 'Rousseau's Pufendorf'. There he charged that Derathé's study was misconceived, 'for if Vaughan attributed to Rousseau the rudiments of a theory he could not have anticipated, still less adopted, Derathé ascribes to him a political philosophy which in large measure it was his intention to refute'.[51] Our assessment of whether the second edition of *Rousseau and the Modern State* marks an advance on the first may well very turn on whether we agree with the line of thought being pressed here by Oakeshott and by Wokler.

The final scholar I want to consider in this chapter is John Plamenatz, whose distinctive methodological claim was that with respect to canonical political thinkers, one could 'learn more about their arguments by

[48] Cf. Rosenblatt, *Rousseau and Geneva*, esp. chs. 3 and 4.

[49] Cobban, *Rousseau and the Modern State*, 2nd ed. (London: G. Allen & Unwin, 1964), 30.

[50] Michael Oakeshott, review of Gierke *Natural Law and the Theory of Society*, in *The Concept of a Philosophical Jurisprudence*, 97–98.

[51] Wokler, 'Rousseau's Pufendorf', 377. For a slightly fuller discussion, see also Wokler, 'Natural Law and the Meaning of Rousseau's Political Thought: A Correction to Two Misrenderings of His Doctrine', in Giles Barber and C. P. Courtney, eds., *Enlightenment Essays in Memory of Robert Shackleton* (Oxford: Voltaire Foundation, 1988), 319–335.

weighing them over and over again than by extending our knowledge of the circumstances in which they wrote'.[52] When it comes to the study of Rousseau, there is a great deal in fact to be said for this method, especially since much of the scholarship considered above did not actually turn on an especially close reading of Rousseau's texts, let alone on any serious 'weighing' of his arguments. The most egregious case, of course, is Isaiah Berlin, but he is by no means the only one.[53] A writer like Vaughan was quite happy to ignore those bits of Rousseau's project that didn't fit his overarching interpretation of what he considered his political thought to be really all about. 'Strike out the state of nature and the contract from the opening pages of the treatise', he had written.

> Replace them by the idea of a gradual growth from barbarism to what may fairly be called the 'civil state' ... Make these changes in Rousseau's argument, and its inconsistencies, its other inherent blemishes, will have largely disappeared.[54]

A scholar like Cobban may have evinced a grip on a wide range of Rousseau's texts, but he rarely subjected particular passages of argument to sustained analysis, and it is striking, for example, that the best example of forensic attention to textual matters from Cobban concerns questions of translation rather than of theoretical analysis or interpretation.[55] The German *émigré* scholar Leo Strauss was offering his own close readings of canonical authors, of course, on the other side of the Atlantic in this period, but Plamenatz had little time for his project, and he reviewed *Natural Right and History* quite dismissively for the *Philosophical Review* in 1955. He didn't in general like the book much – 'Dr. Strauss is not really fair to the position he attacks', 'Dr. Strauss ... can be a very careless reasoner', and so on – and he was in particular dismissive of the interpretation of Rousseau that was offered: 'If space allowed, it would be possible to show that Dr. Strauss has also seriously misinterpreted Rousseau's ideas about freedom.'[56]

[52] John Plamenatz, *Man and Society: A Critical Examination of Some Important Social and Political Theories from Machiavelli to Marx* (London: Longmans, 1963), vol. 1, x.

[53] On the question of the relationship between liberty and coercion encapsulated in Rousseau's notorious remark about being 'forced to be free', compare, for example, Berlin, *Political Ideas in the Romantic Age*, 103–145 with Plamenatz, 'Qu'on le forcera d'être libre', *Annales de Philosophie Politique*, vol. 5 (1965), reprinted in Maurice Cranston and Richard S. Peters, eds., *Hobbes and Rousseau: A Collection of Critical Essays* (New York: Anchor Books, 1972), 318–332.

[54] Vaughan, *Political Writings*, vol. 1, 115; see also Wokler, 'Rousseau's Pufendorf', 375–377.

[55] J. H. Burns and A. Cobban, 'Rousseau's *Du Contrat Social*: Some Problems of Translation', *Political Studies* 10.2 (June 1962), 203–207.

[56] Plamenatz, review of Leo Strauss, *Natural Right and History*, in *The Philosophical Review* 64.2 (April 1955), 300–302.

Space might not have allowed it on that occasion, but I think nevertheless that it is possible to reconstruct what the disagreement to which Plamenatz was referring might have been. In *Natural Right and History*, Strauss had mentioned Rousseau's triple distinction from *Social Contract* I.8 between 'natural', 'civil', and 'moral freedom', but then remarked that 'it is also true that he blurs these distinctions', arguing that 'natural freedom remains the model for civil freedom, just as natural equality remains the model for civil equality', and that, 'Civil freedom, in its turn, being in a way obedience to one's self alone, certainly comes very close to moral freedom.' 'The blurring of the distinctions between natural freedom, civil freedom, and moral freedom', he concluded, 'is no accidental error.'[57] When Plamenatz offered his own exposition of Rousseau's ideas about freedom in a 1965 article, he agreed that there might be an overlap between civil and moral freedom, insofar as 'it is part of Rousseau's creed that the rules imposed by the community on its members are also, when certain conditions hold, imposed by each member on himself'. But if civil and moral freedom had to be understood in terms of rules, natural freedom, or 'men's not being dependent on one another', could not be, and so a view like Strauss's about how natural freedom provides a 'model' for civil freedom could not be sustained.[58]

Plamenatz's major engagement with Rousseau was published in the two volumes of *Man and Society* in 1963.[59] There was also a posthumous three-volume edition in 1992, which was revised by Robert Wokler and M. E. Plamenatz, his widow, and which included more contextual material than was to be found in the first edition.[60] The changes to the Rousseau chapter, however, were entirely cosmetic, and the reason for preferring the first edition for the purposes of this chapter is that the second edition re-keyed the textual references to the Pléiade edition, which had the effect of concealing Plamenatz's extensive debt to the Vaughan edition of the *Political Writings*, on which the discussions of the original edition of *Man and Society* were clearly based. Those discussions of Rousseau were organised around Plamenatz's exploration of two large questions of interpretation: what does he mean by the natural goodness of man, and what does he mean by the general will? The first of these

[57] Strauss, *Natural Right and History* (Chicago: University of Chicago Press, 1953), 281–282.

[58] Plamenatz, 'Qu'on le forcera d'être libre', in *Hobbes and Rousseau*, 324.

[59] Plamenatz, *Man and Society*, 2 vols. (London: Longmans, 1963). The discussion of Rousseau fills pages 364–442 of the first volume. Unless otherwise indicated, subsequent references to *Man and Society* are to this edition.

[60] Plamenatz, *Man and Society*, revised ed., ed. Robert Wokler and M. E. Plamenatz, 3 vols. (London: Longmans, 1992). The discussion of Rousseau fills pages 123–207 of the second volume.

questions was broken down into a handful of sub-questions, concerning the genealogy of the passions, the goodness of the good passions and the evil of the evil ones, the nature of conscience, and so on. The second question was considered in terms of a set of plausible conditions relating to everyone's entitlement to take part in decision-making, the question of 'partial associations', the problem of representatives, and the separation between 'sovereignty' (the making of the laws) and 'government' (their administration). Concerning the general will, although he was fairly critical of some of Rousseau's formulations along the way, his judicious conclusion was that, 'Whether or not these doctrines are true, is open to dispute, but they are, I think, intelligible; and, though they are not simple, they are free from every taint of mysticism.'[61]

The treatment of self-love – *amour de soi* and especially *amour propre* – shows off Plamenatz's approach at its best. In contrast to most of the writers surveyed in this chapter so far, he takes the subject quite seriously, and sees very clearly its importance to Rousseau's wider project. The examination of self-love takes in *Emile* as much as it does the *Discourse on the Origin of Inequality* – but also striking is Plamenatz's interest in chasing the argument beyond even these two texts, and a lengthy footnote chases the puzzle of the genesis of *amour propre* out of *amour de soi* from *Emile* into the later *Dialogues* (but even there, he notes, 'Rousseau's description is by no means clear').[62] Although Plamenatz sticks to the once-traditional translation of *amour propre* as 'vanity' and insists that *amour propre* is 'nearly always' evil,[63] he does nevertheless indicate his awareness that 'Rousseau attributes to vanity some good effects as well as many bad ones', and he offers a useful comparison of pride, and how we might 'distinguish it from and prefer it to vanity'.[64] 'It must be admitted', he concludes, 'that Rousseau never succeeds in making it clear just what he means by vanity and just why he condemns it' – though even here the verdict is qualified by his recognition of Rousseau's awareness that, 'unless men were moved by the desire to be well thought of, they would not be educable'.[65] Plamenatz's discussion indicates what he thinks the difficulties with Rousseau's account are – above all, that it is hard to reconcile the account of *amour propre* he offers with his overall thesis of the natural goodness of humankind. From our vantage point, half a century on, in the face of the problems Plamenatz describes, one is struck again by the achievement of Nicholas Dent in providing a new framework for thinking about Rousseau's moral psychology and the nature of *amour propre*, which was both faithful to the relevant

[61] Plamenatz, *Man and Society*, vol. 1, 409. [62] Ibid., vol. 1, 376–377.
[63] Ibid., vol. 1, 380. [64] Ibid., vol. 1, 421. [65] Ibid., vol. 1, 422.

texts and which also allowed such tensions to be reduced, or perhaps even eliminated altogether.[66]

All things considered, Plamenatz's close work with the texts he is examining serves him well. It nurtures his scepticism towards anachronistic readings, and he pushes back against not only the more obvious targets, such as Talmon's totalitarianism thesis,[67] but also against those readings of Rousseau, such as Ernst Cassirer's, which were more heavily inflected by German idealism.[68] The juxtaposition of Rousseau's arguments with relevantly similar passages from his near-contemporary Hume – with whom Rousseau perhaps had more in common than is generally recognised – is a useful expository device.[69] And just as Cobban rightly recognised the general character of Rousseau's economic doctrine, it is striking that Plamenatz identifies him as an advocate of the 'property-owning democracy' in a book published in 1963, appearing the year before James Meade's slim volume on *Efficiency, Equality and the Ownership of Property* popularised the use of this expression among economists and political theorists.[70]

***

The generation of Rousseau scholars with which I have been concerned in this chapter began to shuffle off the stage in the late 1960s. Alfred Cobban died after a long illness in April 1968, and the following year Michael Oakeshott retired from his chair at the LSE. 1969 was also the year that a young Quentin Skinner published his famous manifesto on 'Meaning and Understanding in the History of Ideas'. This essay not only included a short but destructive passage on the 'totalitarian' interpretation of Rousseau, with Talmon and J. W. Chapman squarely in Skinner's sights, it also took a swipe at Plamenatz's discussion of method.[71] Skinner's paper is often taken to mark the emergence of a new research programme in the

[66] The briefest presentation of the relevant argument is '*amour propre*', in Nicholas Dent, *A Rousseau Dictionary* (Oxford: Blackwell, 1992). For the significance of this new interpretation of *amour propre* in contemporary Rousseau scholarship, see Axel Honneth's chapter in this book (Chapter 11).

[67] Plamenatz, *Man and Society*, vol. 1, 435.

[68] Ibid., vol. 1, 409; also the footnote on 367. [69] E.g., Ibid., vol. 1, 366.

[70] Ibid., vol. 1, 401. James Meade, *Efficiency, Equality and the Ownership of Property* (London: G. Allen & Unwin, 1964).

[71] 'The problem is rather that we need to understand what strategies have been voluntarily adopted to convey their meaning with deliberate obliqueness. And the point is that it is hard to see how any amount of reading the text "over and over again," as we are exhorted to do, could possibly serve as the means to gain this understanding.' Quentin Skinner, 'Meaning and Understanding in the History of Ideas', *History and Theory*, 8:1 (1969), 32. Mark Philp observes that Plamenatz's injunction was not to read and re-read the texts, but to weigh and re-weigh the arguments, which may not be the same thing. See his 'Introduction' to *Plamenatz, Machiavelli, Hobbes, and Rousseau*, ed. Philp and Z. A. Pelczynski (Oxford: Oxford University Press, 2012), xiii.

history of political thought, conventionally labelled 'the Cambridge School'. But, as David Thomson had indicated in 1939, and as I noted above, many of the moves characteristically associated with the distinctive 'Cambridge' approach – of broadening the 'canon', in particular, and of reading texts in context – had already been made on the terrain of British Rousseau studies, even if they were not pursued with quite the vigour that would mark some of the later scholarship.

The work of my generation of British Rousseauists was not quite done by the later 1960s. Only a dozen volumes of the Leigh correspondence edition, for example, had been published by 1970, but these had already covered the period of the production of Rousseau's major works, taking the story down to the climactic summer of 1762, when he was driven into his Swiss exile following the publication of *Emile* and its condemnation in Paris. And even if 'Meaning and Understanding' might have knocked a dent in his reputation, Plamenatz wrote his final manuscript on Rousseau in the form of a course of lectures to be delivered at Cambridge, where he had agreed to teach in place of Skinner, covering part of the latter's period of leave at the Institute for Advanced Study in Princeton, where he was writing *The Foundations of Modern Political Thought*. Those lectures were never delivered, however, as Plamenatz died in February 1975; they were finally published in 2012.[72]

Even if the work of this generation was not quite over by 1968 or so, this does nevertheless mark a good point at which to bring this survey to a close, with the rise of a new generation of scholars. Quentin Skinner and John Dunn at Cambridge might have been the most spectacular new intellects to make themselves felt on the British history of political thought scene in the 1960s, though neither worked on Rousseau. But there was a new wave of Anglophone Rousseau scholarship that was beginning to appear. From the United States, there were books by Judith Shklar and Roger Masters.[73] In Britain, Maurice Cranston – who had succeeded to Oakeshott's chair at the LSE – was increasingly preoccupied with Rousseau, as he worked towards the production of his three-volume biography (the final volume of which was left unfinished when he died in 1993).[74] And there were

[72] Ibid.

[73] Judith N. Shklar, *Men and Citizens: A Study of Rousseau's Social Theory* (Cambridge: Cambridge University Press, 1969); Roger D. Masters, *The Political Philosophy of Rousseau* (Princeton: Princeton University Press, 1968). On Shklar's interpretation of Rousseau (and its impact on her Harvard colleague John Rawls), see Céline Spector's contribution in this volume (Chapter 9).

[74] Maurice Cranston, *Jean-Jacques: The Early Life and Work of Jean-Jacques Rousseau, 1712–1754* (London: Allen Lane, 1983); *The Noble Savage: Jean-Jacques Rousseau, 1754–1762* (London: Allen Lane, 1991); *The Solitary Self: Jean-Jacques Rousseau in Exile and Adversity* (London: Allen Lane, 1997).

younger voices, too. John Charvet's book on *The Social Problem in the Philosophy of Rousseau* was published in 1974;[75] and, above all, there was Robert Wokler, who had studied under Oakeshott in London, and under Plamenatz and Berlin in Oxford, and who in the 1970s completed his remarkable doctoral dissertation on the development of Rousseau's thought in the period between the First and the Second Discourses and kicked off his publishing career in Rousseau studies with a pair of long essays on his complicated engagements with Diderot and Rameau.[76]

[75] John Charvet, *The Social Problem in the Philosophy of Rousseau* (Cambridge: Cambridge University Press, 1974).

[76] Wokler's dissertation was eventually published as *Rousseau on Society, Politics, Music and Language* (New York: Garland, 1987). 'Rameau, Rousseau and the Essai sur l'origine des langues', *Studies on Voltaire and the Eighteenth Century*, CXVII (1974), 179–238. 'The influence of Diderot on the political theory of Rousseau', *Studies on Voltaire* CXXXII (1975), 55–111.

# 9 Rousseau at Harvard

## John Rawls and Judith Shklar on realistic utopia

*Céline Spector*

What remains today of Rousseau's theory of political justice? As a precursor of the Kantian concept of autonomy, Rousseau seems to be one of the main inspirations for John Rawls's *A Theory of Justice* and *Political Liberalism*.[1] As Rawls put it, 'Kant's main aim is to deepen and justify Rousseau's idea that liberty is acting in accordance with a law that we give to ourselves.'[2] The original position, which conceives of all people as morally free and equal, can be traced back to Rousseau through Kant, who 'sought to give a philosophical foundation to Rousseau's idea of the general will.'[3] In his stated wish to round off the tradition of Locke, Rousseau, and Kant, Rawls also cites the *Social Contract* as one of the sources for his theory of a 'well-ordered society,' arguing that it opened the way for him to combine a contract-based theory of justice with a reflection on the stability of a just society.[4]

In *A Theory of Justice*, Rousseau's contractualism is instrumental in clarifying how the concept of *equality* is bound up with the concept of *liberty*; it accounts for the formation of the motives that will enable

[1] John Rawls, *A Theory of* Justice (Oxford: Oxford University Press, 1972), henceforth *TJ*; *Political Liberalism*, expanded edition (New York: Columbia University Press, 2005). In *Au prisme de Rousseau. Usages politiques contemporains* (Oxford: Voltaire Foundation, 2011), I devote a chapter to the profound engagement with Rousseau in Rawls's major works. See also John C. Hall, *Rousseau: An Introduction to His Political Philosophy* (Plymouth: Macmillan, 1973), 140–146; Patrick Neal, 'In the Shadow of the General Will: Rawls, Kant, and Rousseau on the Problem of Political Right', *The Review of Politics* 49.3 (1987), 389–409; Johnny Goldfinger, 'Rawls and Rousseau's Political Projects: Two Sides of the Same Coin?', Paper presented at the annual meeting of the Midwest Political Science Association, Chicago, 12 April 2007 (www.allacademic.com/meta/p197887_index.html); Grace Roosevelt, 'Rousseau versus Rawls on International Relations', *European Journal of Political Theory* 5.3 (2006), 301–320; Robert Jubb, 'Rawls and Rousseau: Amour-Propre and the Strains of Commitment', *Res Publica* 17.3 (2011), 245–260; Christopher Brooke, 'Rawls on Rousseau and the General Will', in *The General Will: The Evolution of a Concept*, ed. David Lay Williams and James Farr (Cambridge: Cambridge University Press, 2015), 429–446.

[2] *TJ*, 256. [3] Ibid., 264.

[4] On the contractualist interpretation of Rousseau, presenting him as a liberal, see B. Barry, *Political Argument* (Berkeley: University of California Press, 1965); Hall, *Rousseau: An Introduction (op. cit.)*.

institutions to survive in the long term. Rawls does not merely fasten onto Rousseau's idea that the basic structure of society lies in its economic, social, and political institutions: he partly situates the origins of his theory of the 'sense of justice' (which enables reasonable agents to understand and follow principles of justice) in *Emile.*[5] Far from being a source of totalitarianism or a gravedigger of liberty, as he was depicted in a certain Cold War liberal tradition,[6] Rousseau thus appears as the advocate of a just and stable society, conceived as the essential prerequisite for true freedom. For the first time in the history of political thought, Rousseau is considered by Rawls as a forerunner of political liberalism.[7] Rousseau's definition of autonomy as obedience to law that one has laid down oneself is at the heart of modern political theory.

But one needs to be clear as to *which* Rousseau is the ally of Rawls's political liberalism. This chapter will focus on the reading outlined in Rawls's *Lectures on the History of Political Philosophy*, given to Harvard undergraduates between the second half of the 1960s and the second half of the 1990s, and more precisely on the final version (1994) edited by Samuel Freeman in 2007.[8] In these synoptic courses, covering the period from Hobbes to Marx (taking in Locke, Hume, and Mill, and a few others), Rawls ventures a bold interpretation of Rousseau in terms of 'realistic utopianism';[9] the *Social Contract*'s well-ordered society is not a mere utopia but a realistic one. Following Judith Shklar, his colleague and friend at Harvard who inspired his reading of Rousseau,[10] Rawls

[5] *TJ*, §69, 462.

[6] See especially Isaiah Berlin, *Freedom and Its Betrayal*, ed. Henry Hardy (London: Pimlico, 2003), 27–49; J. L. Talmon, *The Origins of Totalitarian Democracy* (London: Secker & Warburg, 1952); L. Crocker, *Rousseau's* Social Contract*: An Interpretative Essay* (Cleveland: Western Reserve University Press, 1968). On this tradition, see also Christopher Brooke's contribution in this volume (Chapter 8).

[7] 'This concept of justice [as fairness] is closely related to the theory of the social contract; in particular there are close similarities, as I have only recently come to realize, to Rousseau's concept of the general will in *Le Contrat social.*' (J. Rawls, 'Constitutional Liberty and the Concept of Justice', *Nomos VI: Justice*, ed. C. Friedrich and J. Chapman (Atherton Press, 1963), 100, n. 1, in *Collected Papers*, ed. S. Freeman (Cambridge, MA: Harvard University Press, 1999), 74.

[8] Rawls, *Lectures on the History of Political Philosophy*, ed. S. Freeman (Cambridge, MA: Belknap Press, 2007), 140, 152, 155 (henceforth *Lectures*). The text was also intended as a historical introduction to Rawls's *Justice as Fairness: A Restatement* (Cambridge, MA: Belknap Press, 2001). Rawls stopped teaching in 1995.

[9] See Rawls, 'Some Remarks about My Teaching', quoted in *Lectures*, xii–xiv. See M. Frazer, 'The Modest Professor', *European Journal of Political Theory* 9.2 (2010), 218–226.

[10] Rawls's heavily annotated copy of Shklar's *Men and Citizens* is in the Harvard Archives (HUM 48.1, Box 9). These notes and Rawls's reaction to Shklar's book – evidence of a lively dialogue – require further investigation. I am grateful to David Armitage for this insight.

denies the opposition between realism and utopianism.[11] But contrary to her, he insists on the procedural dimension of Rousseau's theory of justice. The result is a Kantian reading of the *Second Discourse* combined with an ultra-rationalist interpretation of the general will in the *Social Contract*, which eventually lay some of the conceptual foundations for *A Theory of Justice*.

## I A Kantian reading of the state of nature

As a Harvard professor, Rawls devotes several masterful lectures to Rousseau, who is presented as a turning point in modern political philosophy after Hobbes, Locke, and Hume. Rawls does not conceal his admiration for the *Social Contract*, presenting it as the key work in French, comparable in significance to the *Leviathan* in English. Indeed, Rousseau's work is regarded as being unequaled in its combination of speculative power and literary talent.[12] Rawls discusses two fundamental texts: the *Discourse on Inequality* (*Second Discourse*) and the *Social Contract*. His course naturally had to fulfill the pedagogic function of introducing Rousseau's political thought to students within the wider framework of an introduction to modern political philosophy. Therefore, the sequence from the *Discourse on Inequality* to the *Social Contract* is reduced to a sketch – one of the aims of the course being to resolve the apparent contradiction between the pessimistic picture of social oppression in the first text and the utopian optimism in the second.

Rousseau's account of the state of nature is the first highlight. Mainly inspired by N. H. Dent's work after its publication in 1988, Rawls distinguishes between two senses of self-love: a broad *desire for recognition* and a narrower *desire for preference*.[13] The bare concept of *amour propre* is simply the demand for recognition and acknowledgment as a being of

[11] Political theory had a strong tradition in Harvard, represented by Judith Shklar, Harvey Mansfield, and Michael Walzer in the Government Department, and in the Philosophy Department by John Rawls and Robert Nozick. The intellectual relationship between Rawls and Shklar has yet to be studied. See Bernard Williams, *In the Beginning Was the Deed: Realism and Moralism in Political Argument* (Princeton: Princeton University Press, 2005), chap. 5; Seyla Benhabib, 'Judith Shklar's Dystopic Liberalism', *Social Research* 61.2 (1994), 477–488; Shaun Young, 'Avoiding The Unavoidable? Judith Shklar's Unwilling Search For An Overlapping Consensus', *Res Publica* 13.3 (2007), 231–253; Katrina Forrester, 'Judith Shklar, Bernard Williams, and Political Realism', *European Journal of Political Theory* 11.3 (2012), 247–272.

[12] Rawls, *Lectures*, 191.

[13] Rawls had previously been relying mainly on the idea of natural goodness of man. See the hand-written text of a lecture from the 1979 course called 'Rousseau: His Aims + View of Society' in the Rawls papers at Harvard's Widener Library; Brooke, 'Rawls on Rousseau'.

intrinsic worth. While this demand may be manifested as a desire to prove one's worth by establishing one's superiority over others and eliciting their admiration and esteem, this is not the only form it can take. There is also, according to Dent, a 'positive and constructive' form of *amour propre*, which can be opposed to the competitive and aggressive one.[14] This is not a minor distinction: its effect is to highlight, beneath the corrupt self-love geared toward exclusive preferences, a natural self-love that pursues equal recognition of our needs and desires. This original self-love, unlike its corrupt form, is compatible with equality and reciprocity. Rawls is aware that he holds a 'strong' interpretation, which 'rescues' the consistency between Rousseau's two major works.[15] If it is the case that only the second guise of self-love is perverted, then the politics of the *Social Contract* can fit with the anthropology of the *Discourse on Inequality*. Since self-love originally involves a desire for equality, because it is compatible with reciprocity and does not necessarily degenerate into vanity, scorn, and envy, it can be the foundation for a well-ordered society.

This interpretive choice reveals a deeper commitment to a Kantian reading of Rousseau: Kant is supposed to be 'best interpreter of Rousseau.'[16] In order to justify his interpretation of self-love, Rawls hinges on a passage of *Religion within the Boundaries of Mere Reason* in which Kant distinguishes between a natural desire for equality and cultural ('diabolical') vices associated with competition.[17] Kant mentions here a human predisposition to self-love, in the sense that man can consider himself happy or unhappy only in comparison with others. This generates a desire to be valued by others, which is initially a desire for equality, a wish not to be dominated or surpassed, but which gives rise to an unjust craving to gain superiority over others. Envy and rivalry

[14] N. J. H. Dent, *Rousseau* (Oxford: Blackwell, 1988), chap. 3; *A Rousseau Dictionary* (Oxford: Blackwell, 1992), 33–36; both quoted in the bibliography of Rawls's *Lectures*, 212. See also J. Cohen, 'The Natural Goodness of Humanity', in *Reclaiming the History of Ethics: Essays for John Rawls*, ed. A. Reath, B. Herman, and C. Korsgaard (Cambridge: Cambridge University Press, 1997), 102–139; F. Neuhouser, 'Freedom, Dependence, and the General Will', *Philosophical Review* (1993), 363–395 (376 ff.), and *Rousseau's Theodicy of Self-Love: Evil, Rationality, and the Drive for Recognition* (Oxford: Oxford University Press, 2008).

[15] Dent, *Rousseau*, 71.

[16] Rawls, *Lectures*, 199–200. This reading is very different from other Kantian readings of Rousseau, such as Ernst Cassirer's or Andrew Levine's (*The Politics of Autonomy: A Kantian Reading of Rousseau's* Social Contract (Amherst: University of Massachusetts Press, 1976).

[17] Rawls, *Lectures*, 199–200; Kant, *Religion within the Boundaries of Mere Reason*, ed. Allen Wood and George di Giovanni (Cambridge: Cambridge University Press, 1998), 51.

emerge in this way, and the greatest vices are grafted onto these negative passions.[18]

Rawls applies this distinction to the *Discourse on Inequality*: corrupt self-love is not grounded in human nature. Rather, it is a consequence of corrupt social relations, which account for the genealogy of cultural vices. It will also have decisive consequences for Rawls's interpretation of the *Social Contract*, where his scant attention to Books III and IV reveals his disregard for the work of history (the continuous striving of the particular will, the government's natural tendency to degenerate and usurp sovereignty). Yet the desire for preference remains at work in the 'well-ordered society.' By omitting the enduring tension between particular will and general will, Rawls therefore leaves out one of the main driving forces of the *Social Contract* which makes it something other than a utopian fantasy: namely, its remarkable way of handling the issue of evil in history.

In Rawls's *Lectures*, this Kantian vision of Rousseau provides the ground for an optimistic reading. Underlying his analysis is an *a contrario* argument that, unless self-love is interpreted as an original desire for equality rather than superiority, Rousseau's vision would be profoundly pessimistic, and the city of the contract completely utopian. Thus, the project of a just and stable society would fall apart unless the desire for equality has its roots in human nature. The analysis of the *Social Contract* keeps this premise in mind: its well-ordered society is not a true utopia but a 'realistic utopia.'[19]

Like Judith Shklar, Rawls does not think that the commonplace contrast between realism and utopianism, between the practical and the impossible, is relevant to Rousseau.[20] According to Shklar, this opposition was only at work during the nineteenth and twentieth centuries. Rousseau provides an example of the use of utopia as a device to express such political ideas as 'self-revelation' and 'self-vindication.' Utopia expresses the distance between what is and what ought to be: 'Rousseau shared the typical utopian sense of the distance between the probable and the possible.'[21] Both the Spartan model and Clarens (in *La Nouvelle Héloïse*) offer the image of another possible world in order to inspire men to get rid of their chains. Utopia is just a fiction; it is not designed to be actually realized. It is conceived as a challenge to corruption and to

[18] On the complex issue of mutual social recognition in Rousseau and its interpretation in Kant's work, see also the contributions by Axel Honneth (Chapter 11) and Alexander Schmidt (Chapter 3) in this volume.

[19] Rawls, *Lectures*, 193.

[20] J. Shklar, *Men and Citizens: A Study of Rousseau's Social Theory* (Cambridge: Cambridge University Press, 1969), 2.

[21] Ibid., 3.

the fragility even of republican institutions: 'Utopia is therefore a protest against history and a challenge to its madness, not in the name of eternity, but in response to the spectacle of unremitting human suffering.'[22] According to Shklar, Rousseau – who was 'the last of the classical utopists' – was also a political realist: even when he contemplated utopia, his wisdom was in resignation or the acceptance of the limits of the possible.[23]

Rawls shares this vision of Rousseau as a political realist. Yet he does not limit utopia to a 'device for condemnation': the ideal provided by the *Social Contract* is not only the 'present political order reversed' – rather, it has a true normative value.[24] In *The Law of Peoples,* Rawls describes his 'ideal theory' as an account of the world that is *utopian* in so far as it does not reflect existing social arrangements but envisions them as they ought to be, and *realistic* in so far as it does not contravene anything we know about human nature.[25] Following Rousseau's opening thought in the *Social Contract,* Rawls assumes 'that his phrase 'men as they are' refers to persons' moral and psychological natures, and how that nature works within a framework of political and social institutions.'[26] To say that *human nature is good* (a proposition that Rawls himself endorses) therefore means that citizens who grow up under just institutions will act to make sure that their social world endures. Thanks to Rousseau, we know now that 'the limits of the possible in moral matters are less narrow than we think.'[27]

## II From individual liberty to personal freedom: A reassessment of the general will

In this context, Rawls's subsequent argument aims to show that the principles of justice operating through the mechanism of the general will are perfectly compatible with human nature and man's 'fundamental interests,' provided that these are also reflected in the 'basic structure' of society and the legislator's work.

As far as the contract is concerned, Rawls situates Rousseau's theory within a rational choice paradigm (the one that Rawls himself adopts in *A Theory of Justice*).[28] The contract specifies the terms of the cooperation,

[22] Ibid., 12. [23] Ibid., 1. [24] Ibid., 8.
[25] See again J. Cohen, 'The Natural Goodness of Humanity'.
[26] J. Rawls, *The Law of Peoples* (Cambridge, MA: Harvard University Press, 1999), 7.
[27] Ibid.; see Rousseau, *SC,* 110; *OC* III, 425.
[28] See also Joshua Cohen, 'Reflections on Rousseau: Autonomy and Democracy', *Philosophy and Public Affairs,* Summer 1986, 275–297 (esp. 276–279); *Rousseau: A Free Community of Equals* (Oxford: Oxford University Press, 2010). On neo-contractualist

which are to be enshrined in the institutions of society. Such cooperation in no way sacrifices the interests of the members of society: on the contrary, the idea is to enable each person's 'fundamental interests' to be satisfied as well as possible, that is, in a way that is both reasonable and rational. This distinction between *the rational* (referring to instrumental rationality, structured in accordance with interests or preferences) and *the reasonable* (including a disposition to equitable cooperation) is crucial: it accounts for the union of interest and justice in the category of 'fundamental interests,' which are not the interests of actual individuals in a society corrupted by inequality but the natural interests of man.[29] By contrast to Hobbes, Rousseau does not identify these interests with the drive for self-preservation and acquisition, nor does he identify them with property (goods, life, and liberty), in contrast to Locke. According to Rawls, both *amour de soi* and *amour propre* can find optimal expression in society, not in the sense that individuals can achieve the maximum of well-being (Rawls excludes such a possibility), but in the sense that both freedom and perfectibility (on the *amour de soi* side) and the egalitarian desire for recognition (the *amour propre* aspect) can develop within it.[30] A society based on the social contract promotes the flourishing of the intellectual and moral capacities specific to humanity. It enables people driven by uncorrupted self-love to find satisfaction, while allowing others what they wish for themselves. Finally, the well-ordered society encourages people to accept the necessary restrictions required by social life, so long as others consent to them too. Unlike Hobbes's view, for Rawls the *mutual* and *reciprocal* character of social cooperation espoused by Rousseau is thus rooted in man's original predispositions.[31]

The consequence of this move is both interesting and problematic. In Rawls, Rousseau's politics are incorporated and translated into a new terminology. For instance, it is now because all agents have an equal capacity for and an equal interest in liberty (understood as a capacity to act freely for 'valid reasons,' according to what they think best in terms of their own ends) that the social contract offers them the best possible – the most rational and the most reasonable – solution.

In his *Lectures on the History of Political Philosophy*, Rawls thus takes a strong stand against the liberal anti-totalitarian reading of Rousseau. In his view, the problem addressed in the *Social Contract* is how *not* to sacrifice our freedom, i.e. how to satisfy our fundamental interests under conditions that provide for the development of our civil and moral

readings of Rousseau, see Lélia Pezzillo, *Rousseau et le* Contrat Social (Paris: Presses Universitaires de France, 2000), 40–53.

[29] Rawls, *Lectures*, 226. [30] Ibid., 217–218. [31] Ibid., 87, and cf. 66.

freedom. Rousseau's solution is encapsulated as follows: given the fact of social interdependence, a form of association must be sought in which it is both reasonable and rational for equal persons driven by *amour de soi* and *amour propre* to consent to it. Hence the contract by no means supplies the premises for a totalitarian society; the 'total alienation' of the agent and all her rights to the community does not presuppose the sacrifice of her interests or the complete regulation of social life. All that is required for the stability of society is a 'sense of justice,' which is a capacity to understand and to follow the principles of justice based on the contract.[32] This dimension was missing in Hobbes's analysis, whereas Rousseau, without resorting to a Lockean natural law, offers the best way of conceiving it (according to Rawls).

Political liberalism can, therefore, lay claim to the authority of Rousseau. Rousseau's definition of autonomy as obedience to a law that one has laid down oneself is at the heart of modern political theory. Rousseau understood that dependence on society is required while dependence on other individuals gives rise to servitude. Only total dependence on the body politic makes it possible to escape dependence on particular agents.[33] In this view, by establishing equal conditions and equal respect for all, the contract is far from an unnatural device; it corresponds to the fundamental human yearning for autonomy. Consequently, the resulting society does not frustrate individual interests; rather, it corresponds to the fundamental interests of the individual as a *person*. Conversely, citizenship in society makes it possible to pass from instinct to morality, forming human beings with the capacity to obey the laws that they institute for themselves.[34] Not only does the social compact provide the essential social background conditions for civil freedom ('assuming that fundamental laws are properly based on what is required for the common good, citizens are free to pursue their aims within the limits laid down by the general will'),[35] it accounts for our moral freedom, since the general will is our own will, our true will. In this context, the fact that 'each of us places his person and all his power in common under the supreme direction of the general will' does not entail either that we dissolve into an organic whole or that we give up our true *individual* freedom; it means that we give ourselves the capacity to fulfill our *personal* freedom.[36]

In this powerful line of interpretation, Rawls seems to share much with Judith Shklar's influential reading. For Shklar, the general will is first and foremost a faculty which frees men from the evil of *amour propre*:

[32] Ibid., 219. Shklar too mentions this 'sense of justice' (*Men and Citizens*, 178–180).
[33] Rawls, *Lectures*, 222. [34] Ibid., 219.
[35] Ibid., 235; cf. Rousseau, *SC*, 49–51; *OC* III, 360–362. [36] Ibid., 235.

> The general will, like any will, is that faculty, possessed by all men, that defends them against the dangers of *amour-propre*, the empire of opinion and institutionalized inequality. Everyman's overriding self-interest is to prevent inequality and his will is pitted against all these forces within and outside itself that promote it.[37]

Shklar dismisses some of the usual criticisms against Rousseau: far from ignoring individual feelings in order to promote public ends, the *Social Contract* takes into account the people's interests. The good of the whole is related to the well-being of its members.[38] If Rousseau's new vision of the social world starts from the deprived, its politics are not totalitarian: the general will pursues 'nothing but a hard personal interest,' even if it is an interest that all citizens share. Nor is its content vague: it always tends to equality. In other words, the general will 'is general because the prevention of inequality is the greatest single interest that men in society share, whatever other ends they might have.'[39] Its aim is to promote the interest of man in general against those 'particular' wills that lead men to seek privileges. Finally, the general will is the will of 'man in general,' a will to impersonality and to fairness toward all.[40]

Yet Rawls brings back into the picture the constructivist and procedural dimension of the general will: the general will is based upon deliberation among individuals, conducted under conditions of fairness (the general will must spring from all and apply to all).[41] For sure, the general will is understood as abstracted from any particular determination or interest. That is why the general will wills justice: 'equal rights, and the notion of justice they produce, derive from the preference that everyone accords to himself: hence, from the nature of man.'[42] As in Shklar, the general will wills equality first, because of the nature of our fundamental interests, including our interest in avoiding the social conditions of personal subjection (equality is necessary for liberty). But *pace* Shklar, it cannot be conceived without an institutional background: 'only reasons based on the fundamental interests we share as citizens should count as reasons when we are acting as members of the Assembly in enacting constitutional norms or basic laws.'[43] The people are not conceived any

[37] Shklar, *Men and Citizens*, 166. [38] Ibid., 16.

[39] Ibid., 169; Shklar, 'Rousseau', in *Dictionary of the History of Ideas*, ed. P. Weiner (New York: Scribner, 1973), quoted in Rawls's *Lectures*, 223. Besides Shklar, Rawls also cites Patrick Riley, *The General Will before Rousseau* (Princeton: Princeton University Press, 1986). For a thorough discussion of both views, see Samuel Affeldt, 'The Citizen as Legislator: The Conversation of Constitution in Rousseau's *The Social Contract*', in *Constituting Mutuality: Essays on Expression and the Bases of Intelligibility in Rousseau, Wittgenstein, and Freud*, PhD Dissertation, Harvard University, 1996, and 'The Force of Freedom: Rousseau on *forcing to be free*', *Political Theory* 27.3 (1999), 299–333.

[40] Shklar, *Men and Citizen,* 191. [41] Rousseau, *SC,* II, 4, 34; *OC* III, 373.

[42] Rawls, *Lectures,* 232; see again Rousseau *SC*, II, 4, 34; OC III, 373. [43] Ibid., 230.

more as a passive body politic, consenting to the legislator's law.[44] Only deliberation leads to the formation of a general will among a people, by eliminating sources of individual bias or preference.[45] The fundamental interests take absolute priority over our particular interests when the people actually vote for fundamental laws and consider basic political and social institutions. In turn, these institutions will secure the social conditions necessary to realize their fundamental interests, on terms all would agree to.

Meanwhile, Rawls sketches an ultra-rationalist reading of the general will. The general will relies on a certain set of *valid reasons*, and what citizens deem to be valid reasons for their political decisions are the measures that best enhance the common good. A little later, the *Lectures* defines the general will from the point of view of 'public reason.' To vote in accordance with the general will means to accept as valid only a certain kind of reasoning in public deliberation, the kind that corresponds to Rawls's own conception of public reason: 'Rousseau's view contains an idea of what I have called public reason. So far as I know the idea originates with him.'[46] Building on these premises, the fact that the general will is always *straight*, *constant*, *unalterable*, and *pure* does not make it either a transcendental idea or a dictate of the sovereign power. The general will is conceived as a form of deliberative reason exercised by each citizen; it is what remains after we take away the particular interests which incline us to partiality.[47]

Finally, Rawls makes it clear that Rousseau's analysis of the relationship between justice, equality, and freedom inspires his own theory of justice as fairness. Regarding the thesis that the particular will naturally tends toward preference whereas the general will tends toward equality, he contends that 'this remark of Rousseau's is an ancestor of the first reason why, in justice as fairness, the basic structure is taken as the primary subject of justice.'[48] The whole of his ensuing demonstration confirms the main interpretative guidelines analyzed above: the principles of justice are based on the contract; the contract implies that certain values have to be realized in the basic structure of society; and, in a

[44] Compare to Shklar, according to whom people's sovereignty 'is a condition free from personal oppression' but 'is not self-determination in a politically active sense' (*Men and Citizens*, 182).

[45] The deliberation may be understood as individual or collective. On the legacy of this argument, see C. Girard, 'Jean-Jacques Rousseau et la démocratie délibérative: bien commun, droits individuels et unanimité', *Modernités de Rousseau*, ed. C. Spector, in *Lumières* 15 (June 2010), 199–221.

[46] Rawls, *Lectures*, 231. See also his *Political Liberalism*, 448f.

[47] Ibid., 227.

[48] Ibid., 234. Rawls makes reference here to his *Justice as Fairness*, §3, 4, 15.

well-ordered society, the interest in freedom and the interest in perfectibility are part of a people's fundamental interests.

## III The lawgiver

Yet it might be objected that Rousseau's theory of the lawgiver provides evidence of his authoritarian, or even totalitarian, tendencies. Surprisingly, however, far from fearing that Rousseau's republicanism is destructive of freedom, Rawlsian political liberalism exonerates him of any such charge.[49] For Rawls, the legislator who dares to set about constituting a people is by no means the same as a demiurge creating a 'new man' from scratch. The lawgiver makes it possible to express the social nature of human beings, and brings them to recognize the fundamental interests they have in common. Citing the controversial section of the *Social Contract* on the need to transform human nature, Rawls debunks the liberal 'anti-totalitarian' interpretation.[50] The wish to shape human beings in conformity with the goals of society appears sound, since there really is a need to face the critical issue of stability in the just society, and therefore to shape the *social spirit* necessary for the institutions that apply its principles to survive in the long term.

In his comment, Rawls therefore pays a fine tribute to the 'extraordinary' section in the *Social Contract* that used to fill liberals with such dread. Aware that the powers we acquire in society can be used only in society, and only in cooperation with the powers of others, Rousseau presents the legislator as the founding and mediating figure that comes forward at the moment required by society.[51] There is nothing mysterious about this, nor anything destructive of freedom. Once again, Rawls comes quite close to Shklar's interpretation. For her, the legislator testifies to Montesquieu's influence on Rousseau: the character of a people must be taken into account for the sake of stability.[52] Rawls takes the idea one step further: the legislator does not preclude political autonomy. To illustrate his point, Rawls even uses the example of the principles of equality, liberty, and tolerance that were established at the end of the European religious wars. Far from infringing on the liberty of human

[49] Michael Sandel reproaches Rousseau here mainly because of the spirit of unanimity required by the *Social Contract*. See Sandel, *Democracy's Discontent: America in Search of a Public Philosophy* (Cambridge, MA: Harvard University Press, 1996), 319–320. On this issue, see also Philip Pettit's contribution to the present book (Chapter 10).

[50] Rousseau, *SC*, 69; *OC* III, 381–82. On the indictments levelled at Rousseau by Berlin, Talmon, and Crocker, see Chapter II of Spector, *Au prisme de Rousseau*, and Christopher Brooke's contribution in the present volume (Chapter 8).

[51] Rawls, *Lectures*, 240. [52] Shklar, *Men and Citizens*, 174.

beings, the legislator enabled it to become effective; and, in the historical sequel, the initial act of persuasion gave way to a stable balance of institutions. These political institutions were able to shape the people who would subsequently preserve and defend them.[53]

Needless to say, Rawls's overly rationalistic interpretation of the role of the legislator in Rousseau's *Social Contract* also ignores the duplicity involved in the initial consent of the people to the laws. Rousseau is explicit that consent cannot be obtained at this founding moment on the basis of rational persuasion: the lawgiver presents the laws as emanating from divine authority. This manipulation should be troubling for a liberal reading of Rousseau.[54]

As far as the social contract, the general will, or the fiction of the legislator are concerned, Rawls's analysis thus overturns the anti-totalitarian reading of Rousseau, which condemned him for wanting 'to force men to be free.'[55] In Rawls's view, once this phrase is placed in context, it gives no cause at all for indignation. On the contrary, it amounts to a commonsense notion that lies at the heart of a properly conceived theory of justice: if laws lacked the coercive power to command obedience, some people would be able to operate in society as 'free riders,' enjoying its benefits without making any contribution of their own. The point is that if people could enjoy their rights without fulfilling their duties, this would undermine the conditions for mutually advantageous cooperation and thereby compromise the liberty of all. Moreover, to force a recalcitrant individual to discharge public obligations while enjoying social benefits is in effect to *make him free*, where what is at issue is a moral freedom that goes beyond the satisfaction of instincts and reaches true self-mastery. Once again, Rawls follows closely Dent's interpretation: the concept of moral liberty enables us to understand Rousseau's claim that agents are as free after the contract as they were before it (albeit in radically different ways). To force agents to be free is to remove them from relations of domination and subordination and to place them within relations of mutual respect.[56]

[53] Rawls, *Lectures*, 241. [54] I would like to thank Ruth Grant for this insightful remark.

[55] Ibid., 242–243. Shklar still has a negative vision of this phrase (in 'Positive Liberty, Negative Liberty in the United States', in *Redeeming American Political Thought*, ed. Stanley Hoffmann and Dennis E. Thompson (Chicago: University of Chicago Press, 1998), 111–126, here 125). On the uses that the 'humanist' republican tradition associated with Luc Ferry and Alain Renaut (and in a different register, with Tzvetan Todorov) has made of the passage in question, see J. T. Scott and R. Zaretsky, 'Rousseau and the Revival of Humanism in Contemporary French Political Thought', *History of Political Thought* 24.4 (2003), 599–623.

[56] N. H. Dent, *Rousseau*, chap. 5.

## IV From liberty to equality: The difference principle

There is another aspect of Rawls's interpretation of Rousseau worthy of consideration: overall, the liberal philosopher finds in him a major ally in his critique of utilitarianism. The 'common good' that is the object of the general will concerns the social conditions underpinning the people's common interests; the aim in question here, therefore, is not 'the greatest happiness of the greatest number,' even at the price of sacrificing some members of society. Rawls recalls the passage in Rousseau's *Discourse on Political Economy* that refuses to accept the sacrifice of a single innocent person for the security of the whole.[57] Rather, the body politic is supposed to provide for the preservation of the humblest of its members with as much care as all the others.[58] Anticipating and rejecting the arguments of utilitarianism, Rousseau maintains that the fundamental laws of society do not rest upon a principle of interest aggregation; his distinction between the 'general will' and the 'will of all' involves a refusal to see the common interest as a sum of individual interests. The freedom of some cannot be subordinated to the happiness of others. Voting on the fundamental laws of the state means expressing one's opinion about the laws that will best establish the social and political conditions for everyone to advance, on a basis of *equality*, their shared fundamental interests.

For Rawls, then, Rousseau constitutes an integral part of the liberal tradition.[59] In the *Social Contract*, the 'basic structure' of society is there to ensure both liberty and equality, the latter bolstering the former. This is why Rawls chooses Rousseau, rather than Locke, as his main source (with Kant) for contractual theory. Not only does his thought not endanger liberty, it conveys the idea of the reduction of social-economic inequalities as its indispensable foundation.

Finally, the *Lectures on the History of Political Philosophy* draw on Rousseau for the arguments justifying the difference principle. Since social inequalities give rise to dependence, fueling arrogance and scorn on one side and servility and deference on the other, they must be fought in so far as they do not strictly contribute to public utility. Shklar had put forward this dimension of Rousseau's political thought: the fight against inequality is at the core of a non-oppressive society. Compassion is thus transformed into a political force.[60] Without mentioning compassion

[57] Rousseau, *Discourse on Political Economy,* in *SC*, 17; *OC* III, 256.

[58] Rawls, *Lectures*, 229–230.

[59] This view is widely disputed: see, for example, Pierre Manent, *An Intellectual History of Liberalism* (Princeton: Princeton University Press, 1994), chap. 5.

[60] Shklar, 'Jean-Jacques Rousseau and Equality', in 'Rousseau for Our Time', *Daedalus* 107.3 (1978), 13–25, here 13. See also, in the same volume, Carl G. Hedman, 'Rousseau on Self-Interest, Compassion and Moral Progress', 181–198.

(which does not appear in the *Social Contract*), Rawls follows this line of interpretation. For him, Rousseau argues that social and economic inequalities should be limited to ensure the conditions under which citizens can be independent and the general will can achieve adequate expression: 'Does it follow that it [inequality] should not at least be regulated? It is precisely because the force of things always tends to destroy equality that the force of legislation must always tend to maintain it.'[61] Rawls takes this remark as an inspiration for his reasoning on why the basic structure of society is the primary subject of justice. The difference principle can find justification here, while assisting the principle of the maximization of equal liberties for all; the limitation of inequality is required to ensure both the conditions for liberty as well as the conditions for the highest level of *equal respect* are present. It is thanks to limits on social and economic inequality that citizens think of themselves as really equal; they are endowed with the same fundamental interest in ensuring liberty and pursuing their goals within the limits of the law, and with the same capacity for moral freedom. According to Rawls, Rousseau's true originality is most apparent in this social dimension of his doctrine, drawing out the necessity of an *equal respect* to which material equality is supposed to be instrumental.[62]

*

Can Rousseau be saved from the liberal anti-totalitarian critique? This is one of the intentions underlying Shklar's and Rawls's approach to his work. According to a recent commentator, 'what Shklar's realism challenged was not utopia, nor hopeful politics, but the expansion of the realm of the possible beyond what we sensibly know to be true.'[63] The value of Rousseau's theory of citizenship, in this respect, is immense. Consequently, Rawls shares Shklar's admiration for Rousseau's theory of autonomy, which can even correct some of the shortcoming of Kant's idealism.[64] But where Shklar discarded the contractualist theory itself, Rawls puts it back in the forefront.[65] In Rawls's view, the *Social Contract* develops a non-utilitarian theory of justice in which the common good results from seeing oneself as a member in a cooperative enterprise, rather than from incremental addition. It conceives of the well-ordered society

[61] Rawls, *Lectures*, 233–234; Rousseau, *SC*, 79; *OC* III, 392.
[62] Rawls, *Lectures*, 247–248.
[63] Forrester, 'Judith Shklar, Bernard Williams and Political Realism', 260.
[64] Neal, 'In the Shadow of the General Will'.
[65] According to Shklar, 'it is the ordinary people, 'the all' whose will rules, that matters most'; 'sovereignty thus personifies the most important interest of all'; 'the great question of politics is how to protect the people against its own incompetence, and against fraud and usurpation' (*Men and Citizens*, 177).

as protected from relations of dependence and domination. For these reasons, Rousseau is fully part of the liberal, egalitarian tradition into which *A Theory of Justice* is itself inserted. After all, Rousseau's conception of justice in the *Social Contract* is a freestanding view – not justified in terms of any particular religious or moral perspective. It is also a political, not a metaphysical conception of justice.

There is a risk, however, that in trying to paint Rousseau as a modern liberal one might distort his thought. In a sense, the special use that Rawls makes of Rousseau in *A Theory of Justice* is already contained *in nuce* in his *Lectures*. In his Kantian interpretation, Rousseau's positive vision of self-love prior to its corruption makes it possible to reconcile interest and justice, instrumental rationality and higher social goals. Yet Rousseau never offered such an optimistic vision of *amour propre*: as soon as human beings prefer one love partner to another, they too crave to be preferred, and this dynamic is a far cry from the wish to be treated equally. The competitive aspect of *amour propre* is central to Rousseau's account of socio-political decline and corruption, and is the ground for the deep pessimism emanating from his work in the eyes of critics. Besides, Rousseau also never thought that the tension between the particular will and the general will could be definitively overcome, or that the stability of society could be established once and for all on the ruins of the particular will. Rousseau's interest in *mœurs* and the 'law of opinion' goes beyond any attempt to formalize the principles of justice and the legal institutions that would implement these principles. To take men *as they are* means to take into account their passions and beliefs, which cannot be reduced to their higher-order interests.[66]

In his *Constitutional Project for Corsica* and in his *Considerations on the Government of Poland* (two works Rawls never mentions), Rousseau suggests institutional and moral devices to reshape human passions. To be sure, love of country is the end citizens should pursue; it can never be reduced to any reasonable and rational interest. In the *Social Contract* itself, citizens are not only motivated by their desire for freedom and perfectibility (which is unknown to them before the compact); they are primarily motivated by their desire to survive and to retain their agency. Yet after the society is born, the object of this desire becomes the motherland – an expansion of *amour de soi* to encompass the enlarged self of the country. The emphasis is put on national solidarity, an attachment to a distinctive way of life, and on the demanding requirements of civic

[66] See Axel Honneth's discussion of the same problematic issue in his contribution to this book (Chapter 11).

virtue.[67] Shklar, by the way, was fully conscious of this 'Spartan' dimension of Rousseau's thought.[68]

Therefore, Rawls can pursue his ends only by endowing Rousseau with a particular, partly deformed face in order to make him an ally against the utilitarian mainstream. It is a Rousseau without passions, a Rousseau without tensions, who lays bare the depravities of society in order to offer a more rational path to a 'realistic utopia.'[69]

[67] J. Cohen tries to reconcile this 'communitarian' line with the 'liberal' strand of Rousseau; see his *Rousseau: A Free Community of Equals* (introduction).
[68] Ibid., 12–21.
[69] Rawls, *The Law of Peoples*, 11f. For a discussion of this work, see G. Roosevelt, 'Rousseau versus Rawls on International Relations', *European Journal of Political Theory* 5.3 (2006), 303–322.

# 10 Rousseau's dilemma

*Philip Pettit*

## Introduction

In his *Social Contract* (1762), Jean-Jacques Rousseau developed a theory of freedom and government that built upon a long tradition of republican thinking, which by most accounts goes back to the time of the classical Roman republic.[1] The heroes in this tradition are Polybius, Cicero and Livy in ancient Rome; Machiavelli in the Renaissance; English writers like James Harrington and Algernon Sydney in the seventeenth century; and radical Whigs in the eighteenth century like the authors of *Cato's Letters*, the English defenders of the American cause such as Richard Price and Joseph Priestley, and of course American writers such as the authors of the *Federalist Papers*, in particular James Madison.[2] The tradition also had fellow-travellers who endorsed many of the guiding ideas in the tradition but are remembered for the novelty of their claims rather than their fidelity to a recognizable tradition; these, by my reckoning, include John Locke, the Baron de Montesquieu and Adam Smith.

Rousseau belongs to this tradition insofar as he joins all the figures mentioned above in endorsing a conception of freedom which requires not being subjected to the will of another agent or agency, even one that displays restraint and indulgence. But he breaks with that tradition, as do some of the fellow-travellers mentioned, in arguing against the institutions associated with the mixed constitution: the sort of arrangement that

I am grateful for the helpful discussion of the ideas in this chapter that followed my presentation of them at a Rousseau conference at UCL (University College London) in April 2012, at a conference on Kant and Republicanism in Hamburg in March 2014, and at the Political Theory Workshop in Columbia University in December 2015. I am also grateful for helpful comments received from Avi Lifschitz.

[1] Zera S. Fink, *The Classical Republicans: An Essay in the Recovery of a Pattern of Thought in Seventeenth Century England* (Evanston, IL.: Northwestern University Press, 1962); J. G. A. Pocock, *The Machiavellian Moment: Florentine Political Theory and the Atlantic Republican Tradition* (Princeton: Princeton University Press, 1975); Quentin Skinner, *Liberty Before Liberalism* (Cambridge: Cambridge University Press, 1998).

[2] John Trenchard and Thomas Gordon, *Cato's Letters* (New York: Da Capo, 1971); James Madison, Alexander Hamilton, and John Jay, *The Federalist Papers* (Harmondsworth: Penguin, 1987).

was exemplified in the minds of Roman and neo-Roman thinkers by the constitution of Rome. That constitution looked for a number of mutually constraining, multiply representative centres of power rather than allowing 'the accumulation of all powers', as Madison put it, 'in the same hands, whether of one, a few, or many'.[3] The message, in a medieval slogan, was: *Ubi multa consilia, ibi salus*; where there are many councils, there is safety – in particular, safety from subjection to an alien will.[4]

In the *Social Contract*, Rousseau rejects the mixed constitution in favour of a single assembly of all the citizens, breaking with the institutional recommendations, if not the guiding ideals, of the older tradition. He argues that the best arrangement or constitution for enabling people to enjoy freedom in the republican sense is one under which citizens unanimously agree to be bound, each in their own case, by the majoritarian determinations of a collective, sovereign assembly. While this conceptual innovation appealed greatly to those of a Romantic political bent – and Rousseau, of course, was one of the inspirers of the Romantic movement – it did more harm than good, by my lights, in the redirection it gave to republican thinking. I try to illustrate the difficulties that confront his approach in this chapter by showing that his new departure created a serious dilemma that he lacks the resources to escape.

The chapter is divided into five sections. In the first two, I look at Rousseau's ambiguous connection with the older, Italian-Atlantic republicanism: his endorsement of the received view of freedom on the one side, and his rejection of the mixed constitution in favour of an absolute sovereign on the other. In the two following sections I look at the pair of challenges to freedom that his approach raises and, as he thinks, resolves: the first arises from the fact that, no matter how benign, every sovereign subjects citizens to an independent will; the second arises from the fact that the sovereign may not actually be very benign from the perspective of many citizens. Finally, the fifth section identifies the dilemma that his responses to those two challenges create for his approach.[5]

[3] Madison et al., *Federalist Papers*, 303.

[4] Daniel Philip Waley, *The Italian City-Republics*, 3rd ed. (London: Longman, 1988), 38–39.

[5] In this chapter I shall concentrate on the *Social Contract*. Despite that fairly narrow compass, however, I have been unable to develop the argument, as would have been ideal, while interacting with the voluminous literature on Rousseau's views. I am particularly aware of the different views argued, for example, in works such as Robert Wokler, *Rousseau on Society, Politics, Music and Language* (New York: Garland,1987); N. J. H. Dent, *Rousseau* (Oxford: Blackwell, 1988); Tracy Strong, *Jean-Jacques Rousseau: The Politics of the Ordinary* (Lanham: Rowman and Littlefield, 2002); and Joshua Cohen, *Rousseau: A Free Community of Equals* (Oxford: Oxford University Press, 2010). One mitigating consideration is that the secondary literature rarely focuses, as I do here, on the tension between Rousseau's endorsement of the republican way of conceiving

## 1 Rousseau in support of freedom as non-domination

### *Freedom as non-domination*

The conception of freedom that I associate with the long republican tradition casts it as requiring the absence of subjection to another's will, or at least the absence of subjection in the exercise of those choices that came to be viewed in the tradition as fundamental liberties.[6] These are best seen as choices that can and ought to be protected for all citizens under the law and custom of the society.[7] By contemporary standards – and so in any neo-republican doctrine – the citizenry should include all adult, able-minded, more or less permanent residents. But in the older tradition they were always restricted to males and often to those who were minimally propertied and culturally mainstream.

In classical Roman usage, subjection to the will of another was described as *dominatio:* subjection to the will of a *dominus* or master.[8] Hence it is useful to describe it as a conception under which freedom requires non-domination.[9] The contemporary rival to this conception casts freedom as non-interference. That ideal dates from the work of Jeremy Bentham in the 1770s, and became the hallmark of classical liberalism in the early nineteenth century. The difference between the two ideals is revealed in the fact that freedom as non-domination has two implications that freedom as non-interference does not support.

The first implication of the ideal of freedom as non-domination is that you are not just unfree when someone actively interferes with you by imposing restrictions on what you can choose; you are also unfree when someone who has the power of interfering at will – someone who possesses the knowledge and resources required for interference – happens to stay their hand, thereby exercising restraint and displaying indulgence. In that case you are still subject to the will of the other, and still suffer domination, for you depend for being able to choose as you wish on the state of their will towards you: in particular, on their remaining indulgently disposed. This observation led traditional republicans to argue that

of freedom on the one hand, and his endorsement of the absolutist rejection of the mixed constitution on the other.

[6] John Lilburne, *The Legal Fundamental Liberties of the People of England, Asserted, Revived, and Vindicated* (London, 1646).

[7] Philip Pettit, *On the People's Terms: A Republican Theory and Model of Democracy* (Cambridge: Cambridge University Press, 2012); *Just Freedom: A Moral Compass for a Complex World* (New York: W. W. Norton and Co., 2014).

[8] Frank Lovett, *A General Theory of Domination and Justice* (Oxford: Oxford University Press, 2010), Appendix.

[9] Philip Pettit, *Republicanism: A Theory of Freedom and Government* (Oxford: Oxford University Press, 1997); *On the People's Terms; Just Freedom.*

you could not enjoy freedom under any master, however gentle or indeed gullible they may be; you could not enjoy freedom, for example, under a benevolent master.

The second implication of the ideal of freedom as non-domination is that you are not unfree if you suffer the interference of another agent or agency but enjoy a suitable degree of control over the interference practiced. How much control must you have in order not to be made unfree by the interference imposed? That may be a cultural variable, as I have suggested elsewhere, so that you have enough control when by the toughest local standards you can look that agent or agency in the eye without reason for fear or deference; you can pass the so-called eyeball test.[10] But however the idea is to be developed, it led most traditional republicans to think that the interference of statutory and indeed customary law – say, its interference in determining and defending people's basic liberties – is not dominating to the extent that citizens share more or less equally in controlling how that law is shaped and applied.

Those who espouse the ideal of freedom as non-interference are not committed to support such implications; on the contrary, they routinely oppose them. Thus, as against the claim that domination without interference reduces freedom, Bentham's close associate William Paley wrote in 1785 that an 'absolute form of government' may be 'no less free than the purest democracy'.[11] And as against the claim that interference without domination – say, the interference of good laws – does not take away freedom, Bentham himself insisted that 'all coercive laws . . . are, as far as they go, abrogative of freedom'.[12]

### *Rousseau's endorsement of the republican idea*

Perhaps the deepest divide between the classical republican notion of freedom and the classical liberal alternative – and it remains the deepest divide between neo-republicanism and neo-liberalism – lies in their respective views of the relation between law and liberty. Classical liberals take freedom not to require law per se, identifying it with the natural liberty that someone, by received lore, might even enjoy out of society.

[10] For the record, I generally use the eyeball test as a rough criterion of whether people enjoy private non-domination, and I invoke a distinct, if related, test to serve as a criterion of whether they enjoy public non-domination; this consists in their being in a position to treat unwelcome public decisions as tough luck rather than the work of a malign will (see Pettit, *On the People's Terms* and *Just Freedom*). Here I stick, for simplicity, to the eyeball test.

[11] William Paley, *The Principles of Moral and Political Philosophy*, ed. D. L. Le Mahieu (Indianapolis, IN: Liberty Fund, 2002), 314.

[12] Jeremy Bentham, 'Anarchical Fallacies', in *The Works of Jeremy Bentham*, vol. 2, ed. J. Bowring (Edinburgh: W. Tait, 1843), 503.

Classical republicans, by contrast, identify it with a civil form of liberty that is available only in society. They also take it to be accessible to citizens only where, first, the laws and the mores of their society are under the equally shared control of all; second, such laws identify a suitable range of basic liberties for each; and, third, they give suitable protection to every citizen in the exercise of those liberties.

Rousseau is clearly on the republican side in this debate, arguing that 'it is only the State's force that makes for its members' freedom' – that is, their freedom in relation to one another – and that in this exercise of force 'the civil laws are born'.[13] The republican character of this ideal of freedom appears in the fact that what it requires, according to Rousseau, is 'that every Citizen be perfectly independent of all the others'. Rousseau is faithful to the older tradition in this insistence that freedom is associated with the non-domination or independence that law can provide for citizens, where law is taken in a broad sense that includes 'morals', 'customs' and 'opinion'.

But there are various forms of dependence on others, ranging from depending on their goodwill for being able to exercise your basic liberties – i.e. dependence as domination – to depending on their collateral preferences for having access to certain options: say, depending on their air travel preferences for being able to fly away for the weekend.[14] It may sometimes seem that whereas the older republicans looked for independence from an alien power and will – 'independency upon the will of another', as Algernon Sidney had put it[15] – Rousseau rails against all forms of dependence. It may seem, in other words, that he assumes more the form of a normative solipsist – better to live a life of self-sufficiency, even perhaps in isolation from others – than that of a normative republican.

This appearance is quite misleading, however. It is clear in *The Social Contract* that what he objects to is 'personal dependence',[16] which he also describes as 'servitude and dependence',[17] where I take those words to express the same idea. This is the condition against which he had railed in the *Second Discourse* of 1755 when he says: 'in the relations between man and man the worse that can happen to one is to find himself at the other's discretion'.[18] It is not the sort of dependence that living with others inescapably entails, only dependence involving domination: subjection to another's will. Rousseau emphasizes in a letter of 1757 that he has nothing against this inescapable form of dependence, acknowledging that

[13] Rousseau, *SC*, II.12.3. [14] Pettit, *Just Freedom*, Ch.1.

[15] Algernon Sidney, *Discourses Concerning Government*, ed. Thomas G. West (Indianapolis, IN: Liberty Classics, 1990), 17.

[16] *SC*, I.7.8. [17] Ibid., IV.8.28. [18] Rousseau, *DI*, 176; *OC* III, 181.

'everything is to one degree or another subject to this universal dependency'.[19]

These remarks should be enough to demonstrate that the freedom that Rousseau values is precisely the sort of freedom hailed in the republican tradition. Thus it is not the freedom that Benjamin Constant had described in 1818 as the freedom of the ancients.[20] This is a form of freedom that consists in being an enfranchised member of a voting community: a community that determines its laws on the basis of voting in a citizen assembly. That notion of freedom may have been endorsed by vulgar Rousseauvians but it was never supported by the master himself.[21]

Not only does Rousseau value freedom in the sense of non-domination; he also treats it, like his republican predecessors, as the greatest good that a society can bestow. Distinguishing it from the 'natural liberty' that a person might enjoy out of society, as the tradition had routinely done, he casts it as 'civil freedom' and presents it as something that only a suitably organized society can make available.[22] Property or ownership in anything presupposes a law that can protect you against those who would take it away, thereby vindicating your claim; it does not consist merely in having the natural power to maintain possession. And similarly, he suggests, civil freedom presupposes a law that can guarantee your claim to take this or that course of action – presumably, in exercise of a basic liberty – by protecting you against opponents. A person's natural freedom 'has no other bounds than the individual's forces', as brute possession is also 'merely the effect of force'. While people may be able to enjoy natural liberty and brute possession outside society, then, they cannot enjoy the counterparts. Both civil freedom on the one side, and ownership or property on the other, presuppose a suitable rule of law. They are made possible under and by laws that transcend the rule of force, giving a person what Rousseau calls 'positive title'.[23]

These remarks should not suggest that Rousseau thinks of freedom and property as distinct ideals. He thinks of the institution of property as an

[19] Jean Starobinski (ed.), 'A Letter from Jean-Jacques Rousseau (1757)', *New York Review of Books*, 15 May 2003, 31–32.

[20] Benjamin Constant, 'The Liberty of the Ancients Compared with That of the Moderns', in *Political Writings*, ed. Biancamaria Fontana (Cambridge: Cambridge University Press, 1988), 308–328.

[21] Jean-Fabien Spitz, *La Liberté Politique* (Paris: Presses Universitaires de France, 1995). This is to imply that while Rousseau stressed the value of self-legislation in the assembly, he took this to be of heuristic or epistemic rather than constitutive significance; it was a sign – although, as we shall see, a fallible sign – of the presence of the general will. More on this later.

[22] *SC*, I.8.2

[23] Ibid., I.8.2. For the tension in Rousseau's works between civic equality and the defence of property, see Jean-Fabien Spitz's chapter in the present book.

arrangement under which, if it assumes a suitable form, people are given a certain civil freedom: a title to acquire and trade things under the conventions it establishes. The arrangement will assume a suitable form, however, only to the extent that 'all have something and none has too much of anything'.[24] No citizen should 'be so very rich that he can buy another, and none so poor that he is compelled to sell himself'.[25]

For Rousseau, then, civil freedom is the most general, appealing status that society is capable of conferring on its citizens. And so it is no surprise that, like his republican forebears, he represents it as the ideal that the laws of a society should aim at fostering. 'The greatest good of all', he says, and 'the end of every system of legislation', involves 'two principal objects, *freedom and equality*'.[26] And in effect it consists in freedom alone, since he immediately adds that equality is attractive only 'because freedom cannot subsist without it'.

## 2 Rousseau in support of absolute sovereignty[27]

### *The absolutist idea of sovereignty*

The two most important figures in the development of the idea that each state has to have a unitary, absolute and indivisible sovereign – an idea that was designed to undermine the republican notion of a mixed constitution – were Jean Bodin and Thomas Hobbes. Bodin wrote his major anti-republican work, *The Six Books of the Republic*, just a few years after the St Bartholomew's Day massacre of Huguenots in 1572, at a time of great religious and civil strife in France. Hobbes wrote his equally anti-republican tracts in or around the 1640s – *The Elements of Law, De Cive* and *Leviathan* – in Parisian exile from an England beset by civil war.

Prompted by the fear of civil strife, both argued vehemently that whatever individual or body holds power – or at least the supreme power, as they saw it, of legislation – it has to operate as a unitary agent or agency, it cannot embody separate, mutually checking elements and it has to enjoy unchallenged authority. Each believed that in the absence of such a unitary, indivisible and absolute sovereign, there is bound to be continuing dissension and, as Hobbes famously stated it, a relapse into a war of all against all: a state of nature in which no one owes any obligations to others and life is 'solitary, poor, nasty brutish and short'.[28]

[24] Ibid., I.9.8, footnote. [25] Ibid., II.11.2. [26] Ibid., II.11.1.

[27] This section draws on material in Philip Pettit, 'Two Republican Traditions' in *Republican Democracy: Liberty, Law and Politics*, ed. Andreas Niederberger and Philipp Schink (Edinburgh: Edinburgh University Press, 2013), 169–204.

[28] Thomas Hobbes, *Leviathan*, ed. Edwin Curley (Indianapolis: Hackett, 1994), 13.9.

While Hobbes built on Bodin's work, the case he made for a unitary, indivisible and absolute sovereign was quite original.[29] He argued that we should think of the commonwealth, whatever form it assumes – monarchical, aristocratic or democratic – as a corporate body on the model of 'a company of merchants'.[30] In a monarchy – the constitutional form that he, like Bodin, prefers – the multitude of the people are incorporated into a body for which, by unanimous consent, the king or queen speaks. In an aristocracy or democracy, they are incorporated into a body for which, again by unanimous consent, an elite or popular assembly speaks, determining what it says on the basis of majority voting. Prior to incorporation, according to Hobbes, the people in a country constitute just a multitude of dissonant voices: an 'aggregate' or 'heap' of agents, 'a disorganized crowd', a 'throng'.[31] After incorporation, the people comes into existence as a proper agent. It forms a will and assumes the status of an agent or person via the single authorized voice of its spokesperson. This may be the individual voice of a monarch or the majoritarian voice of an assembly.[32]

This spokesperson operates as a unitary agency and gives the unity of a corporate entity to the multitude personated or represented: 'it is the unity of the representer, not the unity of the represented, that maketh the person one ... and unity, cannot otherwise be understood in multitude'.[33] And since the people or commonwealth assumes that corporate existence only in virtue of the sovereign, it cannot continue to exist in the absence of a sovereign. It is 'an error', Hobbes says, to think 'that the people is a distinct body from him or them that have the sovereignty over them'.[34] Or, as he puts the point elsewhere, 'the sovereign, is the public soul, giving life and motion to the commonwealth, which expiring, the members are governed by it no more than the carcass of a man by his departed (though immortal) soul'.[35]

[29] Philip Pettit, *Made with Words: Hobbes on Language, Mind and Politics* (Princeton, NJ: Princeton University Press, 2008), ch. 5.

[30] Hobbes, *On the Citizen*, ed. Richard Tuck and Michael Silverthorne (Cambridge: Cambridge University Press, 1998), 5.10.

[31] Hobbes, *Human Nature and De Corpore Politico: The Elements of Law, Natural and Politic*, ed. J. C. A. Gaskin (Oxford: Oxford University Press, 1994), 21.11; *On the Citizen*, 7.11; *Leviathan*, 6.37.

[32] Hobbes, *Leviathan*, 16. As a matter of record, the members of an assembly could not operate satisfactorily under straight majoritarian decision-making; such an arrangement would be hostage to inconsistency in group judgements and policies; see Pettit, *Made with Words*, ch. 5, and appendix; Christian List and Philip Pettit, *Group Agency: The Possibility, Design and Status of Corporate Agents* (Oxford: Oxford University Press, (2011). I ignore this problem, which arises for Rousseau as well as Hobbes, in the present context.

[33] Hobbes, *Leviathan*, 16.13.

[34] Hobbes, *Human Nature and De Corpore Politico*, 27.9.

[35] Hobbes, *Leviathan*, 29.23.

But not only does each state or commonwealth have to have a unitary sovereign in this sense; according to Hobbes, this sovereign also has to be indivisible. What this means, in effect, is that it cannot exist or operate under a mixed constitution. Hobbes thinks that the mixed constitution – 'mixarchy', as he mischievously calls it – cannot establish the unitary sovereign that every commonwealth requires.[36] It would support 'not one independent commonwealth, but three independent factions; nor one representative person, but three'.[37] His argument is straightforward: 'if the king bear the person of the people, and the general assembly bear also the person of the people, and another assembly bear the person of a part of the people, they are not one person, nor one sovereign, but three persons, and three sovereigns.'[38]

In this Hobbesian view, which closely resembles the earlier image developed by Bodin, the unitary, indivisible sovereign also has to have a third property: it must enjoy absolute power. This means that the sovereign must be unconstrained by the law on the one side, and must be incontestable by subjects on the other.

The argument for why the sovereign is above the law reflects a line of reasoning in Bodin and is remarkably simple.[39] Law is command and the sovereign is the commander who gives the law. But no one can give a command to himself: 'he that can bind, can release'.[40] And so the sovereign cannot be subject to the laws he establishes: 'having power to make, and repeal laws, he may when he pleaseth, free himself'. Thus, by this account, it would make no sense to posit a sovereign at the origin of law and hold at the same time that that sovereign ought to be constrained by the law itself.

The argument for why the sovereign is beyond challenge from citizens is a little more complex but still readily intelligible. Assume that the people, as distinct from the multitude, exists only in virtue of being incorporated by covenant under a single sovereign. If individuals were to contest what the sovereign does, that would be to allege a breach of covenant on the sovereign's part. But this would amount to rejecting the role of the sovereign as the unique spokesperson on what should hold under the covenant; there is no super-sovereign, after all, to resolve such a contest. And, in rejecting the sovereign's role in this regard, they would

[36] Hobbes, *Behemoth; Or, The Long Parliament*, ed. Ferdinand Tönnies (Chicago: University of Chicago Press, 1990), 16.

[37] Hobbes, *Leviathan*, 29.16; see too *On the Citizen*, 7.4, and *Human Nature and De Corpore Politico*, 20.15.

[38] Ibid.

[39] Jean Bodin, *Six Books of the Commonwealth*, ed, M. J. Tooley (Oxford: Blackwell, 1967), I, 8, 395.

[40] Hobbes, *Leviathan*, 26.6.

be acting as if they were still in a state of nature: a war of all against all. Hobbes puts forward this argument in commenting on the essentially restricted place of subjects in a commonwealth:

> if any one or more of them pretend a breach of the covenant made by the sovereign at his institution, and others or one other of his subjects, or himself alone, pretend there was no such breach, there is in this case no judge to decide the controversy: it returns therefore to the sword again.[41]

But what of the case where the whole people, and not just one individual or subgroup, contests what the sovereign does? Would this be possible within the Hobbesian vision? No, it would not. Individuals contract with one another to have a sovereign and it is only in virtue of establishing such a spokesperson that they can act as a single body. Thus they cannot act as a single body in contesting the very spokesperson on whom they depend for so acting. They can only act as the members of a mob or multitude: that is, act as if they were still in a state of nature.[42]

### *Rousseau's endorsement of the absolutist idea*

Rousseau follows Bodin and Hobbes in taking the legislative authority, rather than executive or judicial officers, to be the sovereign, on the grounds that the work of any such agency is the 'application of the law', not the making of law.[43] Moreover, also following their lead, he allows that there is a difference between sovereignty and administration and that the sovereign need not lead the administration or government.[44] Like Bodin and Hobbes, he describes a regime in which the assembly of the people serves as both legislative and administrative authority as a democracy and, as we shall see, rejects democracy in that sense. What he espouses is a 'mixed government',[45] as he calls it, in which the sovereign is the people and the administration is delegated to appointed magistrates. This ideal of a mixed government is consistent with the existence of an unmixed legislative sovereign, however, and should not be confused with the ideal of a mixed constitution.

Rejecting the ideal of a mixed constitution, Rousseau joins Bodin and Hobbes in arguing for a unitary, indivisible and absolute sovereign. For him, as for Hobbes, the existence of a state, as distinct from enslavement to a despot,[46] presupposes association or incorporation. This incorporation has to come about via 'unanimous consent'[47] to a primitive contract that gives the assembly of the people 'its unity, its common *self*, its life and its will'.[48] The sovereign in this vision is that assembly itself, and its unitary

[41] Ibid., 18. [42] Ibid., 18.14. [43] *SC*, III.2.3. [44] Ibid., III.7.4. [45] Ibid., III.7.3.
[46] Ibid., I.5.1. [47] Ibid., IV.2.5. [48] Ibid., I.6.10.

character appears in the fact that it always operates through the voice of the majority. 'Except for this primitive contract, the vote of the majority always obligates all the rest; this is a consequence of the contract itself'.[49]

Rousseau is particularly insistent on the need for this sovereign assembly of the people to be indivisible, railing as strongly as the earlier absolutists against those who would defend the mixed constitution. He thinks that the very idea of a state presupposes a single sovereign – a single source of law – and that 'whenever one believes one sees sovereignty divided, one is mistaken'.[50] And he deploys all his rhetorical skills against theorists of the mixed constitution, prominent though they were in the republican tradition:

> they turn the Sovereign into a being that is fantastical and formed of disparate pieces; it is as if they were putting together man out of several bodies one of which had eyes, another arms, another feet, and nothing else. Japanese conjurors are said to carve up a child before the spectators' eyes, then, throwing all of its members into the air one after the other, they make the child fall back down alive all reassembled. That is more or less what our politicians' tricks are like; having dismembered the social body by a sleight-of-hand worthy of the fairground, they put the pieces back together no one knows how.[51]

Not only does Rousseau follow in the steps of Bodin and Hobbes in developing the case for a unitary, indivisible sovereign, he also follows their path when he goes on to argue that the unitary, indivisible sovereign assembly that he envisages has to enjoy absolute power: it has to be unconstrained by law, and incontestable by individual citizens.

Upholding the claim that the sovereign should be unconstrained by law, he argues that 'it is contrary to the nature of the body politic for the Sovereign to impose on itself a law which it cannot break';[52] here he is presumably assuming that no body can give a command to itself. Thus he maintains that the assembly is 'above judge and law',[53] and that there is no 'kind of fundamental law that is obligatory for the body of the people'.[54]

Upholding the claim that the sovereign should be beyond challenge from individual members, Rousseau invokes the explicitly Hobbesian thought that there is no super-sovereign, no higher judge, that might make it possible for individuals to challenge their sovereign within the terms of the social contract. He says that 'if individuals were left some rights' – presumably, rights of contestation – 'there would be no common superior who might adjudicate between them and the public';[55] 'where interested private individuals are one of the parties, and the public the other', he maintains, 'I do not see what law should be followed or what judge should pronounce judgment'.[56] Thus, 'each, being judge in his own

[49] Ibid., IV.2.7. [50] Ibid., II.2.4. [51] Rousseau, *SC*, 58; *OC* III, 369–370.
[52] Ibid., I.7.2. [53] Ibid., II.5.7. [54] Ibid., I.7.2. [55] Ibid., I.6.7. [56] Ibid., II.4.6.

case on some issue, would soon claim to be so on all', and 'the state of nature would subsist' or obtain.[57] The lesson is that since there is no further judge of a dispute under the social contract, it can make sense for an individual or individuals to contest the sovereign's claims. However, if they were to insist on contestation, they would be retreating to a state of nature, denying the sovereign its proper role.

We saw earlier that Rousseau remains faithful to the republican tradition in taking freedom as non-domination to be the supreme ideal in politics: the end, as he puts it, of every system of legislation. But we now see that this fidelity to republican ideals went hand in hand with a rejection of the institutions of the mixed constitution that, in some version, almost all republicans espoused. This gives its distinctive character to Rousseau's republicanism but it also creates a difficulty for republican doctrine. In the remaining sections of this chapter I distinguish between two distinct problems of freedom that Rousseau's scheme requires him to address, and then I argue that they give rise to a problematic dilemma that he lacks the resources to resolve.

## 3 The first problem for freedom and Rousseau's response

In Rousseau's vision of social and political order, each of us is subject to the mastery of an unconstrained, incontestable sovereign. And so the first issue that he confronts, as he looks at this order from the point of view of freedom, is how it can be consistent with thinking that people remain free. 'Man is born fee, and everywhere he is in chains', he remarks in the beginning of the first chapter of the *Social Contract.* And then he poses two questions, one historical and unanswerable, the other normative and, as he thinks, quite tractable. 'How did this change come about? I do not know. What can make it legitimate? I believe I can solve this question'.[58]

The task Rousseau confronts in addressing the normative question of legitimacy is to explain how social order could appear without compromising the freedom of those who live under that order. He has to find 'a form of association' that would make it possible that 'each, united with all, nevertheless obey only himself and remain as free as before'.[59] 'This is the fundamental problem', he says, and he immediately adds that 'the social contract provides the solution'.

His image of the social contract is developed on lines that Hobbes had already explored. Prior to publishing *Leviathan* in 1651, Hobbes generally suggested that when a state forms by explicit agreement or institution, a democracy will form in the first stage, and then in the second one of two

[57] Ibid., I.6.7. [58] Ibid., I.1.1. [59] Ibid., I.6.5.

things will happen: either democracy will be upheld, with the assembled people retaining the role of sovereign; or that democratic sovereign will cede its sovereignty, giving itself over to the rule of an aristocratic body or a monarch.[60] Rousseau probably did not know *Leviathan*, since it had not been translated in his time, and his vision of the social contract starts from the earlier suggestion.

He assumes, as the early Hobbes had assumed, that all must come together in what Hobbes would have called a democratic assembly in order to form a society. And what they do in coming together is to consent unanimously to follow the outcome of majoritarian voting in making their decisions – or at least, as Rousseau maintains, their decisions about questions of general law.[61] In what way, though, does this solve the first problem of freedom? Why is it that people would not suffer a loss of freedom if society were to be formed in this manner?

The main element in Rousseau's answer is that the social contract he envisages – 'the act by which a people is a people'[62] – 'presupposes unanimity' and is 'the most voluntary act in the world'.[63] Elaborating on this last point, he says: 'every man being born free and master of himself, no one may on any pretext whatsoever subject him without his consent'. But once a society and polity is established, newborn citizens do not have any role in consenting to it. So how do they exercise consent in submitting to the local order? He suggests that a 'free State' will not 'keep an inhabitant in the country in spite of himself', and that under such a regime 'consent consists in residence: to dwell in the territory is to submit to the sovereignty'.[64] This raises a problem, of course, when an inhabitant cannot leave a country because no other state will have him, or he does not have the resources needed to live elsewhere. But we will not dwell on that particular difficulty here.

Is the idea that the citizens of any free state each consent to the rule of majority voting enough on its own to ensure a solution for Rousseau's first and more fundamental problem? By his own lights, not quite.

Where Hobbes had envisaged the possibility of the popular or democratic sovereign transferring sovereignty to an aristocratic committee or to an individual monarch – a view associated in the *Social Contract* with Grotius[65] – Rousseau insists that the sovereignty of the assembly cannot be alienated in that manner. Thus he suggests that submission to a sovereign can preserve the liberty of an individual, and thereby solve the first problem, only if at least two conditions are fulfilled: first, as we have just seen, that the submission must be consensual or voluntary on

[60] Hobbes, *Human Nature and De Corpore Politico*, Ch. 21; *On the Citizen*, ch. 7.
[61] *SC*, IV.2.7. [62] Ibid., I.5.2. [63] Ibid., IV.2.5. [64] Ibid., IV.2.6. [65] Ibid., I.5.2.

the part of each; and second that the sovereign to which each submits in the first place – the assembly of the whole – does not give up its sovereign role to any independent agency. The idea in this second condition is presumably that if the assembly were to give up its sovereign role, then the consent of the individual members to being ruled by the assembly would be worth nothing: they consented to be ruled by the assembly, after all, not to being ruled by any other agency.

But the second condition is not really a problem, in Rousseau's eyes, because he thinks that it is not only impermissible, but also implausible, that the assembly should ever transfer its sovereign powers to another body or to an individual. He argues that for any agent or agency 'it is absurd for the will to shackle itself for the future', tying itself to what someone else 'is going to will tomorrow'; this, he says, would be to deny its own nature as a will.[66] And that premise leads him to an essentially anti-Hobbesian conclusion. 'If, then, the people promises simply to obey, it dissolves itself by this very act, it loses its quality of being a people'.[67] No individual man could give himself to another in this way and still be regarded as being of sound mind. By extension, neither could a whole, incorporated people:

> To say a man gives himself gratuitously is to say something absurd and inconceivable; such an act is illegitimate and null, for the simple reason that whoever does so is not in his right mind. To say the same of a whole people is to assume a people of madmen; madness does not make right.[68]

The two conditions that make submission to the assembly of the whole legitimate have to bear a lot of weight in Rousseau's theory, given that the assembly enjoys absolute power. It is unconstrained by law and incontestable by citizens, thus involving 'the total alienation of each associate with all of his rights to the whole community'.[69] Where Bodin and Hobbes did not have problems with this absolutist vision of the state, however, Rousseau's commitment to republican freedom leads him to try to sugar the pill.[70]

He points out that 'each, by giving himself to all, gives himself to no one',[71] emphasizing that the social contract does not involve accepting dependence on any other particular agent. And then he adds that the social contract has two distinct benefits, 'since there is no associate over

[66] Ibid., II.1.3. [67] Ibid., II.1.3; see also I.7.3. [68] Ibid., I.4.4. [69] Ibid., I.6.6.

[70] It is worth noting, however, that Hobbes (*Leviathan*, 14.29) limits the extent to which individuals can commit themselves to the sovereign, arguing that no one can give up the right to seek self-preservation. Rousseau may be more extremely absolutist on this matter. Thus he writes that under the social contract a citizen's 'life is no longer a bounty of nature, but a conditional gift of the State' (*SC*, II.5.4).

[71] *SC*, I.6.8.

whom one does not require the same right as one grants him over oneself'.[72] The first benefit is that 'one gains the equivalent of all one loses': if others can affect you in their voting as members of the assembly, so you can affect them in that same way. And the second is that one thereby gains 'more force to preserve what one has'.[73] The idea here is that the sovereign body you form with others can give you a status that you could not have given yourself. To return to earlier themes, it can establish your possessions – or at least those that pass muster under the laws – as your property and, more generally, it can transform your natural liberty into liberty of a civil kind.

## 4 The second problem of freedom and Rousseau's response

This attempt to soften the message, however, raises a second problem of freedom for Rousseau. The suggestion is that the social contract offers a good deal in promising to replace natural liberty by civil liberty. But that promise will be discharged only if the sovereign assembly that is established by common consent – and that therefore avoids the first problem of freedom – actually turns out to operate in a distinctively benign manner. The assembly must operate in such a way that 'the characteristics of the general will are still in the majority'.[74] Specifically, it must not allow a particular faction, large or small, to gain control and to use voting as a way of imposing its will on other citizens. Should a faction of this kind gain control, it would no longer be the case that the assembly represented the community as a whole, with each citizen having an equal role and an equal stake in its operations. It would become an arena where some individuals or subgroups lorded it over others.

The second problem of freedom is posed nicely by Rousseau when he asks: 'how can a man be both free and forced to conform to wills which are not his own'.[75] His view, of course, is that there is no problem here if civil freedom is really established for all – a freedom, as we saw, that requires equality – and people are each protected in the same way by the sovereign whole. In that vision of the good society, the idea is that 'every Citizen be perfectly independent of all the others' – that is, enjoy private freedom as non-domination in relation to them – 'and excessively dependent on the City': that is, dependent on the protective, sovereign assembly, and only on that assembly, for protection against others.[76] Traditional republicans would have shied away from the idea that each should be dependent on the goodwill of a single assembly, however comprehensive; that would have

[72] Ibid. [73] Ibid. [74] Ibid., IV.2.9. [75] Ibid., IV.2.7. [76] Ibid., II.12.3.

seemed to guarantee public domination. But Rousseau thinks that this dependence will be innocuous; indeed, that it will do nothing but good for the freedom of individual citizens, so long as it is truly the general will – the will of an un-factionalized, egalitarian assembly – that shapes the law.

Being the will of an un-factionalized assembly, the general will may be expected to track the common interest of citizens, not the interests of this or that individual or subgroup: 'it is concerned with their common preservation, and the general welfare'.[77] Or at least it may be expected to track the common interest so long as there is a legal adviser – unhappily named a 'lawgiver' – to keep the people from falling into error.[78] The general will is essentially the will of the un-factionalized assembly, then, and while it is bound to aim at identifying the common interest, it may sometimes go astray for lack of full information or understanding. Note that according to Rousseau it would make no sense for the citizens to allow someone like the lawgiver to rule over them, since this would be to alienate their sovereignty: 'the people cannot divest itself of this non-transferable right, even if it wanted to do so'.[79] But it would certainly make good sense, he thinks, for them to follow the advice of such a presumptively enlightened counsellor.

The second problem of freedom is that while the general will would establish people in equal enjoyment of their civil freedom, there is no guarantee that majority voting will preserve 'the characteristics of the general will', even in the presence of a lawgiver.[80] The problem is that it is always possible for an assembly of citizens to become factionalized and always possible, therefore, that 'there is no longer any freedom'. People may get over the first problem of freedom by contracting unanimously into forming a society and polity, thereby subordinating themselves to a sovereign assembly. But they may still confront the second problem. They may find that the sovereign assembly that was established without compromising freedom actually operates in a way that fails to deliver the civil freedom that it promised: the sort of freedom that was supposed to compensate for the loss of natural freedom.

The task that Rousseau confronts in facing this second problem is to identify institutions that can ensure that 'the general will is always upright and always tends to the public utility'.[81] He looks for devices, in his own words, that would reduce 'the considerable difference between the will of all' – 'the sum of particular wills' – 'and the general will'.[82] Happily, he thinks that there are 'practicable ways' to achieve this,[83] and he identifies two in particular.

[77] Ibid., IV.1.1. [78] Ibid., II.7. [79] Ibid., II.7.7. [80] Ibid., IV.2.9. [81] Ibid., II.3.1.
[82] Ibid., II.3.2. [83] Ibid., IV.2.10.

In order to avoid faction, to take the first of these devices, it is necessary that in casting his vote, each member of the assembly 'states his own opinion'[84] of what is 'advantageous to the state';[85] he votes according to his perception of the common interest, in other words, not of the interest of his own self or faction. In maintaining that this is essential for the avoidance of faction, Rousseau is claiming in effect that there can be no freedom in a polity, even a polity that is ruled by a plenary assembly of citizens, unless there is a high measure of civic virtue among the citizenry. He rejects the principle adopted by his contemporary David Hume, who had maintained that in 'fixing the several checks and controls of the constitution, every man ought to be supposed a knave, and to have no other end in all his actions than private interest'.[86] In supporting that principle Hume was closer to traditional republicans than Rousseau himself.

Turning to the second of our devices, Rousseau argues in addition that in order to make it likely that citizens will be insulated from the effect of selfish or factional interest, they should be allowed only to consider 'subjects in a body and their actions in the abstract, never any man as an individual or a particular action'.[87] He requires, in other words, that the members of the assembly should only make general laws, and outsource issues of particular policy – that is, issues in which their own interests are likely to be implicated – to appointed magistrates. This means requiring that the republic should have a 'mixed government' (as distinct from a mixed constitution) and not be a democracy in the sense that he, following Bodin and Hobbes, gave to that term. It should not be a body that takes charge of all public decisions, whether of a general or particular nature.

## 5 The dilemma that Rousseau faces

With Rousseau's responses to the two problems of freedom in place, we can readily identify the dilemma opened up by his theory. Put aside the possibility that the sovereign assembly that rules in a community is in error about the common interest; let fallibility not be an issue. The question that his two responses raise is whether people are entitled to reject subordination to their sovereign assembly, if they judge that the assembly is factionalized and that it no longer identifies or implements the general will. Rousseau's answer to this question must be a 'yes' or a 'no', but neither answer is appealing.

[84] Ibid., II.3.4. [85] Ibid., IV.1.6.
[86] David Hume, 'Of the Independence of Parliament', in *Hume's Philosophical Works*, III, ed. T. H. Green and T. H. Grose (London: Longmans, Green and Co., 1875), 117–118.
[87] *SC*, II.6.6.

Suppose that he answers 'yes', arguing that individuals are entitled in the scenario imagined to exit the social contract and to withdraw their consent to community rule. This answer is going to be highly problematic, because it would make political stability unattainable. According to the approach suggested, citizens would each be entitled to withdraw from their community, rejecting the legitimacy of its laws, as soon as they were persuaded, rightly or wrongly, that the assembly is serving the interest of a faction rather than the interest of the whole. This would be a recipe for chaos, since it is a permanent possibility in any society, however perfect the regime, that people will be persuaded that the assembly has been taken over by factional interests.

Suppose, however, that Rousseau answers 'no' to the question raised, arguing that individuals are not entitled to exit the social contract just because they happen to think that the assembly has become factionalized. This answer is even more unappealing, because it suggests that his philosophy may have to condone the coercive subordination of some citizens to a form of rule in which others are really the masters, and not the community taken as a whole. While the first answer would open up the prospect of licensing anarchy, this second answer would hold out the spectre of permitting despotism.

Rousseau does not ever confront the question raised, and it is worth considering where his principles would be likely to lead him. Given that he thinks that 'there is no longer any freedom' in a factionalized assembly,[88] it may well seem that he would have to accept the first answer. He acknowledges, as he says in another context, that there is 'a great difference between subjugating a multitude and ruling a society'.[89] And, adopting this response, he would cast the factionalized assembly as an example of subjugation rather than rule.

But it is hard to believe that Rousseau would take this line. When he talks of the subjugation of a multitude, he has in mind a situation in which 'scattered men, regardless of their number, are successively enslaved to a single man', so that it involves 'a master and slaves' rather than 'a people and its chief'.[90] But in the situation he has in mind, things are very different from how they would be under a factionalized assembly. In this situation, the master 'remains nothing but a private individual', because there has not yet been any social contract: individuals have not yet come together to perform 'the act by which a people is a people'.[91] In the case of the factionalized assembly, the social contract has already occurred, so that we have a people in existence and a body that plays the role of sovereign. Thus Rousseau's remarks about mere subjugation do

[88] Ibid., IV.2.9. [89] Ibid., I.5.1. [90] Ibid., I.5.1. [91] Ibid., I.5.2.

not argue that citizens who believe their assembly is factionalized are entitled to withdraw from the social contract.

But not only does Rousseau lack good reason of this kind for adopting the first answer to our question, thereby accepting the prospect of anarchy, he also seems to have good reason for going along with the second answer and acquiescing in the prospect that, without ceasing to have claims on its citizens, a regime might degenerate into a form of rule, bordering on despotism, in which 'there is no longer any freedom'. He argues that the sovereign assembly is unlikely to require an individual to surrender much of 'his power, his goods, his freedom', on the grounds that this is important for the community. But he observes, crucially, that 'the Sovereign is alone judge of that importance', thereby implying that citizens have no right to contest the sovereign's judgement.[92] This observation reminds us of the principle that, in the absence of a possible judge – a super-sovereign – the sovereign is incontestable by citizens. And it strongly suggests that even if individuals believe that their sovereign assembly has become factionalized, still they are required to submit to its judgements.

If this is right, then Kant may not have broken dramatically with the spirit of Rousseau's republicanism in arguing that no matter how badly it behaves, an existing sovereign cannot be legitimately challenged: citizens may retain 'the freedom of the pen' but they are 'not permitted any resistance'.[93] Indeed, Kant seems to base that position on the very incontestability principle – Hobbesian in origin – that Rousseau defends, suggesting that contestability would presuppose a super-sovereign to judge between the contesting citizen and the contested ruler. He alleges that a constitution would be in contradiction with itself – it would both attribute and deny sovereignty to the ruler – if it allowed contestation. In words that Hobbes or Rousseau might also have used, he maintains that 'the contradiction is obvious as soon as one asks who is to be judge in this dispute between people and sovereign'.[94]

## Conclusion

Insofar as a society is set up by a social contract, it counts for Rousseau as legitimate; and insofar as it operates on the basis of the general will it

[92] Ibid., II.4.3.

[93] Immanuel Kant, *Practical Philosophy*, ed. M. J. Gregor (Cambridge: Cambridge University Press, 1996), 302, 298.

[94] Kant, *Practical Philosophy*, 463; see also 299. Kant sounds an equally familiar sort of note – although he is uncharacteristically sloppy in talking of a contract between people and sovereign – when he writes: 'Even if an actual contract of the people with the ruler has been violated, the people cannot react at once *as a commonwealth* but only as a mob' (ibid., 300, footnote).

counts, we might say, as just. The question we have raised for him is whether a duly constituted society that ceases to be just, according to the perceptions of some citizens, ceases to count for them as legitimate and ceases to have claims on their allegiance. If the answer is affirmative then there is no prospect of political stability: a society can only be as secure as the opinions of its citizenry as to whether factionalism is absent. If it is negative, then there is a real prospect of political injustice: a regime in which some individuals have no choice but to accept the rule of an incontestable assembly, even when they see it as neglecting the common interest and imposing an unjust rule.[95]

It is this spectre of incontestable injustice that really threatens the Rousseauvian vision, for there is no ground on which he can allow individuals to challenge the judgements of their sovereign. And we should note in conclusion that this is the point at which the divide between that vision and more traditional republican doctrine is at its deepest, for in the traditional view citizens are not restricted to their role as lawmakers in an assembly, or as electors to that assembly. On the contrary, this view suggests that even when a regime counts as legitimate, still it is perfectly appropriate for the citizenry to challenge the decisions of the authorities, if not to try to undermine or overthrow the regime.

Rousseau seems to entrench the position of citizens in relation to their state when he insists that they each have to be part of the law-making body, deliberating about what is best for their society and voting in accordance with that judgement.[96] But the *Social Contract* actually weakens the position of individual potentially dissenting citizens in their dealings with government. They are required to go along with the majoritarian assembly and to rest content with having had a vote, albeit a losing vote, on any issue where they think that the decisions of that assembly were the product of an inimical faction. Indeed, they may not even have that consolation available, for they may not be able to get the assembly to vote on laws that they find objectionable: whether there is to be a vote on any issue will presumably depend also on the majority view.

As I understand the older tradition that Rousseau sought to revise, a regime will count as legitimate insofar as its decisions are subject to the equal control of the citizenry in sufficient measure to allow them to pass the eyeball test in relation to government. In this way of thinking we do not look to see if the society is based on past or continuing consent in order to determine whether it is legitimate; we look for whether it is controlled by

[95] On earlier discussions of an absolutist bent in Rousseau's thought, see Christopher Brooke's contribution to this volume (Chapter 8).
[96] Cohen, *Rousseau: A Free Community*.

the citizenry in sufficient measure, and with sufficient equality, to enable them each to look the authorities in the eye without reason for fear or deference. Legitimacy in that sense is consistent, of course, with many public decisions serving sectional rather than common interests, even when those decisions are made by duly elected representatives or citizens as a whole. But the legitimacy of the regime does not require citizens to accept presumptively unjust decisions quietly, treating the legislature and government as an absolute sovereign. It allows them to contest the decisions actively, exercising a right and power that is given to them under the mixed constitution. Indeed, it requires popular contestation to be systematically available and potentially effective, for that is needed to help ensure that the citizenry have a suitable form of control over government. The legitimacy of the regime rules out only extra-constitutional resistance. It requires dissident citizens to operate within the channels of complaint and protest that a mixed constitution would give them, where those channels extend in contemporary terms to include civil disobedience.[97]

The vision of an imperfect republican society that the tradition projects is very different, then, from Rousseau's. He has to envisage a society in which the disaffected submit more or less passively to their assembly's judgements, being restricted to expressing minority views and to casting minority votes within that body. In the traditional republican image, by contrast, even a legitimate regime is likely to be a site of widespread contestation and discord. This is the society imagined by Machiavelli (1965) in the sixteenth century, as he envisages a world like republican Rome in which it is the tumult and challenge of a riotous plebs that keeps the prospect of freedom alive.[98] It is the society that Adam Ferguson presupposes in eighteenth-century Britain when he argues that freedom can only continue to be secured if it is supported by 'the refractory and turbulent zeal of this fortunate people'.[99] It is a society where, in the words of his Irish contemporary John Philpot Curran, people are prepared to impose on government the eternal vigilance – the sustained invigilation – that is the price of freedom.

[97] Pettit, *On the People's Terms* and *Just Freedom*.

[98] Niccolò Machiavelli, *The Chief Works and Others* (Durham, NC: Duke University Press, 1965).

[99] Adam Ferguson, *An Essay on the History of Civil Society*, reprint of the 1767 Edinburgh edition (New York: Garland, 1971), 167.

# 11 The depths of recognition

## The legacy of Jean-Jacques Rousseau

*Axel Honneth*

In 1932, when Ernst Cassirer published his long essay *The Question of Jean-Jacques Rousseau*, he must have been certain that he had finally found the key to an integral understanding of the philosopher's fissured work.[1] Today, however, some eighty-five years later, Cassirer's suggestion is almost forgotten; scholars continue to puzzle over where, if at all, unity can be sought in the seemingly contradictory writings of the great thinker. No other modern philosophical author, with the exception of Nietzsche perhaps, has elicited more starkly opposed interpretations of his work; no other author has therefore remained so constantly the eternally young, always provocative and disturbing contemporary. Depending on the reader's attitude and the contemporary historical context, one could discover in Rousseau the anthropologist invoking a model of human nature, a theorist who stresses feeling and emotion like the English moral philosophers, or a progenitor of democratic self-determination who paved the way for Kant. When the times called for different philosophical emphases, one could also find in Rousseau the pioneer of a totalitarian conception of democracy, the fervent defender of republican equality, or the advocate of an ideal of personal authenticity. As heterogeneous as they might appear, all these interpretations of Rousseau have had to struggle with the same great problem of being able to refer only to some parts of his work while sweeping other, contradicting parts under the rug. Only a few have succeeded like Ernst Cassirer in suggesting a reading that could interpret the philosopher's disparate writings and thoughts as stages in the realization of a single basic idea.

Cassirer saw this convergence point of Rousseau's work in the idea of the human will's capacity for self-determination in spite of all social and political hazards.[2] And yet Cassirer's interpretation soon faced many

I am grateful to Barbara Carnevali for her suggestions and critical questions. This chapter was translated by Mitch Cohen and revised by Avi Lifschitz.

[1] Ernst Cassirer, *The Question of Jean-Jacques Rousseau*, trans. Peter Gay (New York: Columbia University Press, 1954).

[2] Ibid., 104–128.

emphatic challenges from ongoing research. Not only did such a reading, making Rousseau the direct precursor of Kant, seem to place too little emphasis on the collectivist tinge in Rousseau's *Social Contract*, it also seemed to ignore what can be read in Rousseau's other writings on the mutual dependence of subjects, indeed on their being at the mercy of each other.[3] This element of his work, rooted in the notion of *amour propre* or self-love (which is constitutive both for Rousseau's *Discourse on Inequality*[4] and his *Emile*),[5] came increasingly to the fore in more recent interpretations. This, however, did not offer a key to the underlying idea of the whole of Rousseau's work as long as it remained unclear how Rousseau's pessimistic diagnosis of the ever-increasing dependence of the modern subject on the esteem of others could be brought together with the more confident lines of thought developed in the *Social Contract*.[6] After all, where the notion of *amour propre* was the theme in the early writings, it was only in the context of the danger of the complete external control of the subject. However, in the *Social Contract* – the constructive part of Rousseau's work – the same subjects are suddenly conceived as having an irreducible capacity for self-legislation. The breakthrough to a connection between these two elements and thus to an integral interpretation of Rousseau's *oeuvre* did not emerge in the research literature until the concept of *amour propre* was fanned out to include a positive variant as well as the negative. With this suggestion, which we probably owe to the ground-breaking study of N. J. H. Dent,[7] it became possible to conceive of Rousseau's idea of the constitutive dependence of the subject on the other as the fundamental hinge between the two parts of his work by spelling out the negative form of the notion of *amour propre* in his cultural critique and the positive version in drafts of the *Social Contract*.

However, Dent's reinterpretation probably achieved more than he himself originally intended. Giving only a little twist to his interpretation, it was easy to develop from it the thesis that, with his bipolar notion of *amour propre*, Rousseau had become the founder of the whole tradition of recognition theory. The step towards this thesis – which is of downright subversive significance in the history of ideas – was probably first taken by

[3] Elements of such a critique of Cassirer, with a particular view to the wide divergence between Rousseau's and Kant's concepts of history, can be found in George Armstrong Kelly, 'Rousseau, Kant and History', *Journal of the History of Ideas* 29.3 (1968), 347–364.

[4] Rousseau, *DI*, 111–222.

[5] Rousseau, *Emile, or On Education*, trans. Allan Bloom (New York: Basic Books, 1979).

[6] Rousseau, *SC*, 39–152.

[7] N. J. H. Dent, *Rousseau: An Introduction to His Psychological, Social, and Political Theory* (Oxford: Blackwell, 1988).

Frederick Neuhouser in a major study.[8] Neuhouser asserts that the idea that human subjects owe their social agency to the recognition granted by other subjects was not Hegel's invention, as had been assumed hitherto, but can be traced back to Rousseau. The significance of this reformulation and the degree to which it relocates Rousseau's *oeuvre* become clear only in light of its distance from Cassirer's overall reading. While for Cassirer Rousseau stands as a lone precursor to Kant because he is seen as engaging in a lifelong effort to elaborate the active, self-legislative aspect of the human will, those who follow Dent's interpretation see the unifying thread in Rousseau's work in precisely the opposite thesis – that for good or evil, the human will is dependent on the affirmation and esteem of other subjects.

In what follows I would like to elaborate on this second thesis, first showing where it is justified and then highlighting its limits. As I would argue, throughout his life Rousseau was too uncertain about the real significance of intersubjective recognition in the structure of social life to be able to clearly make this intersubjectivity the foundation of his entire theory. Specifically, the first section of the chapter addresses Rousseau's intellectual development to the point where he becomes aware of the necessity of a socially sustainable, egalitarian form of mutual recognition against the harmful forms of *amour propre*. From here it will be easy to survey the enormous influence Rousseau's bipolar conception of social recognition has had on modern philosophical discourse. In the second section I discuss how the negative aspect of this conception, that is, the human need to surpass one's fellow creatures in social esteem, is reinterpreted in Kant's writings on the philosophy of history as a driving force of human progress, and how Fichte and Hegel further develop its positive variant of mutual respect among equals in the direction of a recognition theory of law and an ethical social life. Not until the third section of the chapter will I proceed to address the scepticism that Rousseau always exhibited (increasingly towards the end of his life) towards the dependence on others inherent in *amour propre*. In his late writings, as earlier in the *Discourse on Inequality*, he plays again with the idea that it might be advantageous for people's peace of mind if they became fully independent of intersubjective recognition. In this respect, Rousseau's works exhibit

[8] Frederick Neuhouser, *Rousseau's Theodicy of Self-Love: Evil, Rationality and the Drive for Recognition* (Oxford: Oxford University Press, 2008). See also Honneth, 'Die Entgiftung Jean-Jacques Rousseaus. Neuere Literatur zum Werk des Philosophen', *Deutsche Zeitschrift für Philosophie* 4 (2012), 611–632. Independently of Neuhouser, Barbara Carnevali too has attempted to present Rousseau as a theoretician of recognition: see her *Romantisme et reconnaissance. Figures de la conscience chez Rousseau*, trans. Philippe Audegean (Geneva: Droz, 2011).

two fundamental philosophical motifs that stand in constant conflict with each other: the Stoic idea of personal independence from all external attachments and the intersubjective idea of a deep-seated dependence on others.

## I

The motif from which Rousseau initially draws his central concept of *amour propre* emerges more clearly in his early critique of theatre than anywhere else. Already in the *First Discourse*, he subjects what he derogatorily refers to as 'play-acting' to an extremely negative analysis;[9] this critique matures in his *Letter to d'Alembert*. For Rousseau, the theatre is not merely one cultural institution among others, in which an enlightened audience learns through the contemplation of or engagement with works of art. He regards the stage and the theatre hall as a special instance where the behaviour of actors can infect the audience with the virus of 'mere appearance'. In contrast to the museum or the concert hall, where the viewer might at least imagine in the presented work of art the authentic intention of the artist, Rousseau regards the theatre-going audience as initially confronted solely with a form of behaviour through which the actor wants to reveal his skill at 'putting on another character than his own'.[10] But the still-innocent audience is thereby encouraged to practise gestures and expressions that serve no other goal than disguising their true character. From such critical observations, Rousseau draws the far-reaching conclusion that the creation of theatres does great harm to any republican commonwealth because the arts of disguise presented in the theatre undermine precisely those attitudes and behaviours that are necessary for political institutions built on the will of the people – duty, honesty, and civic pride. As Rousseau puts it in the *Letter to d'Alembert*, the actor develops 'by profession the talent of deceiving men'.[11]

Admittedly, Rousseau believes that the danger of infection from the play-acting on the stage merely reinforces a cultural tendency already powerfully operative in a wide variety of places. Four years before the *Letter to d'Alembert* was published, Rousseau, in his *Discourse on Inequality*, already sought to analyze the genealogy of those new behaviours of pretentious

[9] Rousseau, 'Discourse on the Arts and the Sciences', in *DI*, 1–28; *OC* III, 1–30.

[10] Rousseau, *Politics and the Arts: Letter to M. D'Alembert on the Theatre*, trans. Allan Bloom (Ithaca: Cornell University Press, 1987), 79; *OC* V, 72–73.

[11] *Letter*, 80; *OC* V, 73. On Rousseau's critique of the theatre and its consequences for his understanding of democracy, see the excellent study by Juliane Rebentisch, *Die Kunst der Freiheit. Zur Dialektik demokratischer Existenz* (Frankfurt am Main: Suhrkamp, 2011), ch. 5.

disguise and the craving for social esteem he experienced so intensively in Parisian society. In searching for the anthropological roots of the individual affectation with prestige that the theatre merely intensifies, he found in his *Discourse* a specific form of the human relation to the self. While he did not regard it as being of natural origin, its cultural proliferation still seemed to establish it as a kind of second nature. Rousseau named this form of behaviour *amour propre*. This concept not only forms the basis of his entire critique of society; it is also the key to understanding what he will contribute to the development of a theory of intersubjective recognition.

In the genealogical logic of the *Discourse on Inequality, amour propre* does not play as prominent a role as its importance for the overall design of that study actually demands. Certainly, Rousseau uses the term now and then when identifying the causes underlying the emergence of social inequality,[12] but he restricts his attempt to clarify its meaning to a single long note whose weight, however, can hardly be overestimated. Here, in note XV of the text, Rousseau outlines the significance of *amour propre* in contrast to *amour de soi-même*, drawing distinctions between the two on the basis of the standard of evaluation that each presupposes.[13] For Rousseau, *amour de soi* is a natural human disposition – a form of self-interestedness that contributes to human self-preservation by letting each human being rely solely on his own individual, vital criteria of the right and the good. In the later and thus somewhat artificial phenomenon of *amour propre*, by contrast, the normative standard of self-interestedness shifts to take the opinion of others as the yardstick of opportune behaviour. Rousseau explains this difference most trenchantly in a remark where he takes from Hume's moral theory the formulation already prefiguring Adam Smith's notion of the impartial spectator: in the feeling or striving of *amour de soi* the subject is the sole spectator of himself, whereas in *amour propre* the subject regards others as judges of his actions and omissions.[14]

If the differences between the two kinds of self-interest are explicated in this way, it initially remains completely unclear why the second attitude, that of *amour propre*, should be at all tied to a tendency toward the negative or problematical. On the contrary, from Adam Smith's perspective, it could be said that, in terms of consideration and appropriateness, orienting one's actions toward the internalized judgment of initially merely external others is far superior to an act that is purely self-referential.[15]

[12] *DI*, 152, 153, 167, 174, *OC* III, 154, 156, 171, 174. [13] *DI*, 218; *OC* III, 219–220.

[14] *DI*, 218; *OC* III, 219.

[15] Cf. Adam Smith, *Theory of Moral Sentiments* (1759), ed. D.D. Raphael and A.L. Macfie (Indianapolis: Liberty Fund, 1984), 110: 'We endeavour to examine our own conduct as we imagine any other fair and impartial spectator would examine it. If, upon placing

But in his commentary, Rousseau focuses on a different aspect of this intersubjectively mediated self-assessment that no longer seems compatible with the wholesome effects of Smith's impartial spectator as described in the *Theory of Moral Sentiments*. For Rousseau, the other who has become the judge of one's actions is not an instance for correcting one's own judgment, not a power fostering cognitive and moral decentralization, but rather a source of constant urging to prove oneself superior to one's fellow citizens. What the *amour propre* of the *Discourse on Inequality* becomes, then, is a form of self-interestedness that transforms into a spur to social esteem, thereby making the activity needed for self-preservation dependent on assessment by others.

Yet even upon closer observation, it is not at all easy to accurately identify where Rousseau's account of the status of the internalized spectator deviates from the description Smith provided only a few years later. This difficulty arises because both authors initially aim at a similar assertion, that the socialized human being usually judges the appropriateness of his actions in terms of a presumed evaluation by a generalized spectator. However, one difference in their readings, serious in its consequences, consists in Rousseau's expansion of this bilateral relationship between the subject and his internalized spectator by adding another, second kind of relationship. This relationship emerges because real, empirical others observe the subject in his attempt to orient his actions toward his intersubjective judge. According to Rousseau, when a subject is confronted with these two perspectives, he is driven to present his action to his internal observer in such a way that it seems superior or nobler than those of the other persons present. Thus, *amour propre*, in contrast to self-assessment by imagining the perspective of an impartial spectator, is the expression of a tripartite set of relations of the socialized human being: once the individual has learned, as an effect of ever denser social interactions, to orient his behaviour toward the judgments of generalized others, he will strive to present himself as favourably as possible in relation to these judgments so that he can expect also to be positively evaluated by those contemporaries. For Rousseau, as he repeatedly notes, what is perfidious about this dependence on others' judgment is not the mere fact that someone pretends to have properties that he does not believe he has; what is disastrous here is that *amour propre* permits individuals to deceive themselves, because they must not only be able to present themselves externally to their fellows, but also to their internal

ourselves in his situation, we thoroughly enter into all the passions and motives which influenced it, we approve of it, by sympathy with the approbation of this supposed equitable judge.'

judge, as persons with the best possible attributes. What an individual driven by *amour propre* desires is not just social affirmation, but self-affirmation – that is, a consciousness of his own worth.[16]

All the social pathologies that Rousseau discusses in the *Discourse on Inequality* have their roots, he argues, in the craving for social esteem arising from *amour propre*. In bourgeois society, people are restlessly at work developing the attributes that might make them appear superior to their contemporaries in the eyes of their internalized spectator. Once set in motion, this 'petulant activity of our *amour propre*' knows no limit;[17] it exhausts every distinguishing trait due to its merely relative character, thus forcing the subject to make new efforts to plausibly demonstrate his superiority. And, as a result of its social spread, every quality of wealth or power or beauty that was the sign of individual superiority yesterday must be trumped today, so that every field of status competition is dominated by a tendency to spiral ever higher in the search for distinction.[18] As we have seen, in this cultural process the theatre merely assumes the role of an institution that intensifies sophistication. The reason Rousseau despises the theatre so much is that here citizens so convincingly learn to feign behaviours associated with status, that eventually they themselves believe in the authenticity of such performances.

Already in *Emile* – which Rousseau began drafting only a few years after publishing the *Discourse on Inequality* – it is obvious that Rousseau is not content with this merely critical diagnosis of *amour propre*. Here the same term appears repeatedly again, but without the same automatic and immediate derogation that was apparent in the context of the earlier cultural critique. If in addition to *Emile* we consider the *Social Contract*, which he was writing at about the same time and which does not speak directly of *amour propre* but does speak of related attitudes, we can make out a trajectory in Rousseau's thinking that reveals a growing effort to differentiate its guiding concept. Dissatisfied with his inability to find a way out of the pathologies of bourgeois society, from the early 1760s onward the philosopher wrestles with the possibility of asserting a beneficial, socially acceptable form of *amour propre*. But it is not easy for Rousseau to shift from a wholly negative presentation of *amour propre* to an account that suddenly sheds a favourable light on this concept. Necessary for such an achievement would be an account of the conditions under which the intersubjectively mediated self-assessment could escape the need to present oneself as superior to one's fellows. *Emile* has a number of formulations that clearly show how Rousseau first struggles

[16] Cf. Neuhouser, *Rousseau's Theodicy*, 34. [17] Rousseau, *DI*, 167; *OC* III, 171.
[18] Cf. Neuhouser, *Rousseau's Theodicy*, 76.

with the difficult task of pinning down such conditions. In every instance where he begins to speak of the unavoidable development of *amour propre* in his tutee, he investigates at the same time (as if in an experimental setup) what measures could prevent the danger of the ensuing striving for prestige.[19]

The solution Rousseau finally offers to this problem is a suggestion that at first glance seems rather puzzling: 'Let us extend *amour-propre* to other beings. We shall transform it into a virtue, and there is no man's heart in which this virtue does not have its root.'[20] This formulation makes sense when one realizes that an extension of *amour propre* would mean seeing every other person orienting his own activity in the same way towards the judgment of a generalized observer. If such a change of perspective is carried out, Rousseau seems to say, we recognize all fellow subjects struggling in the same way for the approval of their internal judge; and then the drive to outdo them in reputation and status must vanish. This reasoning can be understood more clearly if, instead of an inner judge, we regarded subjects as equally depending on a generalized approval from the surrounding society. To speak of the extension of *amour propre* is, then, nothing other than suggesting to the subjects the insight that they reciprocally need each other's recognition and should thus forgo a competitive striving for higher reputation. Rousseau tries to prevent the poisoning of his pupil's *amour propre* by trying, given the need for social recognition that all human beings share, to teach him to be satisfied with social prestige that expresses precisely this mutual dependence. Respect among equals is the formula that expresses a form of social recognition tempered in this way, and that seems to reproduce adequately Rousseau's suggested solution.[21]

Summarizing this way the educational therapy of *amour propre* in *Emile* enables us, for the first time, to make sense of why Rousseau can appear today as a theorist of recognition. From its first introduction in the *Discourse on Inequality*, the concept of *amour propre* apparently meant more than mere human passion to prove oneself superior to others and to struggle for ever higher levels of social esteem. Beneath such forms of striving as a driving force lies the human desire to count as someone in the eyes of members of society in general and to enjoy a kind of social

[19] Rousseau, *Emile* in *OC* IV, 444–445, 453–454, 522–542.

[20] Rousseau, *Emile* (trans. Bloom), 252; *OC* IV, 547.

[21] In relation to this 'egalitarian form' of *amour propre*, and following the pioneering study by Dent, see Joshua Cohen, *Rousseau: A Free Community of Equals* (Oxford: Oxford University Press, 2010), 101–104. Cf. Neuhouser, *Rousseau's Theodicy*, 57–70 (including a critique of Cohen's views) and Avi Lifschitz's contribution in the present book (Chapter 2).

value. Before *amour propre* becomes the desire for prestige and special esteem, it therefore has the innocent form that it would assume in Adam Smith's internal spectator.[22] Its essence is to let us be dependent in our self-esteem and self-image on social recognition from the society around us. For Rousseau, this dependence on the generalized other acquires the negative form of a compulsive drive to compare oneself and feel superior to others only when we neglect the accompanying awareness that we all share the same basic need for social approval and affirmation. In such a case we lose sight of the fact that, together with all other members of society, we are part of that court of an inner judge from which we expect approval of our behaviour. Thus it is only logical that, in his writings on education, Rousseau advises teachers to employ pedagogical measures that convey a sense of social equality to pupils from an early age. For only when an individual learns to understand himself as an equal among equals can he also grasp himself as a contributor to the generalized other, upon whose verdict the satisfaction of his own *amour propre* depends.

This last formulation is manifestly chosen in anticipation of Rousseau's design to solve the problem of *amour propre* in his *Social Contract*. In *Emile* we already find the thought that respect for and from one's peers satisfies the fundamental desire for social recognition, but not yet the much farther-reaching idea that this enables the individual subject to understand himself as the co-author of judgments on which his understanding of himself will thereafter depend. With the concept of the general will, with which Rousseau crowns his *Social Contract*, he clearly hoped to outline such an idea of a standard of judgment for social recognition, a standard created by those subject to it. The self-esteem of citizens in a republic is thus no longer subject to an external instance of the generalized other, because in a previous spontaneous act of consultation they have agreed on a common will – in whose light they now can recognize each other in a way that they collectively hold to be right.[23] Rousseau seems to think that in such a society all those uncontrollable standards of individual worth, forced upon each person and hitherto responsible for the corrupt influence of *amour propre*, will have vanished. Instead, only self-imposed and transparent sources of social recognition will remain.

[22] On the notion of recognition in Adam Smith, see Christel Fricke and Hans-Peter Schütt (eds.), *Adam Smith als Moralphilosoph* (Berlin: De Gruyter, 2008), esp. the contributions by Stephen Darwall and Robert C. Solomon (178–189; 251–276).

[23] The normative limitations imposed by Rousseau on the general will can also be understood from this perspective as attempts, through the elimination of fundamental power asymmetries in society, to deny an individual the acquisition of high esteem at the expense of others' freedom. (Cf. Neuhouser, *Rousseau's Theodicy*, 162–166.)

This would ultimately mean that the members of this society respect each other as free and equal persons.

And yet the final chapters of Rousseau's *Social Contract* also seem to imply that he was not entirely convinced that *amour propre* could be completely satisfied only through this mutual respect. His discussion of civil religion and republican patriotism seems to imply that the individual strives for a stronger sense of self-worth than recognition as a free and equal citizen can provide.[24] In *amour propre* – the need for other members of society to see one as worthy – excessive claims burgeon that are hard to satisfy, even when egalitarianism reigns. Therefore, Rousseau apparently seeks additional resources of social recognition even in a republican community.[25] These other sources must not provide a basis for the easily inflamed version of the craving for recognition; hence they must be sufficiently generalizable in society, but they should also permit individuals to enjoy special esteem for virtuous action. Democratic patriotism, civil religion, and indeed all forms of constitutional patriotism are, for Rousseau, sources of social recognition that supplement the general will. Like other well-known representatives of the republican tradition – for example, Montesquieu and Tocqueville, to name just two – Rousseau believes that even democratic societies always face the ceaseless task of establishing sufficient scope for the satisfaction of the individual's desire for reputation and esteem.[26] But before discussing this further complication of Rousseau's theory of recognition, I would like to briefly outline the enormous impact his thematization of *amour propre* had on subsequent discussions in modern philosophy, for later thinkers have independently taken up and further developed many of the aspects of Rousseau's key concept.

## II

If we look at the very different aspects of Rousseau's *amour propre* so far discussed, it should be no surprise that the most diverse conclusions were drawn from it in the subsequent philosophical discussion. Depending on

[24] Besides a few loci in *Emile*, which Neuhouser mentions (*Rousseau's Theodicy*, 67), the main reference here is the chapter on civil religion in the *Social Contract*, extolling the advantages of a state that fosters 'the ardent love of glory and of fatherland' (*SC*, IV.8; *OC* III, 466).

[25] Neuhouser, *Rousseau's Theodicy*, 166–171.

[26] See Sharon R. Krause's study on Montesquieu and Tocqueville, *Liberalism with Honor* (Cambridge, MA: Harvard University Press, 2002). Unfortunately, Rousseau's works receive hardly any attention in this excellent study, for it is committed from the outset to a one-dimensional reading of *amour propre* (p. 60). On the problematic role of Rousseau within the republican tradition, see Philip Pettit's contribution in the present volume (Chapter 10).

whether one based one's reading upon the negative pole of pure craving for recognition or the positive pole of egalitarian mutual recognition, the notion could support diagnoses with diametrically opposed interests. The great host of Rousseau's successors certainly subscribed to the political programme of the *Social Contract* without seeing, however, that the latter resulted from a complicated reinterpretation of the initially negatively employed notion of *amour propre*. Other successors of the Genevan philosopher tied in exclusively with the *Discourse on Inequality*, whereby their pessimistic diagnoses of the times lacked any prospect of the therapeutic remedies developed only in Rousseau's later writings. But there were also thinkers who were intuitively aware of the whole spectrum of meanings of this notion that was so central to Rousseau's thought, and who could therefore probably envisage the internal connection in his writings – which are so difficult to read consistently. These rather rare exceptions in the history of Rousseau's reception may have included Immanuel Kant. In his work, depending on the particular philosophical interest pursued, the notion of *amour propre* appears either in its positive or in its negative meaning. The differences are already marked in his choice of terms. Whether Kant adequately comprehended the systematic connection of both aspects of the human need for recognition is less important in this context than the astonishing fact that he was familiar enough with both modes of *amour propre* to be able to employ them for his purposes in a targeted way.

Well known, of course, is how much theoretical inspiration for his moral philosophy Kant drew from Rousseau's notion that only those general laws that every individual can recognize as self-imposed may be regarded as valid. Kant even shared with his lifelong role model the ensuing consequence that such a common procedure of self-legislation leads to a relation of egalitarian recognition among those involved, summed up in the term 'respect' (*Achtung*).[27] Less well known, however, is that Kant not only takes up Rousseau's positive reinterpretation of *amour propre* but also designates a precisely determined place for the use of the originally purely negative version of *amour propre*. Beyond many references to the anthropological role of comparative self-love, which clearly bear Rousseau's conceptual stamp, an idea of the social craving for recognition is at work particularly in the drafts for his philosophy of

[27] This impact of Rousseau on Kant's early moral philosophy is clearly apparent (Manfred Kuehn, *Kant: A Biography* (Cambridge: Cambridge University Press, 2001), 131–132); yet it becomes manifestly volatile with his development of the distinction between the factual and the ideal, even if some basic insights are maintained. See Jerome B. Schneewind, *The Invention of Autonomy* (Cambridge: Cambridge University Press, 1998), 487–492.

history.[28] The inspiration for this notion can have come only from an intensive reading of the *Discourse on Inequality*. The role assigned to this exclusively negative notion of *amour propre* in Kant's philosophy of history stems from the aim Kant has for this philosophy of history within his overall work: it has to protect us from despair in the face of the solely transcendental, and hence empirically ineffective, validity of moral laws by tentatively creating a picture of human history (with the aid of the faculty of judgment). This picture contains sufficient clues of progress towards betterment so as to motivate and spur our moral efforts in spite of everything.[29] To achieve this objective, however, Kant has to endow his hypothetical draft of the course of history with at least as many clues of real moral progress as are necessary to ensure that it does not lose all credibility for his contemporaries. Precisely at this point in his philosophy of history, where the empirical plausibility of a moral progression of history is at stake, Rousseau's negative conception of *amour propre* comes into effect in a downright paradoxical way. Entirely against the intention of the *Discourse on Inequality*, Kant attempts to give the craving for recognition (which he too regards as constitutive for humankind) a twist that will explain why moral betterment will arise from this desire after all.

Due to their 'unsocial sociability', human subjects – so the train of thought goes in Kant's *Idea for a Universal History with a Cosmopolitan Purpose* – always strive to distinguish themselves by achievements for which they can find recognition within a social community. At a certain threshold in history, this vanity-motivated struggle for distinction reaches a point where the rivalling subjects retain no other potential for distinction than to attempt special achievements in the domain of moral behaviour and the ability to discriminate.[30] Thus, for Kant, what was initially just a craving for public esteem leads eventually, in the longer run of human development, also to progress in moral relationships, so that we can summon the courage for further moral improvements despite our

[28] See, in the most exemplary and striking manner, Kant's *Religion within the Boundaries of Mere Reason*, ed, Allen Wood, George di Giovanni, and Robert Merrihew Adams (Cambridge: Cambridge University Press, 1998), esp. 45–73.

[29] Honneth, 'The Irreducibility of Progress: Kant's Account of the Relationship between Morality and History', in *Pathologies of Reason: On the Legacy of Critical Theory*, trans. James Ingram (New York: Columbia University Press, 2009), 1–18. Additionally, see the groundbreaking study by Yirmiyahu Yovel, *Kant and the Philosophy of History* (Princeton: Princeton University Press, 1980), 146–151 (without reference to Rousseau but with a preliminary link to Hegel).

[30] Kant, 'Idea for a Universal History with a Cosmopolitan Purpose', in *Political Writings*, ed. Hans Reiss and H. B. Nisbet (Cambridge: Cambridge University Press, 1991), 41–53; esp. the fourth proposition (44–45). On the enduring engagement of Immanuel Kant with Rousseau's questioning of natural sociability and 'artificial' needs, see Alexander Schmidt's contribution in the present volume (Chapter 3).

empirical reservations. Quite ingeniously, Kant has thereby unified the two poles of meaning of *amour propre*, whose internal connection in Rousseau's work he may not have even realized. The positive version of the notion, referring to reciprocal respect among equals, has the task of elucidating the normative aspect of morality, while its negative version has the function of yielding a hypothetical explanation of the path towards this moral standpoint. One could also take a step further and posit that Kant resolved the difficulties resulting from the double meaning of *amour propre* ontologically by relegating its divergent meanings to two different spheres: on the one hand to empirical reality, on the other hand to the noumenal. In the causal realm of history, human self-interestedness appears in the shape of the craving for social recognition; in the rational realm of moral laws, by contrast, it takes the shape of moral respect.

Even Kant himself, however, could not have been entirely convinced by such a simple solution, for in his essays on the philosophy of history he endeavoured to build a theoretical bridge between factual history and the ideal – in order to keep the gap between the two realms from widening. It thus seems more likely that Kant did not generally realize that, at least for Rousseau, both the craving for social recognition and the striving for moral respect could originate from one and the same motivational source, namely from *amour propre*. If Kant had known about this internal connection in Rousseau, he would not have bothered considering the causes for the shift in the underlying human need. Rather, he would have picked up two notions from the writings of his great role model Rousseau, each appearing, independently from one another, to possess such explanatory force that he would have attempted to draw upon them at different places in his work.

Even more difficult, however, is an appraisal of the dependence on Rousseau's notion of *amour propre* in the case of thinkers who wanted to transcend Kant's theory immediately after his death, with the aim of preventing from the outset the emergence of any gap between the two realms of empirical causality and noumenal reason. We can note that at least Hegel, though not Fichte, was intuitively aware of the origins of his own theory of recognition in the heritage of Rousseau's thought. Although Hegel, to my knowledge, does not mention the notion of *amour propre* and also takes his entire terminology of recognition more from Fichte than from Rousseau, many remarks in the *Philosophy of Right* allow the conclusion that Hegel conceived of *Sittlichkeit* along the lines of Rousseau's *volonté générale* – namely as the result of reciprocal recognition among individuals limiting themselves in their subjectivity.[31] If one

[31] On the impact of Rousseau's *Social Contract* on Hegel's intellectual development up to his philosophy of right, see the excellent article by Hans Friedrich Fulda, 'Rousseausche

considers that Hegel traces 'vanity' and 'hypocrisy' to the failure to recognize how the need for recognition binds subjects together, a contextual-notional dependence (if not a direct one) on Rousseau's horizon of thought seems plain. Like the great Genevan, so too the German philosopher perceives the subjective craving for recognition and mutual recognition, that is, vanity and equal respect, as two sides of the same human striving to be acknowledged as a person of social worth in the eyes of other people.[32] But, as in Kant's case, it is extremely difficult to make out the extent to which Hegel really understood the double meaning of *amour propre* in Rousseau's work; although the *Philosophy of Right* makes distinctions similar to Rousseau's between decadent and successful forms of the need for recognition, it is doubtful that Hegel's distinctions originate directly in an adaptation of the notion of *amour propre*. One reason why later generations had such difficulties seeing the whole range of meanings of Rousseau's key notion may be that Rousseau himself never shed a certain reservation concerning the relationship to the self thus designated. To the end of his life he struggled with the question whether, on the whole, it would not be more conducive to a good life to mentally overcome our dependence on others.

## III

Looking back at what we have learned about Rousseau's theory of *amour propre* before this interim overview of the history of ideas, the enormous range of this concept is as striking as its inherent character of constant unease: *amour propre*, as opposed to mere *amour de soi*, is a

Probleme in Hegels Entwicklung', in *Rousseau, die Revolution und der junge Hegel*, ed. Hans Friedrich Fulda and Rolf-Peter Horstmann (Stuttgart: Klett-Cotta, 1991), 41–73, esp. 62 ff.; see also Patrick Riley, 'Rousseau's General Will', in *The Cambridge Companion to Rousseau*, ed. Patrick Riley (Cambridge: Cambridge University Press, 2001), 124–153. It may be that Fichte too follows the pattern of Rousseau's general will; see the notable essay by Georg Gurwitsch, 'Kant und Fichte als Rousseau-Interpreten', *Kant-Studien* 27 (1922), 138–164. However, neither contribution discusses explicitly the authors' debt to Rousseau's insight into the conditions of *amour propre*; in my opinion, the opportunity to explore further these deeper contexts arose only with the publication of Neuhouser's monograph.

[32] This split in the notion of recognition is particularly manifest in the instances of the *Philosophy of Right* where Hegel conceives individual craving for acknowledgment as the consequence of the failure of an established, 'moral' relations of recognition. See, for example, G. W. F. Hegel, *Elements of the Philosophy of Right*, ed. Allen Wood and H. B. Nisbet (Cambridge: Cambridge University Press, 1991), §253 (271–272). Moreover, it seems to me not inappropriate to understand Hegel's design of a morally demarcated market economy as a response to Rousseau's diagnosis of the decay of civil society, as Jeffrey Church suggests in 'The Freedom of Desire: Hegel's Response to Rousseau on the Problem of Civil Society', *American Journal of Political Science* 54.1 (2010), 125–139.

self-interestedness mediated by others. For Rousseau it does not even lose its boundlessness and insatiability when, due to the insight of shared dependence, it has taken the form of a mutual respect among equals. As identified by Frederick Neuhouser, the anthropological realism of Rousseau's thought lies in the fact that, after the loss of contented self-love, the individual retains a constant craving to be recognized as an especially esteemed member of his social community. Thus a socialized individual cannot be satisfied merely by being acknowledged as an equal among equals in a republican community, but must strive beyond that for a social esteem that accrues to skills and attributes that differentiate him from all others.[33] Such an excess in the striving for recognition, which compels Rousseau to seek out additional sources of personal worth and reputation in the *Social Contract,* is itself grounded in the structure of the attitude to the self that is characteristic of *amour propre*. Taking up this relation, we have lost all standards of self-assessment that might have arisen from our natural needs, so to speak; hence we are now able to assess our merit only in the reflection offered by those who, taken together, form 'public opinion' or the 'generalized other'. The uncertainty whether our accomplishments are actually honoured appropriately by such public judgments remains even if, as co-authors of the *volonté générale*, we are involved in achieving universally binding standards of value. To preclude any possible misinterpretations of our personality, even under the condition of equal respect, we thus must still strive for a recognition that makes us stand out from all others. Unlike Adam Smith, who could imagine the external observer as so completely generalizable as to have lost any actual features of arbitrariness and even as identifiable with reason as such,[34] Rousseau cannot believe in the possibility of such a complete rationalizability of the general judge.[35] For him, the extrinsic judgment that the individual is exposed to in the relationship of *amour propre* to the self always contains the danger of remaining unrecognized to the extent that

[33] Cf. Neuhouser, *Rousseau's Theodicy*, 67–70.

[34] This other form of recognition, aimed at individual distinction rather than at equal respect, was related to the category of 'esteem' (*Wertschätzung*) in my study *The Struggle for Recognition: Moral Grammar of Social Conflicts*, trans. Joel Anderson (Cambridge: Polity Press, 1995), Part II, ch. 5. As Neuhouser would later do, I relied there on the now renowned article by Stephen L. Darwall, 'Two Kinds of Respect', *Ethics* 88.1 (1977), 36–49.

[35] On some occasions Adam Smith presents the 'impartial spectator' as generalized to such an extent that he becomes a 'vicegerent of God within us' and even identified with the principles of reason (Smith, *Theory of Moral Sentiments,* 166). Kant would take up this point in order to endow this sum of the principles of reason with transcendental aspects. On the significance of Smith's moral theory in this context, see Ernst Tugendhat, *Vorlesungen über Ethik* (Frankfurt am Main: Suhrkamp, 1993), 282–309.

a pre-emptive pursuit of special esteem is not only widespread, but also culturally justified.

On the other hand, this risk of failure to be recognized, by which Rousseau means not simply a lack of respect for individual merits but the absence of their cognitive perception, is also a constant source of anxiety for Rousseau. He sees the tendency of the social environment to misjudge the true nature of the individual and fail to recognize his special talents as the real danger posed by the moment of civilizing transition from *amour de soi* to *amour propre.*[36] This diagnosis, which may be easily overlooked but consequently emerges as the core of Rousseau's theory of recognition, imperceptibly shifts the reference points of social dependence upon the other from the moral to the epistemic. The internalized authority of public opinion, on which the individual's self-assessment depends, no longer presents itself as a moral but as a theoretical judge, who is to assess the qualities a subject actually possesses. With this transition, of course, there is also a change in how *amour propre* prompts a person to action. Just as a person should be able to demonstrate his social value and individual abilities as long as the generalized other is a moral instance, he must also be able to prove the merits and talents he actually has if he interiorizes an epistemic judge.

A look at Rousseau's writings makes it seem rather improbable that he gave a sufficient account of his own oscillation between a moral and an epistemic understanding of *amour propre*. Wherever he addresses the pathological desire for recognition and recommends as therapy the republican spirit of egalitarian respect, the normative notion of the generalized other predominates. Yet as soon as he begins speaking about the more fundamental harm of being dependent on the other, the epistemic model often presses imperceptibly into the foreground. In this shape of an internalized instance – not of moral evaluation, but rather of theoretical assessment – Rousseau's *amour propre* has had an enormous effect on the development of French philosophy. Up to Sartre and Lacan, we find remnants of the idea that dependence on social recognition is inevitably linked to the cognitive failure to recognize the

[36] In Rousseau's later, autobiographically framed works, one can find an increased number of such statements, where he describes the inter-subjective structure of *amour propre* as dependence on the establishment of facts about one's own qualities and behaviour. As evidence, the following citation from his posthumously published work *Rousseau, Judge of Jean-Jacques* would suffice: 'Should he speak of himself with praise that is merited but generally denied? Should he boast of the qualities he feels he has but which everyone refuses to see?' (Rousseau, *Judge of Jean-Jacques: Dialogues*, ed. Roger D. Masters and Christopher Kelly (Hanover, NH: University Press of New England, 1990), 6; *OC* I, 665.

core of one's subjectivity.[37] For Rousseau, however, the epistemic notion of an 'inner judge' repeatedly provides the occasion to approach theoretically the radical alternative of overcoming as a whole the relationship of *amour propre* to the self. Rousseau's autobiographical writings, in particular, constantly revolve around the possibility of regaining an individual attitude in which the social recognition of one's own merits and capabilities has lost all existential significance. Such considerations exhibit a Stoic motif in Rousseau's thought and unmistakably contradict the view presented so far – that as socialized beings we inevitably need the recognition of our social value.

If we examine the works in which Rousseau discusses his own relationship to himself – less perhaps the *Confessions* than *Rousseau, Judge of Jean-Jacques*, whose title is already quite revealing, and the *Reveries of a Solitary Walker* – what is immediately apparent is how much they renounce any dependence on the judgment of others. Here, the path to the good and proper life is characterized as a constant search for inner harmony that is accomplished only by ignoring the judgmental behaviour of our social environment.[38] That the author Rousseau regards only himself as qualified to judge his alter-ego already shows that he sees a desirable goal in finding a position of independence from others' attributions and from judgments which one cannot affect. If I want to be at peace with myself, my self-esteem and my self-image should be based solely on characterizations of my person, whose author I can consider only myself. A threat to such an ideal of autonomous judging seems to lie not primarily in dependence on the moral judgment of public opinion, but in its judgments about our qualities and activities – for these lead us to deceive ourselves about our true nature and thus to fail to recognize the valuable talents we actually have. It is thus not surprising that, in the famous fifth walk of his *Reveries*, Rousseau describes as the epitome of existential happiness

[37] A separate study is required to substantiate this thesis about the deeply ingrained dependence of French currents of recognition theory on Rousseau's epistemological model. Here I limit myself to indicating a few loci which highlight the extent to which Sartre, Lacan, and other French thinkers saw the danger of a 'cognitive' failure of recognition as the consequence of any act of recognition: Jean-Paul Sartre, *Being and Nothingness*, trans. Hazel E. Barnes (New York: Washington Square Press, 1992), 349–355; Jacques Lacan, 'The subversion of the Subject and the Dialectic of Desire in the Freudian Unconscious', in *Écrits: The First Complete Edition in English*, trans. Bruce Fink (New York: W. W. Norton & Co., 2006), 671–702; Pierre Bourdieu, *Pascalian Meditations*, trans. Richard Nice (Cambridge: Polity, 2000), 164–167.

[38] For an account of these 'Stoic' positions and their critique, see Avishai Margalit, *The Decent Society* (Cambridge, MA: Harvard University Press, 1996), 22–27. An impressive defence of such positions is undertaken in Ernst Tugendhat, *Egozentrizität und Mystik. Eine anthropologische Studie* (Munich: Beck, 2003), esp. chs. 2 and 4.

a state in which the author, through the mere passive observation of natural processes, learns about the qualities he truly possesses and about the worries that really drive him. Because nature cannot speak and makes no judgment of us, in it every impulse of *amour propre* is deprived of its nourishing substance: we become unconcerned with others, and thus can recognize ourselves.[39]

As his late writings make clear, Rousseau wavered all his life between a resolute endorsement and a radical rejection of existential dependence on others. On the one hand, his work enables a fundamental insight to prevail: the idea that human beings owe their self-esteem and their capacity for action to inter-subjective recognition. But on the other hand, he also recognizes the hazards associated with being subjected to the judgments of one's social environment. Even if his own indecision may ultimately be rooted in the fact that he does not distinguish clearly enough between a moral and an epistemic understanding of recognition, he nonetheless initiated a philosophical debate that has not reached its conclusion to this day. There are always spirited partisans at hand of both of the positions he promulgated: the transformation of *amour propre* into symmetrical recognition and the rejection of any dependence on the 'generalized other'. The legacy that Rousseau left to the theory of recognition remains highly double-edged; as with a Trojan horse, those who try to take it up always invite the rival into their own home.

[39] See particularly the fifth walk in Rousseau, *Reveries of a Solitary Walker*, trans. Russell Goulbourne (Oxford: Oxford University Press, 2011), 49–58; *OC* I, 1040–1049. For a brilliant reading of this significant chapter, see Heinrich Meier, *Über das Glück des philosophischen Lebens. Reflexionen zu Rousseaus Rêveries in zwei Büchern* (München: C. H. Beck, 2011), Book I, ch. 4.

# Bibliography

## Editions of Rousseau's works

Rousseau, Jean-Jacques, 'A Letter from Jean-Jacques Rousseau (1757)', ed. Jean Starobinski, *New York Review of Books*, 15 May 2003, 31–32
*Collected Writings of Rousseau*, ed. Christopher Kelly, Roger D. Masters, and Peter D. Stillman, 13 vols. (Hanover, NH: University Press of New England, 1990–2009)
*Confessions*, trans. Angela Scholar, ed. Patrick Coleman (Oxford: Oxford University Press, 2008)
*Correspondance complète de Jean Jacques Rousseau*, ed. R. A. Leigh et al., 52 vols. (Oxford: Voltaire Foundation, 1965–1998)
*Diskurs über die Ungleichheit/Discours sur l'inégalité: Kritische Ausgabe des integralen Textes*, ed. Heinrich Meier, 5th ed. (Paderborn: Schöningh, 2001)
*Emile, or on Education*, trans. and ed. Allan Bloom (New York: Basic Books, 1979)
*Œuvres complètes*, ed. Bernard Gagnebin et al. (Bibliothèque de la Pléiade), 5 vols. (Paris: Gallimard, 1959–1995) *[OC]*
*Politics and the Arts: Letter to M. D'Alembert on the Theatre*, trans. Allan Bloom (Ithaca: Cornell University Press, 1987)
*Reveries of a Solitary Walker*, trans. Russell Goulbourne (Oxford: Oxford University Press, 2011)
*The Discourses and Other Early Political Writings*, ed. Victor Gourevitch (Cambridge: Cambridge University Press, 1997) *[DI]*
*The Political Writings of Jean Jacques Rousseau*, ed. C. E. Vaughan, 2 vols. (Cambridge: Cambridge University Press, 1915)
*The Social Contract and Other Later Political Writings*, ed. Victor Gourevitch (Cambridge: Cambridge University Press, 1997) *[SC]*

## Engagements with Rousseau

(A selective list, reflecting the themes and authors discussed in this volume)

Affeldt, Samuel, *Constituting Mutuality: Essays on Expression and the Bases of Intelligibility in Rousseau, Wittgenstein, and Freud*, PhD Dissertation, Harvard University, 1996
'The Force of Freedom: Rousseau on *Forcing to be Free*', *Political Theory* 27.3 (1999), 299–333

Aubert de Vitry, François-Jean-Philibert, *Rousseau à l'assemblée nationale* (Paris: Rue du Hurepois, 1789)

Bach, Reinhard, 'Rousseau et les physiocrates: une cohabitation extraordinaire', *Etudes J.-J. Rousseau* 10 (1999), 9–82

Barni, Jules, *Histoire des idées morales et politiques en France au dix-huitième siècle* (Paris: Baillière, 1867)

Barran, Thomas, *Russia Reads Rousseau, 1762–1825* (Evanston: Northwestern University Press, 2002)

Bécu, Ricardo Zorraquín, 'El Contrato Social y la Revolución de Mayo', in *Catálogo de la exposición bibliográfica argentina de derecho y ciencias sociales* (Universidad de Buenos Aires, Facultad de Derecho y Ciencias Sociales, 1960), 17–26

Berlin, Isaiah, *Four Essays on Liberty* (Oxford: Oxford University Press, 1969)

Bernardi, Bruno (ed.), *Rousseau et la Révolution* (Paris: Gallimard, 2012)

Blanc, Louis, *Histoire de la révolution française*, 2nd ed. (Paris: Furne et Pagnerre, 1869)

Blum, Carol, *Rousseau and the Republic of Virtue: The Language of Politics in the French Revolution* (Ithaca: Cornell University Press, 1986)

Brooke, Christopher, *Philosophic Pride: Stoicism and Political Thought from Lipsius to Rousseau* (Princeton: Princeton University Press, 2012)

Budai-Deleanu, Ion, *Ţiganiada* (Bucharest: Cugetarea, 1944)

Burns, J. H. '*Du côté de chez Vaughan*: Rousseau revisited', *Political Studies* 12 (1964), 229–34

Carnevali, Barbara, *Romantisme et reconnaissance. Figures de la conscience chez Rousseau*, trans. Philippe Audegean (Geneva: Droz, 2011)

Cassirer, Ernst, *Rousseau, Kant, Goethe: Two Essays*, trans. James Gutmann, Paul Oskar Kristeller, and John Herman Randall, Jr. (Princeton: Princeton University Press, 1945)

*The Question of Jean-Jacques Rousseau*, trans. Peter Gay (New Haven: Yale University Press, 1989)

Charvet, John, *The Social Problem in the Philosophy of Rousseau* (Cambridge: Cambridge University Press, 1974)

Chiaramonte, José Carlos, *La Ilustración en el Río de la Plata* (Buenos Aires: Editorial Sudamericana, 2007)

Church, Jeffrey, 'The Freedom of Desire: Hegel`s Response to Rousseau on the Problem of Civil Society', *American Journal of Political Science* 54.1 (2010), 125–139

Clavière, Etienne, *Opinions d'un créancier de l'état. Sur quelques matières de finance importantes dans le moment actuel* (Buisson: Paris, 1789)

Cobban, Alfred, *Rousseau and the Modern State* (London: G. Allen & Unwin, 1934)

Cohen, Joshua, 'Reflections on Rousseau: Autonomy and Democracy', *Philosophy and Public Affairs* (Summer 1986), 275–297

*Rousseau: A Free Community of Equals* (Oxford: Oxford University Press, 2010)

'The Natural Goodness of Humanity', in *Reclaiming the History of Ethics: Essays for John Rawls*, ed. A. Reath, B. Herman, and C. Korsgaard (Cambridge: Cambridge University Press, 1997), 102–139

Constant, Benjamin, *Political Writings*, ed. Biancamaria Fontana (Cambridge: Cambridge University Press, 1988)
Craiutu, Aurelian, *A Virtue for Courageous Minds: Moderation in French Political thought, 1748–1830* (Princeton: Princeton University Press, 2012)
Cranston, Maurice, *Jean-Jacques: The Early Life and Work of Jean-Jacques Rousseau, 1712–1754* (London: Allen Lane, 1983)
*The Noble Savage: Jean-Jacques Rousseau, 1754–1762* (London: Allen Lane, 1991)
*The Solitary Self: Jean-Jacques Rousseau in Exile and Adversity* (London: Allen Lane, 1997)
Cranston, Maurice and Richard S. Peters (ed.), *Hobbes and Rousseau: A Collection of Critical Essays* (New York: Anchor Books, 1972)
Crocker, Lester G., *Jean-Jacques Rousseau*, 2 vols. (New York: Macmillan, 1969–1973)
*Rousseau's Social Contract: An Interpretative Essay* (Cleveland: Western Reserve University Press, 1968)
D'Aprile, Iwan-Michelangelo and Stefanie Stockhorst (ed.), *Rousseau und die Moderne* (Göttingen: Wallstein, 2013)
Darwall, Stephen L., 'Two Kinds of Respect', *Ethics* 88.1 (1977), 36–49
Dent, N. J. H., *A Rousseau Dictionary* (Oxford: Blackwell, 1992)
*Rousseau* (London: Routledge, 2005)
*Rousseau: An Introduction to His Psychological, Social and Political Theory* (Oxford: Blackwell, 1988)
Derathé, Robert, *Jean-Jacques Rousseau et la science politique de son temps* (Paris: PUF, 1950)
Douglass, Robin, *Rousseau and Hobbes: Nature, Free Will, and the Passions* (Oxford: Oxford University Press, 2015)
Du Bois-Reymond, Emile, *Über das Nationalgefühl; Friedrich II. und Jean-Jacques Rousseau* (Berlin: Dümmler, 1879)
Dumont, Etienne, 'Observations sur le caractère et les écrits de Rousseau', *Bibliothèque universelle de Genève*. Nouvelle série, II (1836), 128–135
'Observations sur le style de J.-J. Rousseau', *Bibliothèque de Genève* II (1836), 298–313
Ferguson, Adam, *An Essay on the History of Civil Society*, ed. Fania Oz-Salzberger (Cambridge: Cambridge University Press, 1995)
Frederick II of Prussia, 'Discours de l'utilité des sciences et des arts dans un état' and 'Essai sur l'amour propre envisagé comme un principe de morale', *Œuvres de Frédéric le Grand*, ed. Johann D. E. Preuss, vol. IX, 99–114 and 195–207
Fricke, Christel and Hans-Peter Schütt (ed.), *Adam Smith als Moralphilosoph* (Berlin: De Gruyter, 2008)
Fulda, Hans Friedrich and Rolf-Peter Horstmann (ed.), *Rousseau, die Revolution und der junge Hegel* (Stuttgart: Klett-Cotta, 1991)
Gourevitch, Victor, 'Rousseau on Providence', *The Review of Metaphysics* 53 (2000), 565–611
Graubard, Stephen G. (ed.), 'Rousseau for Our Time', special issue of *Dædalus* 107.3 (1978)

Grimsley, Ronald, *Rousseau: A Study in Self-Awareness* (Cardiff: University of Wales Press, 1961)

*Rousseau and the Religious Quest* (Oxford: Clarendon Press, 1968)

Guizot, François, *The History of the Origins of Representative Government in Europe* (Indianapolis: Liberty Fund, 2002)

Gurwitsch, Georg, 'Kant und Fichte als Rousseau-Interpreten', *Kant-Studien* 27 (1922), 138–164

Hall, John C., *Rousseau: An Introduction to His Political Philosophy* (Plymouth: Macmillan, 1973)

Harvey, Simon, Marian Hobson, David Kelley, and Samuel S. B. Taylor (ed.), *Reappraisals of Rousseau: Studies in Honor of R.A. Leigh* (Manchester: Manchester University Press, 1980)

Hegel, G. W. F., *Elements of the Philosophy of Right*, ed. Allen Wood and H. B. Nisbet (Cambridge: Cambridge University Press, 1991)

Hobson, Marian, *Diderot and Rousseau: Networks of Enlightenment*, ed. Kate E. Tunstall and Caroline Warman (Oxford: Voltaire Foundation, 2011)

Holley, Jared, '*In verba magistri*? Assessing Rousseau's Classicism Today', *History of Political Thought* 37 (2016)

Honneth, Axel, 'Die Entgiftung Jean-Jacques Rousseaus. Neuere Literatur zum Werk des Philosophen', *Deutsche Zeitschrift für Philosophie* 4/2012, 611–32

*Pathologies of Reason: On the Legacy of Critical Theory*, trans. James Ingram (New York: Columbia University Press, 2009)

*The Struggle for Recognition: Moral Grammar of Social Conflicts*, trans. Joel Anderson (Cambridge: Polity Press, 1995)

Hont, István, *Politics in Commercial Society: Jean-Jacques Rousseau and Adam Smith*, ed. Béla Kapossy and Michael Sonenscher (Cambridge, MA: Harvard University Press, 2015)

'The Early Enlightenment Debate on Commerce and Luxury', in *The Cambridge History of Eighteenth-Century Political Thought*, ed. Mark Goldie and Robert Wokler (Cambridge: Cambridge University Press, 2006), 379–418

Israel, Jonathon, *Democratic Enlightenment: Philosophy, Revolution, and Human Rights 1750–1790* (Oxford: Oxford University Press, 2011)

James, David, *Rousseau and German Idealism: Freedom, Dependence and Necessity* (Cambridge: Cambridge University Press, 2013)

Jaumann, Herbert (ed.), *Rousseau in Deutschland. Neue Beiträge zur Erforschung seiner Rezeption* (Berlin: de Gruyter, 1994)

Jennings, Jeremy, *Revolution and the Republic: A History of Political Thought in France since the Eighteenth Century* (Oxford: Oxford University Press, 2013)

Jubb, Robert, 'Rawls and Rousseau: Amour-Propre and the Strains of Commitment', *Res Publica* 17.3 (2011), 245–260

Kant, Immanuel, *Anthropology, History, and Education*, ed. Günter Zöller and Robert B. Loudon (Cambridge: Cambridge University Press, 2007)

*Lectures on Anthropology*, ed. Allen Wood and Robert B. Louden (Cambridge: Cambridge University Press, 2012)

*Practical Philosophy*, ed. M. J. Gregor (Cambridge: Cambridge University Press, 1996)

*Religion within the Boundaries of Mere Reason*, ed. Allen Wood, George di Giovanni, and Robert Merrihew Adams (Cambridge: Cambridge University Press, 1998)

Kapossy, Béla, *Iselin Contra Rousseau: Sociable Patriotism and the History of Mankind* (Basel: Schwabe, 2006)

Kelly, George Armstrong, 'Rousseau, Kant and History', *Journal of the History of Ideas* 29.3 (1968), 347–364

Lamb, Peter, 'G. D. H. Cole on the General Will: A Socialist Reflects on Rousseau', *European Journal of Political Theory* 4.3 (2005), 283–300

Leigh, R. A. (ed.), *Rousseau after 200 Years: Proceedings of the Cambridge Bicentennial Colloquium* (Cambridge: Cambridge University Press, 1982)

Levine, Andrew, *The Politics of Autonomy: A Kantian Reading of Rousseau's Social Contract* (Amherst: University of Massachusetts Press, 1976)

Lewin, Boleslao, *Rousseau en la independencia de Latinoamérica* (Buenos Aires: Ediciones Depalma, 1980)

Lifschitz, Avi (ed.), *Rousseau's Imagined Antiquity,* special issue of *History of Political Thought* 37 (2016)

Lilti, Antoine, *Figures publiques: l'invention de la célébrité, 1750–1850* (Paris: Fayard, 2014)

'The Writing of Paranoia: Jean-Jacques Rousseau and the Paradoxes of Celebrity', *Representations* 103 (Summer 2008), 53–83

Lovejoy, Arthur, 'The Supposed Primitivism of Rousseau's Discourse on Inequality', *Modern Philology* 21.2 (1923), 165–186

Margalit, Avishai, *The Decent Society* (Cambridge, MA: Harvard University Press, 1996)

Masseau, Didier, *Les Ennemis des philosophes: L'antiphilosophie au temps des Lumières* (Paris: Albin Michel, 2000)

Masters, Roger D., *The Political Philosophy of Rousseau* (Princeton: Princeton University Press, 1968)

McDaniel, Iain, 'Philosophical History and the Science of Man in Scotland: Adam Ferguson's Response to Rousseau', *Modern Intellectual History* 10.3 (2013), 543–568

McDonald, Christie and Stanley Hoffman (ed.), *Rousseau and Freedom* (Cambridge: Cambridge University Press, 2010)

Meier, Heinrich, *Über das Glück des philosophischen Lebens. Reflexionen zu Rousseaus Rêveries in zwei Büchern* (München: C. H. Beck, 2011)

Mercier, Louis-Sébastien, *De J. J. Rousseau consideré comme l'un des premiers auteurs de la Révolution*, 2 vols. (Paris: Buisson, 1791)

Merkel, Garlieb, *Hume's und Rousseau's Abhandlungen über den Urvertrag, nebst einem Versuch über Leibeigenschaft den Liefländischen Erbherren gewidmet* (Leipzig: Heinrich Graeff, 1797)

Michalski, Jerzy, *Rousseau i sarmacki republicanizm* (Warsaw: PWN 1977)

Moreno, Mariano, 'Prólogo a la traducción del Contrato social', in *Escritos políticos y económicos*, ed. Norberto Piñero (Buenos Aires: L. J. Rosso y Cía, 1915), 265–268

Mounier, Jacques, *La Fortune des écrits de J.-J. Rousseau dans les pays de langue allemande de 1782 à 1813* (Paris: PUF, 1980)

Mounier, Jean-Joseph, *De l'Influence attribuée aux philosophes, aux francs-maçons et aux illuminés sur la Révolution de France* (Tübingen: Gotta, 1801)

*Recherches sur les causes qui ont empêché les français de devenir libres et sur les moyens qui leur restent pour acquérir la liberté* (Geneva, 1792)

Nakhimovsky, Isaac, *The Closed Commercial State: Perpetual Peace and Commercial Society from Rousseau to Fichte* (Princeton: Princeton University Press, 2011)

Neal, Patrick, 'In the Shadow of the General Will: Rawls, Kant, and Rousseau on the Problem of Political Right', *The Review of Politics* 49.3 (1987), 389–409

Necker, Jacques, 'Du Pouvoir exécutif dans les grands états', *Œuvres complètes* (Paris: Treuttel et Würtz, 1821), vol. VIII, 1–317

Neuhouser, Frederick, 'Freedom, Dependence, and the General Will', *Philosophical Review* (1993), 363–395

*Rousseau's Critique of Inequality: Reconstructing the Second Discourse* (Cambridge: Cambridge University Press, 2014)

*Rousseau's Theodicy of Self-Love: Evil, Rationality, and the Drive for Recognition* (Oxford: Oxford University Press, 2008)

Nisbet, Robert C., 'Rousseau and Totalitarianism', *The Journal of Politics* 5.2 (1943), 93–114

Oakeshott, Michael, 'Rationalism in politics', in *Rationalism in Politics and Other Essays* (Indianapolis: Liberty Fund, 1991)

Paquette, Gabriel B., *Enlightenment, Governance, and Reform in Spain and Its Empire, 1759–1808* (Basingstoke: Palgrave Macmillan, 2008)

Pettit, Philip, *Just Freedom: A Moral Compass for a Complex World* (New York: W. W. Norton and Co., 2014)

*On the People's Terms: A Republican Theory and Model of Democracy* (Cambridge: Cambridge University Press, 2012)

*Republicanism: A Theory of Freedom and Government* (Oxford: Oxford University Press, 1997)

'Two Republican Traditions', in *Republican Democracy: Liberty, Law and Politics*, ed. Andreas Niederberger and Philipp Schink (Edinburgh: Edinburgh University Press, 2013), 169–204

Pezzillo, Lélia, *Rousseau et le Contrat social* (Paris: PUF, 2000)

Philonenko, Alexis, *Jean-Jacques Rousseau et la pensée du malheur* (Paris: Vrin, 1984)

Plamenatz, John, *Man and Society: A Critical Examination of Some Important Social and Political Theories from Machiavelli to Marx*, 2 vols. (London: Longmans, 1963)

Rahe, Paul A., 'The Enlightenment Indicted: Rousseau's Response to Montesquieu', *The Journal of the Historical Society* 18 (2008), 273–302

Rawls, John, *A Theory of Justice* (Oxford: Oxford University Press, 1972)

*Lectures on the History of Political Philosophy*, ed. S. Freeman (Cambridge, MA: Harvard University Press, 2007)

*Political Liberalism*, expanded edition (New York: Columbia University Press, 2005)

*The Law of Peoples* (Cambridge, MA: Harvard University Press, 1999)

Rebentisch, Juliane, *Die Kunst der Freiheit. Zur Dialektik demokratischer Existenz* (Frankfurt am Main: Suhrkamp, 2011)

Reyes, Raúl Cardiel, *Los filósofos modernos en la independencia Latinoamericana* (Mexico City: UNAM, 1964)
Riley, Patrick (ed.), *The Cambridge Companion to Rousseau* (Cambridge: Cambridge University Press, 2001)
*The General Will before Rousseau* (Princeton: Princeton University Press, 1986)
Romero, José Luis and Luis Alberto Romero (ed.), *Pensamiento político de la emancipación*, 2 vols. (Caracas: Biblioteca Ayacucho, 1977)
Roosevelt, Grace, 'Rousseau versus Rawls on International Relations', *European Journal of Political Theory* 5.3 (2006), 301–320
Rosenblatt, Helena, *Rousseau and Geneva: From the First Discourse to the Social Contract, 1749–1762* (Cambridge: Cambridge University Press, 1997)
Roussel, Jean, *Jean-Jacques Rousseau en France après la Révolution, 1795–1830* (Paris: Armand Colin, 1972)
Rzadowska, Ewa (ed.), *Voltaire et Rousseau en France et en Pologne* (Warsaw, 1982)
Sack, Jörn, *Friedrich der Grosse und Jean-Jacques Rousseau. Eine verfehlte Beziehung und die Folgen* (Berlin: Berliner Wissenschaftsverlag, 2011)
Schiller, Friedrich, *On the Aesthetic Education of Man in a Series of Letters and Related Writings*, trans. Keith Tribe, ed. Alexander Schmidt (London: Penguin, 2016)
Schmidt, Alexander, 'Scholarship, Morals, and Government: J. H. S. Formey's and J. G. Herder's responses to Rousseau's *First Discourse*', *Modern Intellectual History* 9.2 (2012), 249–274
Schneewind, Jerome B., *The Invention of Autonomy* (Cambridge: Cambridge University Press, 1998)
Scott, John T. and Robert Zaretsky, 'Rousseau and the Revival of Humanism in Contemporary French Political Thought', *History of Political Thought* 24.4 (2003), 599–623
Shea, Louisa, *The Cynic Enlightenment: Diogenes in the Salon* (Baltimore, MD: Johns Hopkins University Press, 2010)
Shklar, Judith N., *Men and Citizens: A Study of Rousseau's Social Theory* (Cambridge: Cambridge University Press, 1969)
'Positive Liberty, Negative Liberty in the United States', in *Redeeming American Political Thought*, ed. Stanley Hoffmann and Dennis E. Thompson (Chicago: University of Chicago Press, 1998), 111–126
Simon, Jules, *Inauguration de la Statue de Jean-Jacques Rousseau, Le dimanche, 3 fevrier 1889* (Paris: Firmin-Didot, 1889)
Smith, Adam, *The Theory of Moral Sentiments*, ed. D. D. Raphael and A. L. Macfie (Indianapolis: Liberty Fund, 1984)
Sonenscher, Michael, *Sans-culottes: An Eighteenth-Century Emblem in the French Revolution* (Princeton: Princeton University Press, 2008)
Spector, Céline, Au prisme de Rousseau. Usages politiques contemporains (Oxford: Voltaire Foundation, 2011)
(ed.), Modernités de Rousseau, special issue of Lumières 15 (June 2010)
Spell, Jefferson Rea, *Rousseau in the Spanish World before 1833* (Austin: University of Texas Press, 1938)
Spink, John S., *Jean-Jacques Rousseau et Genève* (Paris: Boivin, 1934)
Spitz, Jean-Fabien, *La Liberté Politique* (Paris: PUF, 1995)

Strauss, Leo, 'On the Intention of Rousseau', *Social Research* 14 (1947), 455–487
*Natural Right and History* (Chicago: University of Chicago Press, 1953)
Strong, Tracy, *Jean-Jacques Rousseau: The Politics of the Ordinary* (Lanham: Rowman and Littlefield, 2002)
Talmon, Jacob, *The Origins of Totalitarian Democracy* (London: Secker & Warburg, 1952)
Terjanian, Anoush Fraser, *Commerce and Its Discontents in Eighteenth-Century French Political Thought* (Cambridge: Cambridge University Press, 2013)
Trencsényi, Balázs and Michal Kopeček, *Discourses of Collective Identity in Central and Southeastern Europe* (Budapest: CEU Press, 2006)
Trousson, Raymond, *Jean-Jacques Rousseau jugé par ses contemporaines. Du 'Discours sur les sciences et les arts' aux 'Confessions'* (Paris: Champion, 2000)
Trousson, Raymond and Frédéric S. Eigeldinger (ed.), *Dictionnaire de Jean-Jacques Rousseau* (Paris: Champion, 2001)
Tugendhat, Ernst, *Egozentrizität und Mystik. Eine anthropologische Studie* (Munich: Beck, 2003)
*Vorlesungen über Ethik* (Frankfurt am Main: Suhrkamp, 1993)
Vallette, Gaspard, *Jean-Jacques Rousseau, Genevois*, 2nd ed. (Paris: Plon-Nourrit, 1911)
Vaughan, C. E., *Studies in the History of Political Philosophy before and after Rousseau*, 2nd ed., 2 vols. (Manchester: Manchester University Press, 1939)
Whatmore, Richard, *Against War and Empire. Geneva, Britain and France in the Eighteenth Century* (New Haven and London: Yale University Press, 2012)
Williams, David Lay and James Farr (ed.), *The General Will: The Evolution of a Concept* (Cambridge: Cambridge University Press, 2015)
Wokler, Robert, 'Natural Law and the Meaning of Rousseau's Political Thought: A Correction to Two Misrenderings of His Doctrine', in *Enlightenment Essays in Memory of Robert Shackleton*, ed. Giles Barber and C. P. Courtney (Oxford: Voltaire Foundation, 1988), 319–335
'Rameau, Rousseau and the *Essai sur l'origine des langues*', *Studies on Voltaire and the Eighteenth Century* 117 (1974), 179–238
*Rousseau: A Very Short Introduction* (Oxford: Oxford University Press, 2001)
*Rousseau on Society, Politics, Music and Language* (New York: Garland, 1987)
'Rousseau's Pufendorf: Natural Law and the Foundations of Commercial Society', *History of Political Thought* 5.3 (1994), 373–402
*Rousseau, the Age of Enlightenment, and Their Legacies*, ed. Bryan Garsten with an introduction by Christopher Brooke (Princeton: Princeton University Press, 2012)
'The *Discours sur les sciences et les arts* and Its Offspring: Rousseau in Reply to his Critics', *Reappraisals of Rousseau*, ed. Harvey et al., 250–278
'The Influence of Diderot on the Political Theory of Rousseau: Two Aspects of a Relationship', *Studies on Voltaire and the Eighteenth Century* 132 (1975), 55–111

# Index